The Advanced Science of Hockey

Horst Wein

translated from the German by Martin Copus, B.A.
revised for English readers by John Cadman

Pelham Books

Acknowledgements

The author is grateful to the following for permission to reproduce photographs in this book:

Bild-Zeitung 62; Carl Coetzee 43; Ger Dijkstra & Zn. 7; Ebrahim Viyani 11; Editoraial Atlanda 6, 28; Dr Joachim Flugel 49, 53, 63, 64; Hermann Hill 46; Hans-Dietrich Kaiser 2, 3; Morley Pecker 23, 29, 32, 36, 58; Rhodesia Herald 17, 39; J. Sanguino 35; Felipe Sevillano 41; Utrechts Nieuwsblad 9, 47; David Vinson 15, 29, 30a, 30b, 31, 33, 37, 40; Werek 44; Wilfred Witters 52.

First published in Great Britain by
Pelham Books Ltd
44 Bedford Square
London WC1B 3DU
1981

British Library Cataloguing in Publication Data

Wein, Horst
The advanced science of hockey
1. Field hockey
I. Title
796. 35′5 GV1017.H7

ISBN 0 7207 1171 1

Typeset by Allset Composition
Printed by Hollen Street Press, Slough,
and bound by Dorstel Press, Harlow.

Contents

Foreword

I was very pleased to learn that Horst Wein had written a new book. It is one which cannot help but improve standards in hockey. In the space of only a few years, Horst Wein has become one of the great experts in our game. His training and coaching methods, and his suggestions for improving the standard of play, are now recognised throughout the world.

He has always maintained that our methods of coaching and, above all, the tactics of hockey, remain behind those of other sports. From an exhaustive study of these other sports, he has derived suggestions for the modern game of hockey.

As President of the International Hockey Federation, I should here like to thank him for his outstanding contribution to the development and prosperity of our game. I am convinced that his new book will lead to much wider adoption of modern coaching and training methods, which will in turn make our sport more attractive to both player and spectator.

René Frank
President of the International
Hockey Federation

1 The many faults that remain in European hockey

There are no slack periods in competitive sport, either for those actively involved, or for the coaches and sports scientists whose job it is to analyse the latest international matches and training sessions, and who must always be on the lookout for ways to improve performance.

Can Europe fulfil the promise it showed at the beginning of the seventies? Is there room for further improvement in performance? The answer to these questions, I feel, is that we have only just begun to use our resources properly and to remove the many flaws in skills, tactics, and physical and technical coaching.

TOWARDS TECHNICAL COACHING

The Olympic competitions of 1972 and 1976, and the fourth World Cup of 1978, showed that the Indians' and Pakistanis' lead in the technical sphere have diminished. The technical ability of many European and Australian players is no longer second to that of the Asians. Indoor hockey (practised most intensively in Germany and the Netherlands), together with the broadening of training schedules, has played a fundamental part in Europe's gain in the skills of hockey.

Photo 1 Pakistan confirmed its supremacy again in January 1980 winning for the second successive time the 'Champion's Trophy'. Here their defence stops a Spanish attack in the very last moment.

Even at the highest level, however, Europeans continue to make many technical errors when they use their skills at maximum speed. This is in contrast to the Indians and Pakistanis. Using special exercises designed to develop speed on the ball (see *The Science of Hockey* pages 207-209)*, combined with technical training under conditions of oxygen deficiency, we Europeans must learn to be able to retain mastery of the most important technical facets of the game even when fatigued and functioning at top speed, and learn to execute movements accurately and successfully in difficult circumstances. These technical facets include scoring, passing, stopping and dribbling under pressure from an opponent as well as stopping inaccurate passes. Along with working to improve speed on and off the ball, we must also learn to use speed to effect, at the correct moment, when dribbling.

A further technical flaw in European hockey is many players' lack of dexterity. In order to improve a player's dexterity, his knowledge of moves must be widened to the extent where he can adapt himself to the changing match situations by making appropriate moves himself. The game of hockey involves an extraordinary range of movement: running forwards, sideways and backwards with or without the ball, sudden stops, feinting, body-swerving, as well as the skills, pushing, hitting, flicking, dribbling, and so on.

Modern hockey requires not only that a player has mastered all these movements and knows how to use them at precisely the right time, but also that he can execute them quickly and accurately. Fit and mobile players who have expanded their skills by practising their moves in match situations thus have a great advantage over players who do not, for example, have the ability to lose their permanent marker or to follow their attacking opponent step for step. For the attacker to lose his defender or for the defender to mark an opposing forward out of the game, first-class running and a certain skill of dexterity and flexibility are needed, in addition to tactical awareness (see *The Science of Hockey* pages 223-228 'Developing flexibility and dexterity').

The weakness of many players (above all in defensive play, but also in attempting to beat a player with a sudden change of direction, and in escaping man-to-man marking) is due to a lack of dexterity, and an underestimation of the importance of these skills when the training plan is drawn up. If the Asians would employ their outstanding skill in a tactical way, enabling them to escape tight man-to-man marking by Europeans, and putting the latter under pressure when they received the ball, then Pakistan would not be the only Asian country with medal chances.

We should also examine the relation between exercises used in elementary hockey coaching, and the practice of the more complex technical and tactical facets of the game. Systematic and progressive technical teaching of the complex moves demanded of players under opposition pressure is frequently forgotten, in both Asian and European club training schedules, i.e.:

* All references in this book refer to the second edition published in 1979.

Escaping tight man-to-man marking and receiving passes from team mates without obstructing the defender (*The Science of Hockey*, pages 147-150).
Preparation and execution of quick counter-attacks (see Chapter 8).
Increased use of the wall-passes (see Chapter 11).

The coaching of many players, especially in clubs, is still too limited. The modern defender ought to be made more familiar with attacking roles, and the attacker with more defensive duties, so that he understands the demands made on his colleagues.

Considering these few technical deficiencies in European hockey so far mentioned, numerous suggestions for exercises to improve training schedules and their content immediately come to mind. Simplified practice games with reduced numbers of players, and training matches against weaker opponents, also have their place in competition-based training sessions, when the skills that have been systematically acquired in skill-training can be put into practice.

TOWARDS TACTICAL COACHING

From 1966 to 1976, for the first time in Europe, tactics dominated skill and fitness. The commanding role played by skill in the early fifties was followed at the end of the fifties by a wave of fitness-fever that was evident in all sports. Since 1966, European hockey players (but notably not the Indians) have recognised that besides good technical and physical training, it is tactical ability which largely determines performance. This realisation, and the resultant training plans comprising an increased consideration of tactics, also explain why leading European national teams can nowadays beat the Indians and Pakistanis on their home territory.

If European hockey players are again to win the three-cornered fight between Asia, Oceania and Europe, as they did in Munich in 1972 and Amsterdam in 1973, then tactics, as well as the unavoidable need for fitness, must be stressed in training whilst still not neglecting the necessary skills.

In order to use available time as efficiently as possible, and to shift the balance of training towards match situations, skills and fitness training ought to be integrated with tactical instruction. Simplified games and tactical exercises will coach skills under match conditions, improving fitness, and developing tactical awareness in varied match situations, in a way that pure skill training cannot do (see Chapter 10).

This emphasis on a tactical training which keeps attack and defence equally in mind can be summed up under the following headings:

a Switching quickly from defence to attack and vice-versa or from man-to-man marking to combined marking.

b Players not in possession of the ball being always available for a pass by means of skilful running into free space.

c Running straight into free space, particularly after a successful pass.

d Quick transfer of pressure by means of long passes (see Chapter 12).

e Attacking from the second or third line including surprise by a defender or middle field player in the attack (see Chapter 10).

f Execution of free hits in any part of the field and in particular near the opponent's circle (see Chapter 16).

THE ORGANISATION OF COACHING

Europe's hockey future also depends on whether a sufficient number of qualified coaches is available in individual countries to attend to both junior and senior hockey players. West Germany, England, and Holland have set a trend for other European countries to follow by arranging annual instruction courses at sports centres. But it is sometimes sadly true that many coaches in the clubs of these countries do little justice to their prominent role. After establishing and explaining exercises, they all too often get involved in matters of organisation rather than carefully observing, and if necessary correcting, players' technical skills and tactical moves. Because of a lack of tactical expertise, the technical and physical training of players is also too rarely combined with tactical exercises.

A further fault is that training intensity is often not high enough in either the final phase of preparation or in the competitive periods of training. Training is 'intensive' if an individual player's period of exercise is as great a proportion as possible of the total training time. Good intensive training does not only provide a high total workload, but also sufficient intensity of individual physical workload during training. There is far too much inaction because of unnecessary pauses and insufficient preparation and organisation on the part of the coach, and this can greatly lower the effectiveness of training.

Furthermore, players ought to be given individual exercises more often than has previously been the case in hockey coaching. Almost everywhere, one sees all players of a team going through the same training schedules, identical in both content and workload. I do not want to demean the value of coaching players together, since all-round instruction is vital, but, as coaches, we must work towards the individualisation of the training of our players (see Chapter 4). Far more than before, we must take into account the specific areas of practice needed to match each individual's part in play, and also consider the stage to which each player has developed in technical and tactical, physical and psychological aspects of play.

THE COACH'S JOB

Coaches, with few exceptions, lack instruction and preparatory training in psychological matters. Many have correct attitudes to individual players without knowing it, but some stand out only because of their poor, unsym-

Photo 2 Schuler (Germany) scores the equaliser against India in Hamburg 1966 (final result 1:1).

pathetic understanding of individuals, giving non-specific instructions to both groups and individuals. This type of coach cannot develop the skills of a player or team fully.

Discoveries are frequently made during practical psychological work with international players. One useful finding is that hockey coaches pay most attention to those skills which are inadequately mastered by players but fail to develop the others, which may yet be improved, although already practised well. As in much education, the principle seems to hold that what is done correctly requires no comment, and solely what is done incorrectly needs criticism and comment. Where blame is more forthcoming than praise, however, players may develop a fear of failure. Where praise is usual, hope generally builds into success. It is of paramount importance for general development of character, as well as of the individual's proficiency as a player, that a positive attitude is developed. According to the coach's attitude, the player may aim for success in both his daily life and in the important matches before him, or may be adversely affected by apprehension to the point of failure.

Top competitive sport is an area of human endeavour in which the smallest error can mean failure. Since only in the rarest cases can total, insurpassable, perfection be achieved there will, to all intents and purposes, always be reason to comment upon an individual's play. The majority of coaches follow this adversely critical pattern in their comments, because they were trained to reduce errors by recognising them and correcting them.

But they ought to strive for a balance between positive and negative criticism in their comments–their own temperament apart–for the benefit of their players. The more that positive criticism is apparent in the negative judgement of a technical or tactical move, the more a player will tend to go into a match looking for success rather than being dispirited. If right at the beginning of collaboration between coach and player only faults are stressed, then pronounced inhibitions and feelings of guilt can soon make themselves felt in the player. Then, each player–and so the team–go onto the field with avoidance of mistakes being a chief aim (see Chapter 18).

Whenever possible (except, of course, during a match), the coach's correction and criticism should be expressed during or immediately after the incident. A quick and most effective method of learning is the immediate boost given to a correctly executed move by comment during that move itself (e.g. praise of a player's attempt to flick at tactically the right moment, or relieve pressure with a long pass). If, however, criticism is made, as is usually the case in a match, at half-time or after the game, then coach and player alike are forced to imagine themselves in the match situation referred to, which is particularly difficult for the player who frequently does not know exactly which move or piece of action is meant by the coach. (Analysis and discussion of video tapes of the game can compensate for this, however, and can be important teaching aids.)

It is not only coaching methods which have evolved in recent years because of scientific study, but also it is equally important to establish whether or not a youngster is predestined to play hockey and if so, where his physical, emotional and mental constitutions set limits.

We ought to initiate youngsters into hockey as early as possible–at between eight and ten years old. Players only become world-class by virtue of the concentrated experience which follows when that talent has been discovered and encouraged early on. In order to recognise talent early, some aptitude test is required, which identifies required motor skills and tests basic physiological and some simple psychological factors (e.g. commitment, powers of concentration), as well as intellectual factors. This can decide whether the young player is endowed with the necessary basic requirements for the game of hockey (see Chapter 23). Before tests and criteria for assessing individual aptitudes can be drawn up, the game of hockey must be analysed and all those main factors necessary for good performance determined.

If Europe succeeds in finding highly talented youngsters each year, channels their skills into hockey at an early age (at the latest, 10 years old), coaches and trains them in skills and tactics both physically and mentally with tried and tested methods, then Europe could soon be one step ahead of Asia and Oceania.

Finally, all countries, and the F.I.H., should hold coaching seminars at regular intervals from which all coaches at club, divisional or national level, could receive new stimuli and ideas. They could then analyse the findings individually, fitting them to their own circumstances, and ultimately developing them further.

Photo 3

2 The planning and direction of a training plan for a national hockey team: a case study of the Spanish Olympic squad 1976

Success in sport at the highest international level is nowadays possible only through long-term systematic coaching. Sports coaching and competition must be preceded by detailed planning, during which aims, contents, style and methods of coaching, and an awareness of efficiency-testing, are established.

After being made responsible for the preparation and management of the Spanish national team by the Real Federación Española de Hockey in April 1973, Juan Antonio Prat (Fitness Coach) and I drew up, forty months before the Montreal Olympic Games, a clear training plan of several years' duration. This plan was co-ordinated with the personal characteristics of the players concerned and was aimed at gradually developing higher levels of performance from the team. The plan was aimed at achieving this in stages, with the World Championships of 1973 and 1975, the European Championships of 1974, and the Olympic Games of 1976 as the markers of each period.

STEP ONE: DIAGNOSIS; STEP TWO: PROGNOSIS

One of the fundamentals of establishing the training schedule of the Spanish team and its subsequent successful direction was the carrying out of an objective diagnosis of the standard of the twenty-five selected players. This was done in May 1973. As far as possible, all important components of technique, tactics, physical fitness, determination and other mental factors were subjected to objective analysis. On the basis of that contemporary state of affairs, there followed a prognosis, or realistic evaluation of the possible development of performance for each individual player and for the team as a whole. The time-span considered was that up to and including the international championships of 1976.

On the basis of the results received from the diagnosis and prognosis three regular members of the Spanish Olympic team of Munich (1972), Juan Amat, Paco Segura and Jaime Arbos were assigned completely new positions in the national team (e.g. a defender became a striker or vice-versa), and were therefore required to develop completely different tactical duties. Other players in the 1972 Olympic team were dropped on the basis of the results in the diagnosis or, more particularly, in the prognosis, or else they decided to announce their retirement from the national team. Many promising youngsters who had repeatedly played well in their club teams and who also had achieved good results in both diagnosis and prognosis, were given their first chance in the national team. Only after proving their worth in practice matches with the national team were they then considered for official international matches. Of course, their debut match would never be part of an important tournament such as the European Championships, the World Cup or the Olympic Games. During the forty months of preparation up to the Olympic Games in 1976, fifteen players were given their first chance to play in a Spanish shirt. Four were finally able to command a regular place, and thus a place in the Olympic Games. Not only were their technical and intellectual capabilities decisive, but also their readiness to train regularly and devotedly, to maintain discipline on and off the field of play, and their desire to improve personal performance.

DRAWING UP THE TRAINING SCHEDULE

The diagnosis and short- and long-term prognosis of possible further improvement in a player's or team's performance were important tasks. The results obtained were to define the aims and content of the training plan. The composition of the training schedule was by no means final. In the months to follow, because of medical examinations, further efficiency testing, squad practice matches and especially international tournaments, (whether the Spanish team had taken part or not, e.g. the pre-Olympic Tournament in Montreal, 1975), there was renewed opportunity to subject the plan to critical examination and, where necessary, to alter it. This constant reviewing of the procedures and their effectiveness meant that optimal planning, direction and execution of the training schedule could always be guaranteed by those in charge.

THE CONTENT AND AIMS OF THE TRAINING PLAN

The aims and content of the training schedule for the Spanish national team were determined principally by the players' lack of certain skills, and by the extent of tactical awareness and fitness. The development of hockey over the next three years to 1976 was also important. The author was able to predict this evolution relatively easily since he had experienced several Olympic sports and had been concerned with the fundamental evolution of hockey between 1967 and 1973.

The Spanish national team of 1973 lacked certain important tactical facets. They were weak, for example, in the use of man-to-man marking, the systematic transfer of pressure, the intuitive execution of a counter-attack, and the readiness to force and then optimally use penalty corners. In addition, a training system had been favoured in which the technical, tactical and physical potential of individual players was not sufficiently used or fully stretched. If the Spanish in 1973 were to be rated in Europe after only West Germany and the Netherlands in terms of skill (despite lacking a mastery of certain important moves), they were only moderately well prepared in fitness terms.

THE PERIODS OF THE TRAINING PLAN

The blocks of the training schedule between 1973 and 1976 were always planned with the international competition calendar in mind. Time was reckoned backwards from the date of the major international championships to allow players to find their peak form and to settle down before the first match of a tournament. The timing of the period of preparation, the level of interim competition and the post-competition training phase of approximately one month, was conditioned each year by the dates of the European Championships and, when applicable, the World Cup and Olympic Games. To ensure smooth and adequate preparation for the national team, avoiding timing conflict with top players' clubs, the R.F.E.H. agreed to bring forward, or postpone as necessary, championship matches in the 'Liga de Honor' and the First Division. They co-ordinated these dates to the dates of the relevant international championships. For example, the national club championship in the Olympic year 1975/6 was commenced two months earlier than usual and was conducted in weekends of two matches each, the format of international championships. Selected players thus had the chance to experience something like the rhythm of Olympic competition ten months before the Olympic Games–granted, though, that there would also be training on Tuesdays, Wednesdays and Thursdays.

Care was always taken that one training session followed on from the immediately preceding session. A 'micro-cycle' of one week or a 'macro-cycle' of a month or more were established to ensure a continuous and systematic plan.

By bringing forward the beginning of the championship matches of 1975/6 by two months, one weekend per month could be reserved for training for the national team, and ultimately the weekends during the months of May, June and July could be used exclusively for intensive Olympic preparation. This timetable also encouraged rapport amongst the national players and with the coaches, manager and team doctor. (Out of twenty-two players and officials, eighteen lived within a radius of twenty-five miles.)

THE FIRST PERIOD OF COMPETITION

After preparative training of three months (October to December 1975), the national team played in Madras at the beginning of the first period of competition for the 'René Frank Gold Cup'. We aimed to examine the contents of the training plan–both that had been carried out up to then, and that still had to be undertaken–and to check the standard of the

Photo 4 Half-time in a training match.

Olympic candidates in international matches, particularly in the technical and tactical sphere. We also aimed to make a provisional selection for the Olympic Games. Finally, we meant to determine and test out the best tactics for the Spanish team in the forthcoming group match in Montreal (against the Indians or Pakistanis).

One month later, in the middle of the first period of competition (28 December to 31 March), with three practice matches against a Pakistan XI in Madrid, there was a further chance to try out and refine the match tactics. In order to be better able to get inside the Pakistanis' sporting mentality and overcome any undue awe at the Asian 'pros', five Spaniards combined with six Pakistanis to form one team for one match, playing against six Spaniards and five Pakistanis.

At the end of the first period of competition, plans were made to take part in the Jubilee Tournament of the Scottish Hockey Association in Edinburgh. Playing three matches against top European teams required players to adjust from one day to the next to various opponents' different systems and tactics. Their ability to adapt and their fitness standards, were tested by their playing three matches in four days—the Olympic rhythm.

THE SECOND PERIOD OF PREPARATION

No transition or rest period was planned to follow the end of the first competition period because the removal of competition stress in the month of May gave the necessary opportunity for relaxation and recovery.

In the second period of preparation, the remaining eighteen Olympic candidates (two players were by now officially named as reserves) were given the chance to build their confidence by playing on artificial turf. Three months remained until the Olympic Games, during which time the players would be shown the methods of play best suited to artificial turf, and be allowed to test and confirm their suitability.

In this respect, the wealth of experience gained at the Montreal pre-Olympic tournament of July 1975, played on artificial turf, was of particular importance. The experience was recorded for the benefit of the national squad in a 36-page booklet entitled *Hockey on grass and artificial turf–a comparative study*. This experience influenced the structure of coaching in the second period of preparation.

During May 1976, the Olympic Squad experienced the different requirements of play on artificial turf with three consecutive weekends at an indoor pitch in Bilbao, which measured 45 by 25 metres (49 x 28 yards), and then, in the following month, they travelled to Paris since there was no full-size artificial pitch in Spain. There we aimed to discover, in one training session and two practice matches against the Indian national team, whether the tactics used so successfully at Madras against the top Asian teams could be used with the same degree of success on artificial turf. On one further weekend in Holland, two matches were played against the 'European' style of the Dutch national team, also on artificial turf.

'EXHAUSTION TRAINING' AND 'OVERCOMPENSATION'

The Olympic squad was given the finishing touches for the time being with four practice matches against the West German club champions R.K. Russelsheim (played to the Olympic rhythm, i.e. two games on two days with one rest day) and with three practice matches against the Dutch national team in Barcelona, twelve days before the first match of the Olympic Games. The workload in this micro-cycle of ten days and seven matches called for a considerable expenditure of energy and resulted in noticeable fatigue in all players. The following five days, immediately before the flight to Montreal, were therefore devoted to active recovery. One additional practice match was played against a team preferring the European style of play–Canada–three days before the first pool match against Pakistan, and a further match was played against India two days before. In neither did the team go flat-out. The aim of these games was not only to keep the players usefully occupied in Montreal, but to accustom them to the atmosphere of the Olympic hockey stadium and provide another chance to experience the artificial surface. The team would also get suitably keyed-up for Olympic competition, being made aware that they were fully prepared.

The players' stores of energy were developed by organising the three weeks prior to the first group match to include exhaustion-training and overcompensation. In this way, by reducing the demands of training at that point, the stores could be replenished, not only back to the level of on the day of departure, but above and beyond this level. Peak form, therefore, was to be expected from the players between the twentieth and twenty-sixth days, i.e. during the pool matches, and this was precisely the time when overcompensation was to be at its greatest, (see chapter 3).

Regular confrontation with the best world-standard teams from December 1975 on served not only to ensure that the training schedule was constantly under critical examination, but also to observe the team and players collectively as their standard improved, and to give them important tactical and technical experience. It convinced players that there were faults still to be eliminated, and, most importantly, showed that even the best national teams had room for improvement. This meant that even the least experienced members of the Spanish team overcame their awe at being faced by the best teams in the world. In my opinion, this was a vital part of players being psychologically prepared and motivated.

INDIVIDUAL SKILL TRAINING IN THE FIRST PERIOD OF PREPARATION

Each season, during the first period of preparation and a good six months before an important international tournament, individual training periods of two months were always undertaken together with fitness training. With the help of a wide range of exercises and games, each player could practise especially difficult technical moves, or learn moves new to him. In 1975, for example, special attention was given to tackling in retreat, man-to-man marking, the flick, the wall-pass and beating a man by a sudden change of direction. These skills, either new to the players or not fully mastered, were put to the test at the end of each training session in special exercises, small games, and practice matches, and were tried out 'for real'. Finally, at the beginning of 1975, the R.F.E.H. approved the coaches' proposition to send a squad to Asia every two years in the first or second stage of preparation. This squad was to be selected from promising young players, but combined with a few regulars from the national team, so as to learn or copy the complex dribbling skills of the Asians. Eight matches in two weeks, with the same number of skill-training sessions, were to contribute fundamentally to improving the technical standard of every Spanish international.

DEVELOPING OVERALL TACTICS

In less than forty months, the Spanish national team learnt to play flexibly with modern tactics, and above all, to play successfully. Following Spain's success at the 2nd World Cup in Amsterdam in 1973 (5th) and a change in offensive tactics that seemed to be successful (Spain scored more goals in its seven World Cup matches than any other team), all Spanish club teams in the 'Liga de Honor' and the 1st Division had within two years adopted a 3-3-3-1 system, with man-to-man marking and with the counter-attack seen as the most important tactical moves in both defence and attack. Even

Photo 5 Eleven of the sixteen Spanish players who took part in the Montreal Olympic Games.

women's and children's hockey were tactically influenced.

The following year, 1974—ending with Spain's success in the European Cup—saw defensive tactics discontinued after a renewed diagnosis, and attacking play was subjected to a gradual tactical restructuring up to the Olympic Games. Both attack and defence tactics employed by the Spaniards in 1976 were proved, by the successes achieved by using them in the Olympic Games, to be the most suited to this national team.

DIAGRAM OF THE TRAINING SCHEDULE

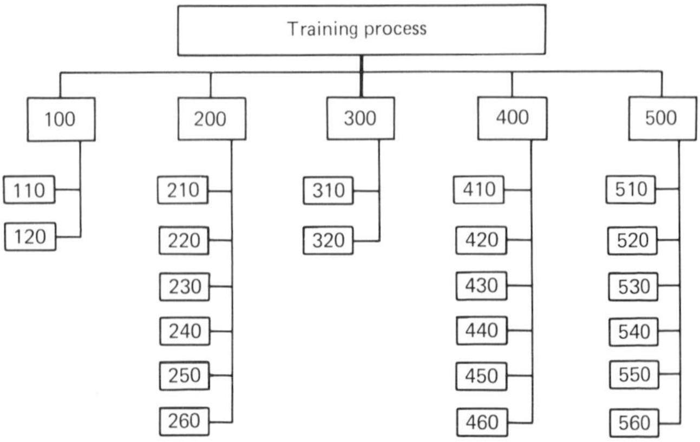

Figure 1

100 Transition period with active recovery

110 Psychological regeneration, with a reduction in the stress level by giving a 'holiday from hockey'.
120 Psychological regeneration developed by general exercises and games.

200 Planning the training schedule

210 Collecting individual performance data from the first performance test and diagnosis.
211 Collecting comparative data and comparison of the results obtained with results obtained previously under identical conditions.
220 Short-term prognosis of performance (i.e. up to the next international championships).
230 Long-term prognosis of performance (i.e. up to the Olympic Games).
240 Setting dates of training days (241), weekends (242), matches or tours (243), and medical examinations (244).
250 Collecting data for the most important international competitions in the next four years.
260 Provision of training schedule.

300 Period of preparation

310 Initial phase of preparation, with collective physical training and individual skill-training, and with specialist exercises and aptitude tests for the twenty-five selected players.
320 Second phase of preparation, with aptitude tests (321), match reports (322), training weekends (323) and nomination of sixteen players plus two reserves.

400 Competitive period

410 Specialist training for individual positions, including execution and defence of corners and penalty-flicks (as in 310), specialist exercises to develop and improve standard of performance, determining fitness since this is not possible in match practice (insufficient workload), practice matches against first-class clubs.
420 Micro-cycle of active recovery.
430 Official international matches, practice matches, training in divisional groups, and courses of instruction with strong international opponents.
440 Micro-cycle of active recovery (overcompensation).
450 Main competitive period.
460 Post-competition phase.

500 Supervision of training and competition

510 Medical supervision with examinations including analysis of results to improve training schedule.
520 Presence of team doctor at courses and matches.
530 Psychological supervision, including identification of psychological

qualities which facilitate players reaching peak performance in matches, preparation of character analysis.

540 Social supervision, including possible assistance with professional work (541), national service (542), personal problems (543) and other difficulties (544).

550 Sociological analysis of the national team.

560 Organisational preparations, with appointment of technical director, fitness coach, manager, team doctor, and joint compilation of list of points to be included in training schedule.

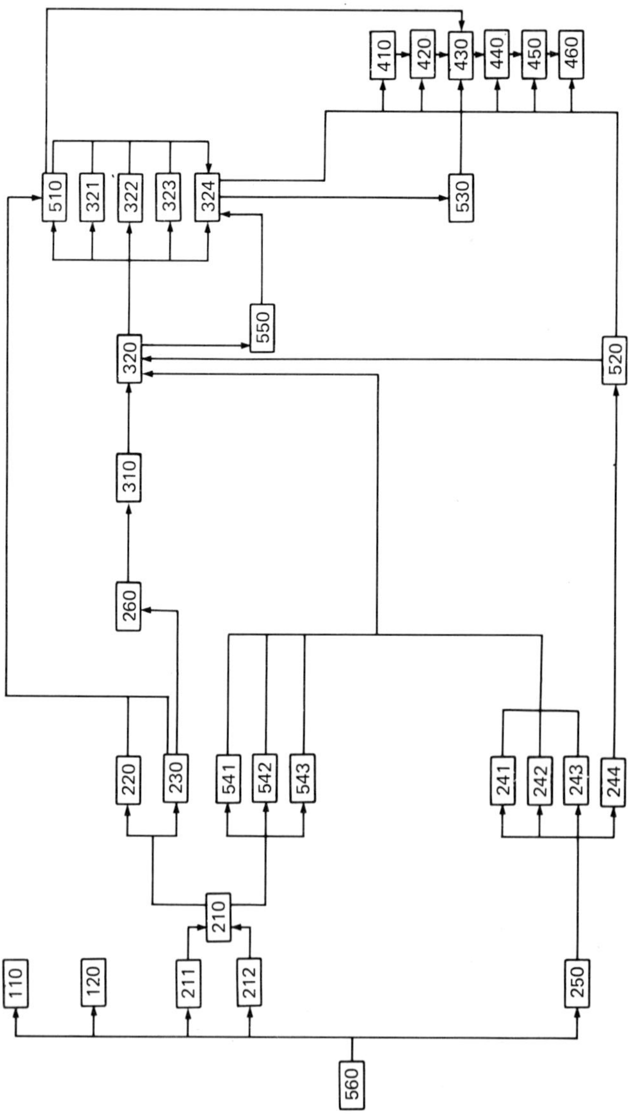

Figure 2

3 Physical fitness preparation for a national hockey team

This chapter is based, in general, on the preparation of Spain for the 4th World Cup in March 1978 in Argentina. Spain was to rank fifth behind Pakistan, Holland, Australia, and West Germany, finishing above India which was sixth. The fitness coach was J. A. Prat.

INTRODUCTORY CYCLE OF THE PREPARATORY PHASE (OCTOBER 1977)

The introductory cycle serves to re-introduce the selected players to systematic training after the summer break. But before development of aerobic and anaerobic stamina, muscular endurance, speed, and agility can take place, the effective training intensity for each individual player–in terms of aerobic stamina and muscular endurance–must first be determined in a maximum test. This should avoid players being trained with too great or too little intensity. The principal aim of the introductory cycle is to develop aerobic stamina and general muscular endurance.

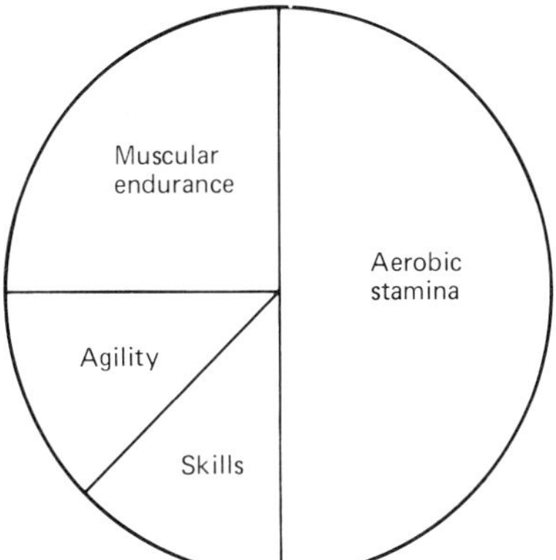

Figure 3

Aerobic and anaerobic training

Aerobic training is that in which no oxygen debt is built up in the muscles, and a steady state of oxygen consumption and supply is reached. In anaerobic training ('without free oxygen'), a heavy oxygen debt is built up, and muscular activity cannot be sustained indefinitely.

Training sessions should be twice per week, never longer than ninety minutes. Both anaerobic stamina and general muscular endurance are main concerns. The weekend includes a competitive match.

Generalised training schedule

1 *Aerobic stamina* is built up through a workload of low to medium intensity, involving distance running at constant speed through woods, across country, or round the hockey pitch, and by Fartlek (interval) training, in which running speed changes according to the terrain and the players' moods and desires.

At the first training session, the run should be of 3¾ miles (6 km) duration, which roughly corresponds to the distance covered by a player in a seventy-minute match. Each week, the distance is lengthened by a mile (1500 m). In the third week of this cycle, at the last (or second) training session, Balke's running test should be carried out for fifteen minutes in order to determine the maximum oxygen intake of each player. The results can be considered as a measurement of the squad's overall performance in fitness or as a combination of the capacity of individual organ systems such as breathing, circulation, blood, etc. According to Balke in *Medical Physics* (1960), there is a correlation between distance (metres covered in one minute) and oxygen intake capacity measured in ml per minute and kg of body weight.

Metres per minute correlate (± 10%) to	*VO_2 ml per minute per kg*
174	41
188	43
201	45
214	47
228	50
241	52
248	53
255	54
268	56
281	58
295	60
302	61

If the figure VO_2 ml per minute per kg is multiplied by the body-weight of the sportsman concerned, then a measurement of the maximum VO_2 intake in litres per minute (l/min) is obtained. Although this largely assessed and calculated figure does not withstand strict scientific examination it may nevertheless provide us with important information, for only when a player has reached a maximum oxygen intake of 3.6 - 4.1 l/min is it advisable to commence training with the intention of building up anaerobic stamina. This fifteen-minute test is to be carried out a second time at the end of the introductory cycle, and for a third and fourth time in the middle and at the end of the intermediary cycle.

2 *General muscular endurance* is improved by a circuit-training with seven or eight different exercises covering all groups of muscles. Since all these general exercises are sufficiently well-known to the players and can be

properly performed, a maximum test can be carried out.

Each player has thirty seconds to perform each exercise as many times as possible without a rest in between. The maximum total achieved by any player in each of the seven or eight exercises is noted down and rated as 100 percent (intensity co-efficient $W_{int} = 1.0$). In this introductory cycle, general muscular endurance is developed according to the intensity co-efficient $W_{int} = 0.6 - 0.8$. The co-efficient is the ratio of the repetitions to be executed to the maximum total possible for that individual.

If, for example, $W_{int} = 0.7$ and the maximum number of repetitions of that exercise was found to be twenty in the maximum test, then that exercise must be repeated fourteen times by the corresponding player within the time limit set.

$$W_{int} = \frac{act}{max} \qquad 0.7 = \frac{act}{20} \qquad act = 14 \text{ repetitions}$$

In the first week of training, an intensity co-efficient of 0.6 should be used for two sessions, one on the Tuesday and one on the Thursday; week two should have a co-efficient of 0.6 and 0.7, week three, 0.7 and week four, 0.8.

The whole group of exercises should be repeated three times at each training session with a break of two minutes between each repetition for recovery exercises. Since there is no recovery time between individual exercises, each series of exercises lasts between three and four minutes according to the number of exercises included, and the whole training schedule aimed at improving general muscular endurance should last a maximum of sixteen minutes including breaks. As has already been mentioned, the maximum test should be repeated after week four in order to check each player's progress and to reassess the training schedule's effectiveness.

After five or six weeks, a circle with new exercises should be drawn up in order to derive maximum effectiveness from physical fitness training and to avoid monotony. The new schedule is to gather information not only about a player's present standard of fitness, but also about the aims of the current cycle (e.g. particular emphasis on exercises which help to improve the muscular endurance of the legs when the team is being trained for a tournament on artificial turf).

Some general comments

1 Irregular appearances at training and laziness during exercises interrupt the progressive development of a player's standard of fitness.

2 In this introductory cycle, with the exception of the goalkeeper, speed is not to be a consideration in any training session.

3 Correct workload is the key to successful training, and leads to the body adapting itself towards an improvement in the standard of fitness. The different workloads are increased gradually, at intervals, by:

a a longer running distance in training for greater aerobic stamina;

b a higher total of repetitions in training for greater general muscular endurance;

c higher running speed in training for greater anaerobic stamina;

d greater resistance or increased weight to be carried in weight training.

INTERMEDIATE CYCLE OF THE PREPARATORY PHASE (NOVEMBER 1977)

The figure below is designed to show the proportion of training given to developing the various physical characteristics. The principal aim of the intermediate cycle is to build up aerobic stamina, with some anaerobic facets, while improving overall muscular endurance.

Training sessions should be three times per week, on Tuesdays, Wednesdays and Thursdays, with or without hockey sticks. At the weekend there should be one, or even two, competitive matches. Training on Wednesday should take place at the training centre together with other squad players.

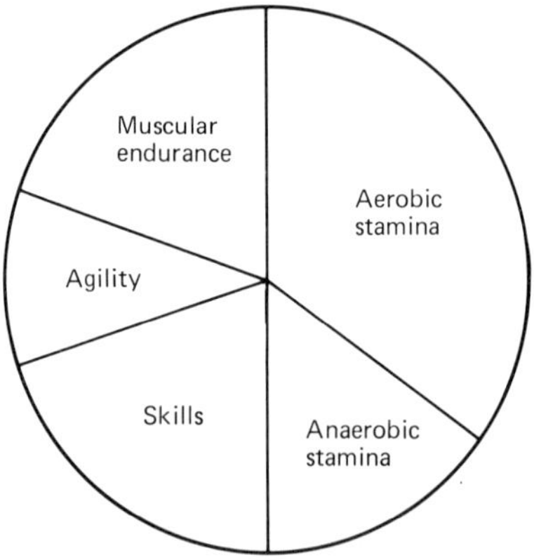

Figure 4

Generalised training schedule

1 *Aerobic stamina.* (See 'Introductory cycle'.) Along with the continuous method, the repetition method is now introduced. This is also to develop the player's *anaerobic stamina.* Applying the repetition method, each player runs round the hockey field for five minutes, and then later on the same occasion for four minutes (always running behind and not in front of the goal-posts), at 60 to 80 percent of maximum intensity (i.e. with an intensity co-efficient of 0.6 to 0.8). On Tuesdays, an intensity co-efficient of 0.6 is recommended, 0.8 on Wednesdays and 0.7 on Thursdays. After each run, recovery should be almost complete, which requires a rest time of between three and five minutes, according to the stage reached in this intermediate cycle, and according to the standard of the player's fitness.

Before the repetition method is first used, a maximum test should be carried out with five minutes running round the pitch (which is, of course, a known distance). According to the result achieved in the test (distance covered in five minutes), each player is given a certain distance to run in the next training session, or a spot on the goal-line or sideline that he must reach after five minutes' running. Immediately after the run, pulse-rate should always be taken and noted since the body's adaptation can be measured not only in distance covered in a certain time, but also by a slower pulse-rate or by a faster speed of recovery of the pulse after a given distance run. These results are to give the coach a basis for determining further points of emphasis for endurance-training and, if necessary, altering the training schedule.

In a repetition or re-examination, all external conditions should be kept as constant as possible, i.e. nature of the running surface, weather conditions and time of day.

2 Training for improving *general muscular endurance* in this cycle is carried out with an intensity co-efficient of 0.75 = 0.85 (see 'Introductory Cycle').

3 The training schedule envisaged in the 'skills' sector (as in the previous cycle) should include the acquisition and improvement of new or as yet unmastered skills, such as flicking a rolling ball over a long distance, flicking a rolling ball at the goal on the reverse, wall-passes while both players involved are on the move, tackling in retreat, beating a player with a sudden change of direction, deflection of balls crossed from the wings towards the goal, feinted passes, and receiving the ball whilst closely marked.

Flexibility, elasticity, and the ability to relax the muscles, are all prerequisites for sound skills and require frequent practice. If these characteristics are insufficiently developed, then the desired amplitude of movement cannot be achieved. Stretching and relaxing exercises must therefore be constituent parts of any training schedule.

CONCLUDING CYCLE OF THE PREPARATORY PHASE (DECEMBER 1977)

The principal aim of the concluding cycle is to increase anaerobic stamina and develop particular strengths.

One training session is to be principally devoted to increasing aerobic stamina while the others are basically concerned with anaerobic stamina.

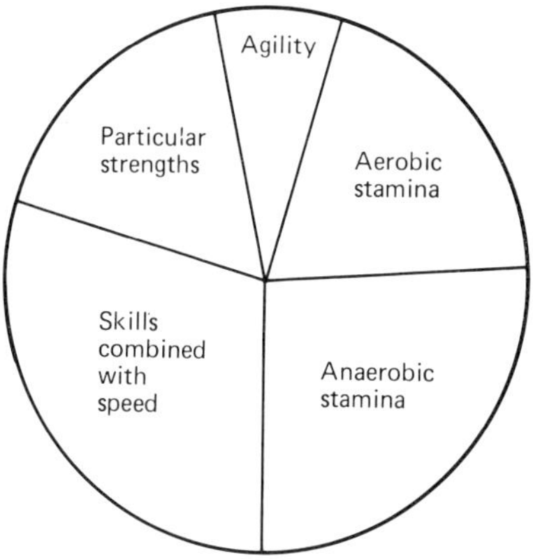

Figure 5

Generalised training schedule:

1 Training sessions should commence with a 1.8 miles (3 km) run with an intensity co-efficient of 0.5 – 0.6 (*aerobic stamina*).

2 Runs of three minutes', two minutes' and one minute's duration are undertaken with an intensity co-efficient of 0.75 – 0.85 to improve *anaerobic stamina*. The rest period between runs should be twice as long as exercise itself. For example: X covered 750 yards in two minutes round the hockey pitch in the maximum test. If on the Tuesday he completes his three two-minute runs with an intensity co-efficient of 0.75, then his distance to cover on that day comes to:

$$W_{int}\,(0.75) = \frac{\text{act}}{\text{max}\,(750)} \quad (\text{act} = 0.75 \times 750 \text{ yards} = 562.5 \text{ yards})$$

That means that, knowing the dimensions of the pitch, the player has to run once around the pitch, one length, one width, and three-quarters of another length until a point between the centre and the 25-yard line.

At the beginning of the cycle, runs of three and two minutes' duration should predominate, while at the end it is rather one and two minute runs, i.e. the player is trained to be markedly 'faster'. The total workload undertaken in one fitness training should remain within the limits of the workload of a competitive match (3½ to 4½ miles). In the final week of the concluding cycle, a test should be carried out as always, with one-, two- and three-minute runs in order to check the effectiveness of the training programme.

3 *Strength training* undertaken in this cycle should not be principally concerned with overall strength, but aimed instead at the specific demands of typical match moves. Moves (e.g. hitting, pushing, and flicking using mini-gym apparatus) are coached under conditions of increased workload, but must undergo no basic alterations of form nor of strength-to-time ratio. This ensures that the muscles or groups of muscles concerned are developed individually and collectively with typical match co-ordination.

4 The skills factor (see 'Intermediate cycle') is now combined with the time factor, i.e. all the skills learnt in October and November and mastered in December should now be carried out accurately at full speed.

PRE-COMPETITIVE PERIOD (JANUARY AND FEBRUARY 1978)

The principal aim of the pre-competitive period is to improve anaerobic stamina and develop speed.

As in previous months, there should be three training sessions weekly, combining fitness, skills and tactics. Weekends should normally include two days of league matches.

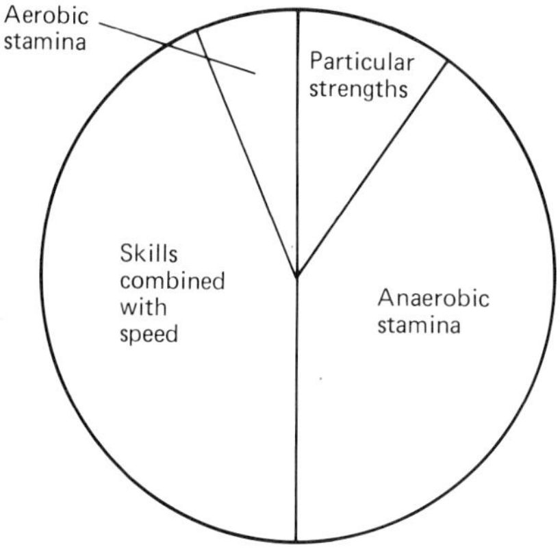

Figure 6

Generalised training schedule:

1 *Aerobic stamina* only forms part of the programme, as a warm-up run of 1.8 miles (3 km) in approximately fifteen minutes to begin each session.

2 In January, *anaerobic stamina* should be built up by means of repeated sprints of sixty, forty-five and thirty seconds' duration, while in February, these runs should last thirty, twenty and fifteen seconds with an intensity co-efficient of 0.8 - 0.9. The total volume of fitness training should correspond to the workload encountered in a competitive match, i.e. 3½ to 4½ miles. Workload should vary between greater and lesser intensity during training. Recovery time between runs should last twice as long as the short but intensive periods of exercise (interval method).

3 Training of specific *strengths* should be carried out only in each third training session.

4 *Speed* is improved with stick and ball. Each player, using his maximum strength and flexibility, should try to reach or better his previous highest speed while maintaining his technical standard. Speed-training is best done when the nervous system is keyed-up, but not tired, so it should not be preceded in a session by any tiring exercise. It should immediately follow the warm-up and encompass five to ten (maximum) runs up to a distance of 50 yards each, with a ball. So as not to overtire players too early in the training session, each sprint with the ball should follow an inactive period of two or three minutes.

PERIOD OF COMPETITION (MARCH 1978)

The principal aim of coaching is to reach the highest possible standard of fitness and skills.

Photo 6 Juan Amat (Spain) about to tackle the Indian forward with a 'jab' in the World Cup match 1978 for fifth place Spain vs India 2:0.

Training sessions should be three per week each, with and without ball. A normal weekend would include two national league matches.

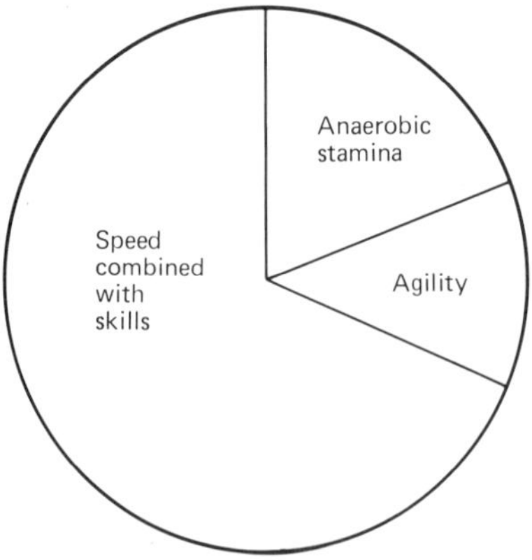

Figure 7

Generalised training schedule:

1 *Anaerobic stamina* should be built up, particularly with interval training (fifteen- and ten-second runs with an intensity co-efficient of 0.85 - 0.95). According to individual players' ability, the fifteen-second runs can be carried out from the corner of the pitch to the opposite corner-flag, right or

left goal-post, or diagonally across to the far corner-flag. Recovery time should be double that of the period of exercise. Along with the interval method, anaerobic stamina can be improved by playing small-scale tactical games which are balanced in both workload and recovery time. Skill-training will now be organised so that the interval method (the repetition of a certain move in a given time under conditions of reduced oxygen intake) will not only acquaint a player with a move and make it an automatic response, but at the same time improve anaerobic stamina.

2 Training in this final cycle is always based on the principle of over- or super-compensation. In the first half of this cycle, which can last from one week to one month, each player needs to build up his energy reserves by rigorous daily training and practice matches against strong opposition. In the second half of this cycle—which also includes travelling to where the international tournament is to be held—he will undertake lighter training and will build up his reserves of energy not only back to his initial level at the start of the final (competition) period, but beyond this level (i.e. over- or super-compensation).

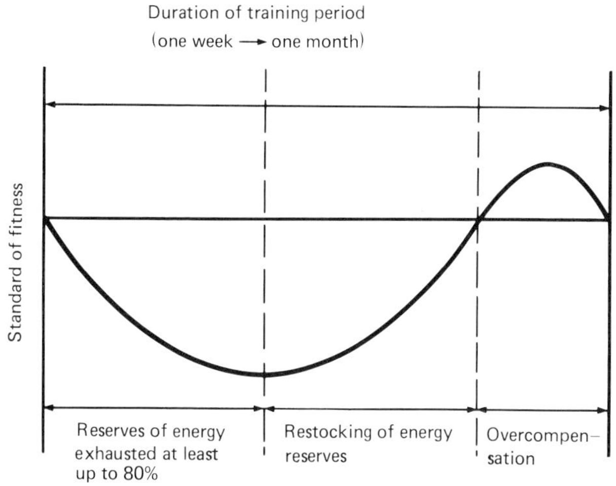

Figure 8

In order that over-compensation can occur, then in the first half of this cycle, energy reserves must be depleted by at least 80 percent. Peak form, which according to plan should be reached during the international tournament, occurs when over-compensation is at its height. The performance curve finally drops back to its initial position.

A training schedule carried out in this way (known as exhaustion-training) is highly tiring, and can be undertaken even by a top player on absolute peak form, only twice a year at most.

4 Standards cannot improve without individual training

The very nature of many sports–athletics, swimming and gymnastics, for example–demands individual training. But in team sports, such as hockey, handball or soccer, where on the whole it is the skilful teamwork of the players that decides victory or defeat, training predominantly takes the form of group-training. The contribution of individual-training (apart from coaching of the goalkeeper) to training as a whole has remained absurdly small in these sports.

THE IMPORTANCE OF INDIVIDUAL TRAINING

While it is right and proper to consider and coach the team as a unit, the coach must never forget that every team is composed of a number of players, each of whom has his own particular individual characteristics.

Group-training, which has until recently dominated hockey, is not on its own sufficient to stimulate further improvement in performance. Since it derives from the *average* standard of the team, and usually provides the same exercises for all players, it can achieve only an average and never an outstanding development in a player's skills or fitness. Individual coaching, taking into account a player's character, potential, and specific requirements of his field, will develop the best physical and mental attributes and the highest technical and tactical skills.

The importance of individual training is not yet generally recognised. Many trainers and coaches are too content to carry on with their sixteen or so players, and many are frightened by the apparent complexities involved in setting up individual training schemes. Whatever the cause of this scant regard for individual training, it hampers the development of the individual hockey player whose skills represent a basic requirement for raising the standard of the team.

THE COACH'S JOB IN INDIVIDUAL COACHING

Individual training makes greater demands on the coach than does group training. The coach must use the observations and assessments he makes during training and matches, not only to evaluate and criticise a player's ability, but also to decide how he may construct an individual training schedule for that player. This presupposes, however, that the coach is able to choose the necessary training methods, and his difficult task does not finish here. Having chosen the exercises required for the particular player, the coach has to persuade the player that his individual schedule and its

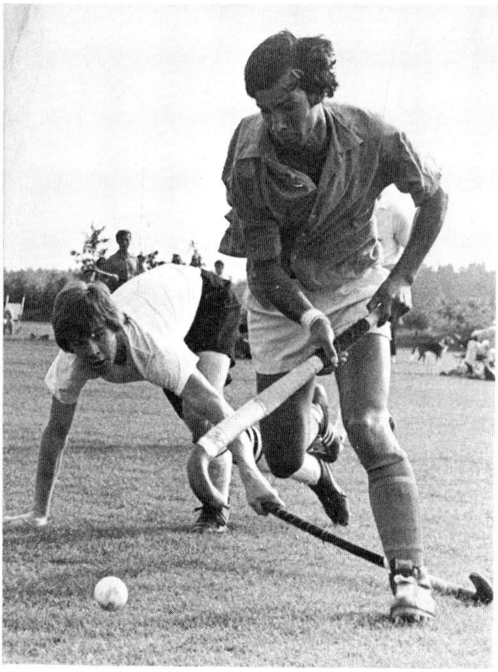

Photo 7 Wouters Leefers, one of Europe's most skilfull players in the 70s; played for the first time for the Netherlands when he was eighteen.

contents are vital to the team's success, and also work on him to eliminate his individual weaknesses and faults.

The player must not leave this task entirely to the coach. He must immerse himself thoroughly in his training. He should assist in drawing up his individual schedule, be aware of its aims, and fully understand the exercises and workload target. The player's own activity and commitments are the final determinants of whether or not that player can make a contribution towards *improving the team's standard of play by improving his own performance*.

Individual training, involving the coach's making a response to specific characteristics of a player, contributes to curing individual faults and weaknesses in technical, tactical, physical and psychological aspects. The particular requirements of a player's field position must be taken into account.

One position in which the importance of individual training is particularly noticeable, (I am ignoring the obvious case of the goalkeeper) is outside left. A left-winger must learn to master hitting across by running past the ball at full speed; he should be able to carry the ball safely even at top speed, be able to beat an opposing defender on his (the winger's) open side, and not show the weakness in tackling that is often evident in this position.

One important task for the coach is to analyse the roles and training requirements of all the positions on the field, and then draw up a list of specific functions of each position. Furthermore he should coach specialists for all set-piece moves—e.g. the accurate and hard-hitting out of corners, and penalty-corners, the hitting of short corners, defence on the goal-line at corners (to be practised with tennis balls), the taking of free hits close to the opponents' circle, taking penalty-flicks or push-ins. These set-piece moves by individually coached 'specialists' can frequently decide a match.

ORGANISING INDIVIDUAL TRAINING

The higher a team's standard, the more urgently must planned individual training be encouraged. A third of training time should be available for individual training. Individual training is most effective if the player trains with the coach since the coach can supervise and instruct continuously. The players can be alone or in groups. In groups, players with related positions (such as left-half and left-wing) or players with the same faults or with different but interdependent or complementary exercises (such as shooting at the goal and defence of the goal, or beating a man and defending), learn faster than if practising such skills alone. If competitions among the players of a group are set up, training intensity and players' willingness to exercise greater effort can be increased. Individual training, however, can also work in a team framework. Once each player, under the general supervision of the coach, has completed his individual exercises, then squad and team exercises can be set up so as to blend individual and team training.

THE SUBSTANCE OF INDIVIDUAL COACHING

The exercises that are best suited to individual training are those which are measurable by stop-watch, tape-measure, points system etc., which can give the player an accurate picture of any change in his performance. For example:

1 Development of speed in dribbling for 35 yards after receiving the ball on the run. The player should improve his speed over three months by about 0.2 secs. The stop-watch is started when the ball is received on the half way line, and stopped after a line 35 yards away is crossed. The ball must never be further than 3 yards away from the stick.

2 Either while standing still, or while running, cross the ball from the right or left wing (from various positions outside the circle between the goal and the 25-yard-line) to the 7 yard spot where the centre striker, running towards the ball from a position opposite the far goal-post, deflects the ball straight into the goal.

3 The centre striker deflects a free hit from outside the circle into the goal. The harder the ball is hit, to within one or two yards in front of the striker on his open side as he stands beside an opponent, the easier it is for

him to score without stopping the ball. The centre striker should always run towards the ball, in order to avoid an obstruction forced by the defender.

4 Use of the wall-pass between the centre striker and a team-mate with the ball, both with and without active opposition (see Chapter 11).

5 Improvement of accuracy in short corner striking and penalty flicking. Out of ten hits (or flicks), seven or nine should be placed in a one yard square that is specified beforehand.

6 Improvement of goal line defence at corners (see photos). Out of ten short corner shots with tennis balls from a distance of 10 yards, at least eight should be saved with the help of the goalkeeper. Shots that miss the goal altogether do not count.

Photo 8 A Polish defender saves a penalty corner hit from Spain on the goal line in the 1975 World Cup pool match Spain vs Poland 4:1.

7 Improvement of stopping on the run with reverse-stick. Out of ten passes that are hit out to the left wing or left half, nine should be stopped perfectly on the run.

8 Improvement of dribbling the ball with a sudden change of direction through 90 degrees, (see exercise 17 Chapter 9).

9 Use of the overhead flick against man-to-man marking at tactically the most opportune moment, without obvious premeditation.

10 Improvement of individual defence work. Ten attackers, one after the other, attempt to beat a defender standing on the 25-yard-line within a prescribed area, so that they are then able to shoot at the goal. Out of ten attacks, the defender should intercept eight. If the defender makes a mistake (or breaks the rules) the attack should be repeated (but play on if the attacker has advantage).

11 Improvement of stopping the ball inside the circle by the centre back. Out of ten crosses from the wings, eight should be stopped and pushed out of the circle within two seconds of receiving the ball.

12 Improvement of dexterity. Between the goal-line and the 25-yard-line, two additional lines are drawn parallel to them, 8 yards away from each. The player stands on the goal-line and at a signal runs to the first line, stops, puts one foot to the far side, and runs back to the goal-line, which he must also step over. He then runs from the goal-line to the second line, back to the goal-line, and finally from the goal-line to the 25-yard-line. The player is to improve his speed by 0.2 seconds in six weeks.

By virtue of the fact that players are given a definite time limit by which they must have achieved the given objectives, they are urged to greater efforts of will, and, faced with not achieving these objectives, to more frequent practice, (see Chapter 6).

A player with lively ambition will also make greater efforts if a second player has the same objective to aim at; the actual objective can be different for each player, but not the increase in performance (e.g. 0.2 seconds or 5 yards). The time limit makes the player take his task seriously and give his all. If a time limit of longer than six weeks is given, then periodical evaluations are to be recommended. Such evaluations are important to a player in training, since they make it possible for him to see his own performance improve. His interest therefore increases, and he will usually take greater pains to improve personal performance.

An individual training programme should only envisage two, or at the most three, objectives to be achieved by one player over a given period. Only when these objectives have been accomplished to the satisfaction of both player and coach, can new training exercises be allocated. If the time limit is reached, a new, but realistic, target date should be set.

Individual training does not consist entirely, as was perhaps to be concluded from the exercises proposed above, in one single exercise which is to be regularly repeated. Since any weakness can derive from many causes (lack of speed in dribbling can, for example, be caused by wrong position of the body, or the wrong position of the ball relative to the body), it is up to the coach, after he has detected the cause of a certain weakness, to overcome the fault by exercises which should be varied both to cover all possible contributary weaknesses, and to maintain interest.

5 Training without actual exercise

Many technical and tactical moves (i.e. penalty-corner hitting, taking penalty strokes, beating a man, and playing wall-passes) can be introduced and worked on without players actually using stick and ball. The visualisation of a move without actual exercise is called 'mental training'.

Mental training concerns 'a deliberately undertaken and systematically repeated imaginary confrontation with the physical objective, without some or all of the movements involved in the physical action being observably carried out', to use Kunze's definition. In this connection, according to Jacobsen, micro-movements can be observed in the appropriate muscles, and, according to Jefinow, blood pressure rises, pulse rate changes, and the peripheral nervous system is aroused. Puni made the valuable observation that mental training was crucial for accuracy, co-ordination of movement, and for perfecting sporting skills.

In hockey coaching, the following three kinds of mental training can be examined and utilised (according to Kunze).

1 Talking to oneself about the move concerned—so-called sub-vocal training. Verbalise the entire move. The player who is doing the mental training should describe the exact course of the move concerned to his coach, so as to prevent possible difficulties whilst doing steps two and three (which follow), which might be restricted by an inability to express the move clearly.

2 In the mind's eye, observing the move carried out by a top class player (inner perception training). Closing his eyes, the player, in his imagination, watches another player who carries out the move perfectly. This process can be supplemented by observation, i.e. directed observation of coaching films or video tapes of the moves concerned.

3 In one's imagination, carrying out the move perfectly oneself (active mental training). The player carries out the move in his imagination, with closed eyes, paying particular attention to the decisive factors involved in the move's success. The player can succeed far more easily in achieving an inward representation of technical or tactical moves when in a relaxed state.

There is still no definite conclusion as to the best duration for these daily exercises, although more than ten minutes per day is not to be recommended. Players who have a specific match-deciding function (e.g. the goalkeeper, the corner-specialist, and the penalty-stroke specialist) should undertake mental training immediately before competition. This should be restricted to one minute because of the high level of concentration required.

A systematic consideration of mental training should be included in a hockey coaching session for the following reasons:

1 Technical ability and tactical capacity can be improved and perfected by mental training. Of course, the effectiveness of mental training depends upon the player's personal experience of match moves.

2 Alternate practical and mental training has the greatest effectiveness.

3 Mental training is more effective than observation (of matches, films or video tapes) and can be undertaken without additional physical workload.

4 Even injured players can train mentally, and thereby avoid being too out of touch with technical and tactical training.

MENTAL TRAINING AIDS

(Running through corner-striking)

In this example, the player runs verbally through corner-striking.

Preparation:

1 I move to the opposition circle—not too hurriedly—relaxing on the way, and persuade myself that I am the best short-corner striker.

2 Having arrived at the circle, I exchange a few words of encouragement with the stopper in order to establish a team spirit.

3 I rely on my great ability as a corner-striker, and then, without facing the goalkeeper I degrade the most important player in the opposition. In doing so, I relax letting my shoulders and arms hang loose.

Run-in:
Almost immediately after the ball is pushed or hit out, I move quickly and decisively from my position towards the ball. In doing so I must be aware of the possible need to vary the last (third) step in order to be sure that my left foot is placed on the ground, to the left-hand side of the ball as it is stopped.

Hitting:
As the ball arrives and remains stationary for a split second I quickly hit it with maximum power and application and try to follow it in its goalward

Photo 9 Ties Kruize, top goal scorer in the early 70s; scores against Pakistan without preventing his team's defeat (1:2).

direction with stick and body. In striking, I take no notice of the speed and position of the runner-out, and try to 'devour' the ball.

Follow-up:
Immediately after the shot, I concentrate on following the path of the ball, and move three yards further into the circle in order to hit a direct follow-up shot should the ball rebound to me from the goalkeeper's pads or from a defender's stick.

6 Instilling commitment amongst hockey players

Every hockey player must have encountered the situation where a team or player simply cannot play as well as they ought on the basis of their technical and tactical ability, or their physical fitness. It sometimes happens, too, that a team or player performs better than expected. Either way, unexpected results frequently occur. It happens equally often that a young player of outstanding talent with a seemingly great future makes no further progress, while an otherwise average hockey player becomes an outstanding adult player who can determine the result of a match single-handed.

These few observations show that psychological factors can decisively affect, either way, the performance of individual players and whole teams. While physiological factors draw relatively definable limits of sporting ability, the day-to-day limits are greatly affected by psychological factors.

Will-power is probably the most significant psychological factor in playing sport. Since the Russian Butenko demonstrated by means of experiments that there is a direct relationship between the intensity of a sportsman's will-power and his speed and accuracy in carrying out moves, no one can any longer doubt that a player's strong or weak will-power is reflected in the quality of his play, and often in the result of a match.

Many hockey players develop strength of will-power only if expectations and objectives, or some other psychological encouragement, can be applied to a match. This encouragement should be appropriate to the psychological and personal attributes of a player's achieving a given objective i.e. winning the next league match, or an entire championship, selection for a representative team, performing better than a team-mate or opponent, justified self-approval from playing well, and sheer enjoyment and commitment to the game. These are all concepts which can affect will-power positively.

On the other hand, there is an equally large number of external and psychological factors which can affect performance and will-power detrimentally. For example, one's oponent, the weather, pitch condition, the crowd or umpires, and excitement, inhibiition, anxiety, fatigue or lack of self-confidence. These psychological pressures, of which the player himself is sometimes unaware, must be recognised, and eventually eliminated, under the influence of the coach, trainer and team-mates. However great this influence, though, it is finally up to the player himself to overcome these negative factors and replace them with more encouraging and positive aspects. This is easier for him to do if he has learnt, during training, to overcome the factors which might adversely affect the standard of his play (e.g. awareness of insufficient preparation, excessive feelings of responsibility, anxiety about his opponent, lack of interest, indifference or laziness) and to turn consciously their effect to positive encouragement.

One requirement for the successful development of a will-power which is able to overcome counter productive ideas and feelings, and realise positive ability, is the readiness to accept a burden. The better a player's physical fitness, speed, muscular endurance, stamina, strength and skill, the greater this readiness will be. If a player is therefore to be coached to develop his will-power for important matches, he must also be pushed frequently to the limits of his physical and psychological ability during training.

Photo 10 A player in training must be pushed to the limits of his physical and psychological ability in order to give a satisfactory performance of commitment in a match.

Will-power emerges only from a constant struggle with inner and outer difficulties and by overcoming them. However, if the encouragement of commitment is only undertaken sporadically in training, no satisfactory performance of determination can be expected in a match.

Players lacking determination are often to be found in teams that win frequently. Since they win easily by virtue of their greater skills or a lack of equally good opponents, few inner or outer difficulties arise which require a solution. It is precisely these players from whom greater determination should be demanded, by training them with teams of similar ability and with a suitably demanding selection of exercises. Their sporting training should also take place in rough conditions—high temperatures, rain, cold, strong winds and on poor pitches. The better the trainer has accustomed his players to handle these difficulties and overcome them, then the more successful they will be in competition, especially if they encounter conditions which are better than those they have learnt to overcome during training.

In addition, the coach should take every opportunity to influence his players' determination by efficiency testing, drawing up an order of merit, and by praise or reprimand. The continuous development of determination by the coach will, in due course, teach players to teach themselves. Teaching themselves determination is easier for players who are in competition with better and more ambitious players, since every player will then strive by increased effort to demonstrate his technical, tactical or physical superiority in comparison with players rated more highly.

Regular efficiency testing, tactical games and a long-term training schedule drawn up by the coach with many objectives to be attained, guarantee a steady improvement in determination.

Since the importance of determination is beyond question for a good match performance, training would be incomplete if determination were not developed systematically alongside the improvement of physical attributes and technical and tactical skills.

It was Puni who defined a series of qualities involved in determination, and the various symptoms of their insufficient development in coaching hockey. We must then try to select the exercises which will assist particularly in developing them, and take note of the principles which underlie them. These are the qualities: singleness of purpose, self-reliance, decisiveness, resolution and keenness, perseverance, stamina, and self-control. (See *The Theory and Practice of Body Maintenance* Book II. U.S.S.R. 1960. Translated by G. Friedrich.)

DETERMINATION IN THE HUMAN BEING

Characteristics of determination	**Symptoms of insufficient development of determination.**
SINGLENESS OF PURPOSE Under this heading is included the ability to give oneself clear objectives and tasks to be carried out.	1 Insufficient activity to achieve objective. 2 Insufficient concentration towards solving each assignment, and towards carrying out each activity which is involved in achieving the objective. Distraction, mind-wandering. 3 Inability to set oneself a higher objective after solving the assignment set and, if the opportunity arises, to change over to new actions necessary to attain this objective

Characteristics of determination	**Symptoms of insufficient development of determination**
SELF-RELIANCE AND DECISIVENESS We are concerned here with the ability to work productively towards the given objective on one's own initiative, thereby developing prudence and creative power and not allowing oneself to be influenced by other people and their actions.	1 Over-reliance on routine moves and unexceptional use of available knowledge, ability and skill. 2 Change of action brought about only with outside help or instruction. 3 Inability to take into account changing conditions of play and to see the necessity for altering one's own moves or those of team-mates. 4 Inability to adapt learned actions to varying conditions. 5 Insufficient flexibility in applying learned actions to moves required in play. 6 Inability to decide for oneself what new actions may be required because of changes in external conditions, and how to do them. 7 Inability to judge the effectiveness of an opponent's or team-mate's action without outside help. 8 Uncritical attitudes towards the advice of others. 9 Uncritical emulation of an opponent's actions. 10 Insufficient confidence in the correctness of one's own decisions, thoughts, plans and moves, and fear of their consequences. 11 Insufficient evidence, or complete absence, of self-criticism. 12 Inability to free oneself from opinions made (or imagined) in advance about one's opponent, one's own ability, and the outcome of matches.

Photo 11 The German forwards Dopp and Seifert miss a centre into the 'Spanish circle' (Germany vs Spain 2:1 in Karachi 1980).

Characteristics of determination

RESOLUTION AND KEENNESS

These we attribute to a person who can solve problems and assignments at the right moment. Resolution requires the ability to accept responsibility even if risks are involved.

Symptoms of insufficient development of determination

1. Hesitation in making decisions.
2. Not making decisions in time.
3. Insufficient consideration in making decisions.
4. Inability to carry out appropriate actions having made decisions.
5. Performing actions too late.
6. Fear of accepting responsibility for decisions.
7. Fear of independent actions at decisive moments.
8. Uncertainty in making decisions.
9. Uncertainty in actions.
10. Inability to overcome uncertainty, doubt and anxiety.

Characteristics of determination	Symptoms of insufficient development of determination
PERSEVERANCE Perseverance shows the ability to carry on a long and decisive struggle to reach the given objective, to retain energy and activity, and to overcome difficulties that arise.	1 Giving up in the face of difficulties that arise in the course of training and matches. 2 Attempting to avoid difficulties in training and matches. 3 Inability to overcome personal shortcomings. 4 Erratic expenditure of energy and activity in a match. 5 Slacking off because of failures or mistakes. 6 Slacking off because of problems of a subjective nature (fatigue, exhaustion, injury etc.). 7 Slacking off because of the appearance of unexpected problems and obstacles.
STAMINA AND SELF-CONTROL Under this heading are included the abilities to maintain clarity of mind, and to control feelings and actions in a state of excitement or dejection, of intense strain, or of fatigue, or due to unexpected problems, etc.	1 State of nervousness at the beginning of a match. 2 State of apathy at the start. 3 Refusal to continue to play when the point of exhaustion is reached. 4 Confusion or even panic at unexpected occurences in the game. 5 Dejection at mistakes in a match. 6 Depression at losing the first match, first half etc. 7 Dejection and confusion if an opponent does well (especially when this is unexpected). 8 Exasperation resulting from interruptions in the match's progress and bad decisions by the umpire.

Characteristics of determination	**Symptoms of insufficient development of determination**
	9 Dejection at growing fatigue especially if it is necessary to fight the contest even more strenuously.
	10 Exasperation or dejection resulting from interruptions by, or from reduction in the contribution of, a team-mate.
	11 Inability to overcome difficult inner problems (for example, a player wants to give a game up because continuing seems hopeless; viewed objectively it is necessary to finish the match with the best result possible).

Even when instructing beginners, coaches must teach the qualities of determination so that players can learn at an early age to deal with inner problems and external difficulties. A consideration of determination early in the training programme is not only important in improving match performances, it is also of educational value.

Exercises that make great demands on a player's technical and tactical skill, on his anaerobic stamina and speed of execution—but the mastery of which remains nevertheless obviously feasible to the player—are especially suited to training will-power. The following exercises are put forward for discussion:

1 During a training or practice match, one (or two) players are given the task of neutralising their personal opponent in his every move over the entire field of play by means of strict man-to-man marking. How often does this opponent touch the ball in fifteen, thirty-five or seventy minutes (apart from at free hits and corners)?

2 Training and practice matches with goals of different sizes, different sizes of circle, or with more players in one team, spur the players to increased involvement and commitment. Qualities of determination can be developed if the coach notes down, in these and other matches, how often individual players lack commitment. Players who lack determination are given special tasks immediately after the match.

3 In modern hockey new assignments or problems arise for the strikers, who are numerically inferior. Two strikers are often forced to take on two,

or more usually three, defenders (see photograph). In order to be equal to such match situations, the striker must be particularly coached in attacking a numerically superior defence. For example, one (or two) strikers attack two (or three) defenders for five minutes on a pitch 22 yards long, or three players have the same task, of holding their own against four defenders. Both teams can score goals, but from less than the normal shooting distance.

Photo 12 In modern hockey forwards are generally numerically inferior to the defenders as the two Spanish strikers are against the defence from Argentina in the 1978 World Cup match (0:0).

4 A further possibility for coaching determination lies in having the players carry out certain difficult technical tasks, e.g. tackling in retreat, or playing technically faultless hockey against a striker, while in a state of extreme fatigue. Eight players consecutively (in a one-to-one confrontation) try to beat a defender inside a 12-yard square, such that they can run over the back line of the square with the ball at the end of the stick. In addition, the defender is instructed to cover the striker to at least a distance of 5 yards, from the centre of the square before he tackles. After sixteen attempts at a defender, whereby each successful tackle by the defender earns him one point, the defender changes places with one of the attackers. The attacks by eight strikers should be carried out in swift succession, i.e. at five-second intervals.

5 Stopping the ball under pressure when short of breath. After successfully stopping the ball and passing it back to the server in front of a line, a player

runs 8 yards back to a marker (e.g. a fence), touches it with his stick, and turns quickly towards the line so that he is still able to stop the next ball, which is played to him in front of the line. How often is he able to stop the ball in one minute?

6 Since evidence of determination shows up particularly in tactical discipline, tactical possibilities must not be 'restricted'. Skills such as running free into space, immediate running into space after a successful pass, or the inside forward (or another team-mate) making himself available for an upfield pass along the touch-line when the winger is in possession of the ball, all provide clear evidence of determination.

7 a Sprint with the ball from the half-way line to the circle followed by a shot at goal. When the ball goes over the goal-line, or the goalkeeper makes a save, the watch is stopped. Which player needs the least time to dribble and shoot accurately at goal? The forward should not forget to follow up his shot.

b As above, but as a sprint race, with a defender who stands 2 yards behind the striker at the beginning of the dribble.

Photo 13 Hanif (Pakistan) about to curve in and cross the way of the Dutch defender who runs a little behind him (Pakistan vs Netherlands 2:1 in 1979).

8 Combination of square-pass and through-pass in pairs from the half-way line to the circle, followed by a shot at goal, timed as in 7a.

9 A player hits ten balls, one after the other, at three-second intervals from the middle of the pitch towards a flag-post goal 13 yards wide, set up on the right or left side-line. The stationary right or left winger has to stretch himself, requiring the utmost determination to stop each ball from going over the side-line and then bring it under control. After ten shots the two players change places. Which of the two players let the most balls through?

10 Three players stand in line, facing a stationary partner 22 yards away. The latter receives the ball from the first player in the line, controls it, hits it straight back to the second player in the line, and runs behind his pass (as the first player has done). When he has stopped the ball for the third time opposite the line of players, the competition, played against other teams of four, is completed.

11 Players, one to one, 30 yards apart, stand between two flag-post goals 15 yards wide, hitting to each other. After each successful stop, the ball must be hit back at the opponent's goal within three seconds. If the ball rises above knee height then the hit does not count, and the opponent is awarded a free-hit in front of the goal-line he is defending. The game is restarted in this way after a goal. Who is the first to score ten goals?

12 Competition with hits. Three against three, over the whole pitch. A goal is scored if the attacking team can hit the ball over the opposition goal-line. After a goal, the game is restarted with a hit from the 25-yard-line. The ball can only be hit from where it was stopped, or from where it went out of play over the side-line. The ball must be hit back within three seconds after the first touch of the ball. Raising the stick above head-height is not allowed. Several teams can compete in a knockout competition, and there should be a neutral umpire for each game.

13 A team of five has two players standing in a flag-post goal 5 yards wide on the opposite side of the field, 40 yards away. Player no. 1 hits the ball firmly and accurately to the stick of no. 2 on the opposite side, while no. 4 stands behind no. 2 and intercepts if the ball is not stopped by no. 2 or bounces off his stick. If no. 2 can control the ball with (or without) no. 4's help, he hits the ball back to no. 3 as quickly as possible. After each hit, the player concerned sprints to the opposite side so that he reaches his place behind the front man in time to cover him as the ball arrives. If a player does not stop the ball clearly, hits it inaccurately, or is too late to assist his partner, then he loses one point.

14 Sprint competition for the ball. Three players stand 2 yards apart on

the half-way line. The man in the middle has the ball. After he has passed into space in the direction of the circle, the two players outside him try to reach the ball first and score a goal. (Variation: the player who can pass the ball back to the middle-man is the winner.)

15 Relay race. The first player in each group of three dribbles the ball from the half-way line to the 25-yard line. After he has dribbled to the right or left around a flag-post set up there, he hits the ball back to the second player. Player no. 2 proceeds as the first player. If the player standing on the base-line (half-way line) stops the ball before it crosses the line, the team concerned is disqualified. Once each player has stopped, dribbled, and hit the ball ten times, the competition is over. One or more teams are given a handicap or have one player less (fig. 9). By means of increased determination, the players of the handicapped teams should try to make up the deficit before the end of the relay. Because they lack a third player, their recovery time between each of the ten runs is reduced.

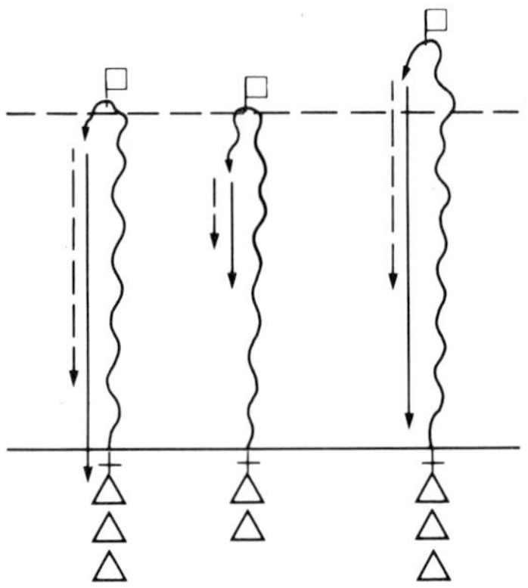

Figure 9

In all these exercises, the coach should apply the principles which make constant demands on a player's will-power. He should:

1 Produce competitive situations.

2 Introduce regular efficiency tests, and draw up orders of merit; e.g. for flicking or pushing the ball as far as possible, for the time taken for a pair to attack from the half-way line up to the goalkeeper making a save, for the number of consecutive successful saves made by a defender against one or two strikers, for the defensive reactions of a goalkeeper at short corners.

3 Strictly supervise the completion of assignments he sets.

4 Praise and encourage, but also give sharp reprimands if determination is lacking.

Again and again after training, and after each match, the coach must ask himself how positive an effect the tasks he has set to coach will-power have had on the determination of individual players, and on the team as a whole. The following considerations may help coaches to determine the current state of their players' determination, and its development:

1 The way a player accomplishes the tasks set by the coach, that is, the number of repetitions of an exercise, speed and accuracy of carrying them out.

2 Whether he completes the tests on his own without renewed encouragement.

3 Whether he makes further efforts to accomplish the demands made of him by the coach in voluntary training.

4 Whether a player is willing to train even in inclement weather (snow and rain, extreme temperatures) and on bad surfaces or when organisation is not all it might be.

5 The way he takes part in training and competition (fighting spirit, resolution, mental attitude, etc.).

6 The way a player adheres to a sportsman's way of life.

These observations give the coach the opportunity to evaluate critically the development of an individual player's determination. On the basis of this evaluation, he can vary the proportion of time spent on determination coaching as necessary.

7 Systematic attack or improvisation?

In hockey, what one generally means by a system is the functional disposition of players on the pitch in order to mount attacks and organise defence. This functional disposition of the players should be in no way static, but elastic, and adaptable to varying situations. In order to have success on the field, one must give players practice in those recurrent match situations which are fundamental to defence or attack.

Whilst systematic play is the basis of all defensive organisation in good hockey teams, the attack is seldom carried out systematically. Particularly in front of the opposition circle, decisions must be made dependent upon the measures taken by the opposition: whether certain set-piece moves are to be used, or whether an improvised move is called for (i.e. a 'free' tactical action as an expression of creative thought).

This question (one which must constantly be asked during coaching) is important not only in field hockey, but is a paramount question in indoor hockey. The answer should not be 'either . . . or', but 'both . . . and'.

REQUIREMENTS FOR SYSTEMATIC ATTACKING

For a team to carry out systematic attacking moves in a match certain requirements must be fulfilled—ones that are not found in all teams:

1 The basic tactical role of each individual player must be established for various match situations and drilled until it is second nature.

2 Tactical discipline must be demanded of the players, in accordance with the tactical principles established.

3 The skills necessary for making tactics work must be mastered at top speed.

4 As well as the ability to make automatic tactical reactions to rehearsed situations, the ability to improvise is required. Thoroughly drilled standard attacking moves should be considered only a safeguard. As soon as a complicated situation arises, analytical perception of the game, and a conscious awareness of possible problems, must be brought into action so that players will select the most appropriate (and hopefully most successful) move from the many practised. Match activity therefore, even if it seems systematic, is still connected with the tactical thinking of players and their own initiative.

Photo 14 Instead of centering the ball on level with the edge of the circle, Hanif (Pakistan) preferred to run through to the goal line, draw the Dutch goalkeeper Sikking and pass the ball back to one of his team-mates who followed up the attack at high speed (Pakistan vs Holland 2:1 in Amstelveen 1979).

DRILLED TACTICAL MOVES ARE ONLY THE FIRST STEP

Here is an example of a systematic attacking tactical move, first practised in training so that it becomes second nature, and then varied. The outside right (or outside left) stands beside the side-line in possession of the ball. While the ball is on its way to the winger, his inside-forward (or link) runs diagonally forward to the side-line, in order to collect the through-pass from the winger past the opposing wing-half, who is coming in to tackle.

If this tactical move (in many cases it can be both usefully and successfully employed) is systematically practised in training without variation, then it will be used automatically by players in a match, even if the inside-forward's marker is shadowing him, or if the opposing 'sweeper' is covering the space behind his half-back. In this case, the winger would no longer be able to adapt to the difficult new situation. If schematic training allows no development of a player's personality, the winger may use a drilled tactical combination move in an inappropriate match situation. The analytical perception of the game necessary for intelligent tactical play and thoughtful reaction to an unexpected situation in actual play may be lacking in a player if this is not developed in the training programme.

It emerges from these observations that the automatic attacking or defensive moves learnt in training represent only a preparatory step in tactical coaching. After the systematic practice of tactical moves (in this case, the square and through-pass combination by the outside-right and link without opposition and then with passive opponents), practice that is relevant to the resultant game situation is a very important step in continuing tactical coaching. In addition, the tactical move should then be practised the outside-right and link with one active opponent, and finally with two active defenders and a 'sweeper'. The most appropriate solution to this match situation will be found according to the actions of the three opponents.

TACTICAL MOVES MUST BE VARIED ACCORDING TO ALTERING CONDITIONS

In tactical coaching, all possible reactions to a match situation, which naturally depend upon the opposition's movements, must be systematically demonstrated to the forwards and practised with them under standard conditions so that they finally become automatic. Practice should be carried out initially without active opponents. Then, in order to develop flair, the tactical moves that have been systematically learnt in the preparatory stage must be varied according to the different moves or play on the part of the opposition.

A player can then choose the most effective move from many skilful individual or team moves 'available' for the given match situation. By such practice, *stereotyped* activity is transcended and develops into *creative* activity. It is absurd to begin with the creative application of a move which has not previously been practised, since a player can only correctly employ what he has previously mastered.

A wing forward who, in the first attack, successfully plays a through-pass along the side-line to his inside-forward, who switches out to the wing, will not necessarily repeat his move in the next attack if an opponent reacts differently. The opposing wing-half might read the intended move by the winger and react quickly; the opposing 'sweeper' might cover the space behind the wing-half near the side-line; or an opposing defender might mark the inside-forward as he tries to run into space, making a pass to him impossible. In this case, the winger must alter the intended move, since a through-pass would now be dangerous. He must analyse the new situation, and carry out a different, appropriate, tactical move, learnt systematically in the first preparatory stage; e.g. a feint as if to make a through-pass followed by a dribble, beating the wing-half inside, or a run into the space left by the inside-forward.

The systematic practice of moves and attack, resulting in firmly drilled tactical moves, does not mean that players are hampered in their development towards independent thought and action. From a consideration of systematic attack or defence, the player learns how he can best act in any likely match problem. Firmly drilled tactical moves, therefore, represent only a kind of preliminary exercise. As soon as a difficult situation occurs in a match, it is up to the player's vision and initiative to react. If he solves the problem appropriately and automatically with a quickly-executed drilled technical move, he frees greater mental reserves for the demands of any subsequent situation but is free also to use a tactical move which requires creative mental activity and flair!

To an outside observer there is no distinction between automatic tactical moves and a move that is the result of flair. The state of a player's development will decide whether one form or the other predominates. A solution which is due to a player's experience and is carried out with little mental exertion can also appear in less seasoned players as a result of original thinking. Here are some examples:

1 A gap in defence requires a through-pass, or a sprint through the gap by the player in possession, and requires a defender to close the gap.

2 Seeing a player unmarked calls for a pass from the player with the ball who is under pressure, and for marking up by the opposing defender.

3 A striker who is free in the circle with the ball must try a shot at goal, while a defender must tackle immediately.

4 Where numerical superiority exists in attack, the forward must attack as quickly as possible, whereas the defender should retreat to slow down the opposing attack.

An experienced player with great tactical knowledge will resolve quickly and economically match situations which require a beginner to summon all his attention in order to make a correct decision quickly and still have mental reserves for further special requirements (e.g. to draw a team-mate or an opponent into a particular position), or for still higher forms of match play (e.g. feinting or concealed passes). If all moves in a match had to be pre-planned, then no high tactical level could ever be reached because match situations in hockey change so fast. It is therefore necessary to make elementary individual and team moves fully automatic both in attack and defence, so that 'conscious' tactical thinking only begins when the exploitation of an opponent's particular weakness or a solution to a new situation are required.

8 The theory and practice of counter-attacks

An open play goal can be scored in two ways—by a counter-attack, or by positional attacking. Although both forms of attack have the same intention, they differ greatly from each other in execution.

The counter-attack is a sudden attack or upfield charge out of defence beginning in one's own half. When the ball is won, space can be covered more quickly by the attack than the opposition can retreat into defence, so superiority of numbers is sometimes gained in attack. When an unmarked forward receives the ball without a defender between him and the opposing goalkeeper, he clearly has the highest possible chance of scoring. Similarly, good scoring opportunities are established with two against one, three against two, or four against three. Achieving numerical superiority is the aim of counter-attack and positional attack.

COUNTER-ATTACKS ARE PLANNED IN THEIR INITIATION BUT MAINLY IMPROVISED IN THEIR EXECUTION

Since neither the place nor moment at which the ball is won are ever approximately determinable in advance, the initiation of counter-attacks should be planned in advance through certain individual and collective actions (e.g. giving up midfield without a struggle; leaving one or two strikers in front on the same side where the opposition is attacking; anticipation of beginning an attack at the end of a successful defensive manoeuvre), while their execution remains mostly improvised. The tactical advantage of an improvised counter-attack lies in the element of surprise. Since the players themselves decide both their own running direction and the path of the ball corresponding to the move concerned—and thus remain for the most part independent of systematic planning—the counter-attack is hardly perceptible to the opposition until it happens. Nevertheless, a great deal of training time is necessary for players to be able to effect an improvised counter-attack in an economical and efficient way.

THE EXECUTION OF THE COUNTER-ATTACK

An unsuccessful attack by the opposition always precedes a team's counter-attack, i.e. the opposition conclude their attack with a technical error or a missed shot at goal. Any defender who gains the ball or is awarded a free-hit after an opponent's mistake must endeavour to begin an attack as quickly as possible. A successful counter-attack is started either by a dribble on the

Photo 15 Govinder (India) starts a counter-attack against the Netherlands 1976 in Montreal (1:3).

burst by a defender sprinting out of defence, or by means of a long upfield pass where a forward has already lost his marker while his defender was winning the ball in defence. A long pass can be played either directly by the defender concerned, or else by a team-mate nearby to whom a short pass is played first. Just at the moment when it is clear that the pass out of defence will reach the striker upfield, two or three further players must come out of defence in order to make pass possibilities available, and to gain superiority or at least equality of numbers. If the attacker with the ball, who has good control and is difficult to tackle, has seen the defender being drawn towards him, the best chance of a successful attacking move is to pass to a supporting player in space. The difficulty of counter-attacking lies in the requirement not only of rapid exploitation of numerical superiority, but also in the surprisingly quick instigation it requires immediately the ball is won. Thus, both before and during a defensive action, each defender should be sure of the position of his forward and the positions of his own and opposing defenders in order to start the counter-attack (without too much risk of losing the ball), at any time that he gains possession.

If numerical superiority is achieved by rapidly bridging the midfield area, the superiority must be reduced, so that the probability of success is enlarged. A reduction in comparative numbers succeeds because the player with the ball draws an opponent to him (see exercise on pages 94-106). In a four against three situation, therefore, three attackers are to take on two defenders; in a three against two, only two attackers are to take on two defenders; in a two against one situation, the ultimate intention of an attack with superiority in numbers is brought about—one attacker ends up free, with the ball, in an unmarked position. Counter-attacks are usually carried out with three forwards who should avoid attacking in a line. The weakness of this form of attack without depth lies in the danger of losing the ball without the chance of the forwards tackling back, thus giving the opposition the chance to counter-attack.

THE DIFFERENCE BETWEEN THE COUNTER-ATTACK AND POSITIONAL ATTACK

During a counter-attack, each player has to solve each problem spontaneously, and therefore greater freedom of action and decision is open to him, while every player in a positional attack fulfils the role ascribed and appropriate to him (see exercises in Chapter 29). Moves in a positional attack are instigated by a relatively slow transfer of the ball, in a situation of equal or superior numbers, where the path of the ball and the direction in which players are running (and their positions) are mostly planned in advance. The aim of the positional attack is to use well-drilled, collective means (e.g. hard passing between defenders while a team-mate without the ball continually runs into space) to beat man-to-man marking by opponents up to their goal.

CONDITIONS FOR THE COUNTER-ATTACK

For a successful counter-attack, not only are anticipation and speed of reaction in the switch from defence to attack crucial, but, above all, the basic requirement is that the technical elements of passing, stopping, and dribbling are mastered, even at full speed. The higher the standard of play, the more technical mistakes in stopping or passing the ball are exploited by the opponents. If technical skills and tactical ability are not thoroughly coached, the failure of a counter-attack will be due to mistakes of the attacking team, rather than to good defensive work by the opposition. The success or failure of counter-attacks is a good indicator of the standard of coaching of the players taking part.

If any value is to be derived from observations made in the last few years, then greater consideration must be given by coaches to counter-attacking. Evidence in recent matches shows that success from counter-attacks, against positional attacks, is high. In training, therefore, one should try more than has until recently been the case, to bring about the necessary physical, technical and tactical conditions for employing the counter-attack.

METHODICAL EXERCISES AND GAMES FOR DEVELOPING THE COUNTER-ATTACK

1 a Solo attack from the half-way line into the circle followed by a shot

Photo 16 Samiullah, Pakistan's and the World's fastest winger to date, beats Taylor (Great Britain) finishing his individual counter-attack with a spectacular goal (Pakistan vs Great Britain 6:1 in Karachi 1980).

at goal. The ball must be touched at least six times on the way to the circle. The time between crossing the half-way line and the ball hitting the backboard is taken with a stop-watch. Who takes less than five (or six) seconds to dribble and shoot?

b Ditto, with one defender who stands 2 yards behind the forward on the half-way line and has to try to tackle him.

2 a A ball is played towards the opposing goal by a team-mate on the half-way line, timed so that a forward starting from the half-way line can reach it before the 25-yard line and then, at full speed, shoot at the goal. Time is taken on a stop-watch. This can also be practised with a goalkeeper.

b Ditto, with one defender standing on the half-way line (with the forward and his team-mate). His intention is to prevent a shot at goal after the pass is made.

3 a A combination of two attackers starting from the half-way line and finishing with a shot at goal. Which pair requires the least time for the shot? At least two passes must be made.

b Ditto, with one defender waiting behind the two attackers and chasing after them from the half-way line.

4 a Combination of two attackers against one defender (timed exercise).

b Ditto, with one full-back 'already beaten' two yards behind the forwards (no time limit).

5 a A wing-half positioned close to the side-line tries to beat his opposing wing-forward in the opposing half of the field. The winger wins the ball and starts a fast solo attack. The stop-watch is started as soon as the half-way line is crossed, and stopped when the ball hits the backboard.

b Ditto, with a passive (then active) sweeper, who must be beaten on the route to the goal. As in a, the wing-half remains passive after losing the ball.

c Ditto, with sweeper and goalkeeper.

d As in a, except that *both* players (winger and wing-half) are now actively involved, and each should try to beat the other and score a goal despite his efforts in chasing his opponent to the circle.

6 a 'Hit and run' (see fig. 10). A hit-out team of four stands in the circle while an attacking team, also of four players, lines up behind the half-way line with the intention of controlling the ball as quickly as possible and scoring a goal. After the hit-out, all players of the 'defending' team must run to the half-way line, touch it, and try to retreat into the circle before the ball enters the goal. They must not interfere with the attacking team's progress! When returning into the circle the trainer blows his whistle. Every time a player from the hit-out team successfully makes the circle before the ball is in the goal, he scores one point. Only the hit-out team can score points. After all the players in the hit-out team have played the ball once, the teams change over. A hit-out does not count if the ball goes out of play before crossing the half-way line. If the hit-out team in any way interferes with the attacking team, they score no points. With children or women's teams, the hit-out should be taken from the 25-yard line instead of just outside the circle.

b Ditto, but with a neutral goalkeeper.

c As in a except that the ball can be passed once before it is hit in the direction of the half-way line. The pass should always be parallel to the 25-yard line. The player who hits the ball towards the half-way line has had his turn in doing so.

d Ditto, but with a neutral goalkeeper.

e As in a. The player hitting the ball now stays in defence as sweeper, while his team-mates run to the half-way line but have no defensive duties (see fig. 11).

f Ditto, but with a neutral goalkeeper and offside rule.

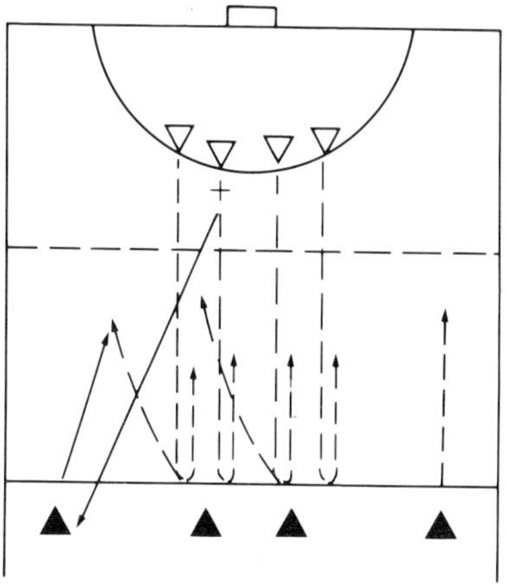

Figure 10

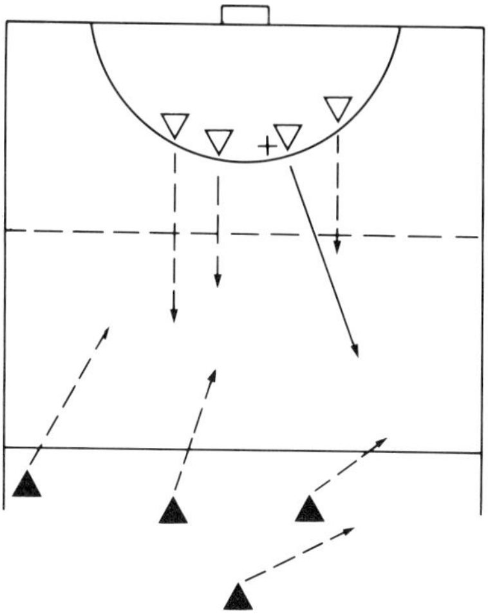

Figure 11

g As in c, except that now both players involved in hitting the ball out stay back as defenders, i.e. only two members of the hit-out team run to the half-way line in order to score points.

h As in a except that the player hitting the ball out has to run to the half-way line, while his three team-mates try and delay the counter-attack until their runner has regained the circle. This should be played without neutral goalkeeper or offside rule.

7 a Five (or six) backs defend in their own half against four (or five) strikers, who after losing possession of the ball should try to prevent any defender making a quick pass to a team-mate running free into the other half of the field. How many seconds elapse between the defence hitting the ball out and a goal being scored by their attacking team-mate? The strikers are not allowed to enter the other half of the field.

b Ditto, except that the strikers can now enter their half of the field once the ball has crossed the half-way line.

c As in a except that the backs play with a forward upfield who is marked by a fifth striker.

d As in c, with two forwards upfield, and one defending striker in the other half.

9 Advanced games and exercises for improving the Indian dribble

In Chapter 2 of *The Science of Hockey*, under 'The Indian style of dribble', the basic theoretical and practical methods for the beginner were given. This chapter, which is considered to be a continuation and gives further exercises and games as a means of mastering the fundamental exercises for coaching the Indian dribble, will gradually help the advanced player towards ultimate co-ordination and consolidation of these skilful movements.

1 Dribble the ball in stationary position in front of the body along two parallel lines 2 feet apart. Each time the ball is played on the backhand from outside the left line to outside the right line, one point is awarded. If the ball is touched with the stick between two lines, then the subsequent point does not count. How many points can a player score in thirty seconds?

The aim of this exercise is for the player's body to follow approximately the movement of the stick and ball, i.e. body, ball and stick should form a unit in dribbling, a fact that is of importance for the perfect execution of this manoeuvre especially at higher levels when beating an opponent with stick feints or body swerves.

2 a Dribbling the ball whilst walking or running slowly. The slower the player runs with the ball, the more he must try to bring his centre of gravity nearer the gound (see photo). The knees are bent forward such that the player can no longer see his toes. Only a relatively strong bend in the knee-joints will allow a quick sidestep to either side, and thus facilitate the dummy. The upper body is in a slight bend forwards to facilitate good vision.

b Ditto, with sudden bursts while the ball is played 3 or 4 yards square to one side or the other, and brought back after a powerful push off the far leg.

3 Timed dribbling of the ball in front of the body, followed by a shot at the goal. In this exercise, players learn to carry the ball as far as possible in front of the body, a fact greatly neglected in the exercises laid out in *The Science of Hockey*. Carrying the ball even further away from the body (where both arms are practically straight at the elbows):

a enhances peripheral vision and thus one's overall vision of play,

b prevents the ball from touching the foot if it misses the stick,

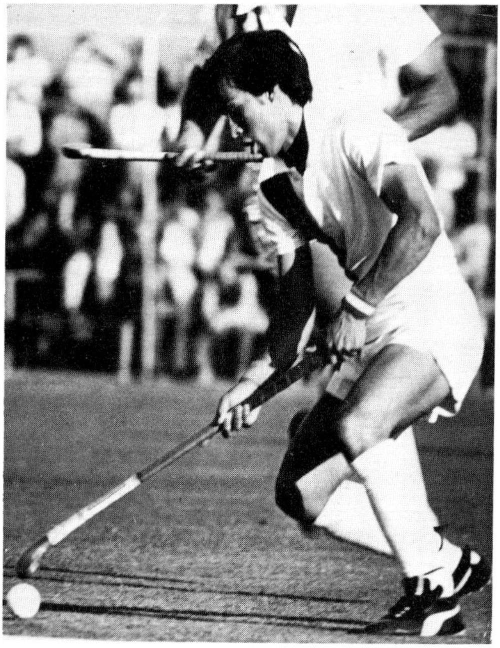

Photo 17 Leefers, Netherlands, here playing in the colours of 'Los Caracoles', with perfect positioning of trunk and limbs while dribbling the ball at low speed.

c allows the player to feint with both stick and body, and

d allows fast running with the ball.

Which player requires the least time to dribble from the half-way line to the circle and shoot?

To allow rapid movement, the player has to dribble in a more upright position, but with the upper part of his body inclined further forwards than in exercise 2.

4 Dribbling the ball in front of the body in a slalom of eight flag-posts (set 6 yards apart) *with* oncoming players. The flag-posts are set up one behind the other in a line.

5 Dribbling round flag-posts which are erected in a very curved line 2 or 3 yards apart (similar to ski-ing), such that even an agile and nimble player has difficulty in running through the slalom course as quickly as possible without touching the flag-posts. Because of the many sudden changes in direction, the player has to dribble the ball in a 'stooped ski-ing position'.

6 Dribbling in pairs (between 4 and 10 yards apart) with hard surprise passes with both forehand and backhand into the partner's path, who then proceeds with an Indian dribble on receiving the ball. This can be practised

with two balls simultaneously, which develops not only speed, but also vision.

7 *'Demonstrate and imitate'.*
Two players each have a ball, and the second must imitate the movements of the first player running in front of him, who is allowed only to dribble at half speed, with as many changes of direction as possible.

8 *'Cops and robbers'.*
Two 'cops' chase the 'robber', who has 5 yards' advantage inside the field between the 25-yard and the half-way line. Each player has a ball. The 'cops' must try to touch the 'robber' with their sticks (or free hand) as soon as possible, while keeping perfect control of their ball. Which 'robber' can avoid the 'cops' for the longest time?

9 *'Tag' in a restricted area, one against three.*
By changing speed and direction, three dribbling players try, without leaving a 12-yard square, to avoid being 'tagged' by the stick of a fourth player, who is dribbling a ball. When a player is 'tagged'–the catcher keeping control of his ball at the same time–then he too becomes the catcher, but cannot 'tag' his predecessor. Any player who loses his ball whilst running from the catcher becomes the catcher.

10 *'Cat and mouse' as a team competition (fig. 12).*
Instead of in one area, the game is now played in two areas of equal size set next to one another, with in each three 'mice' being chased by two 'cats' from the other team. Only when both 'cats' have 'tagged' two of the three 'mice' in their restricted area ('tagged' players carry on dribbling) are

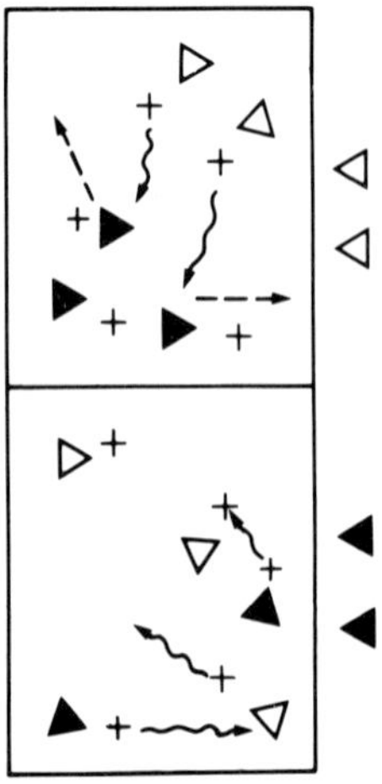

Figure 12

they allowed to return to the base in order to let the next two 'cats' in. Which of the two competing teams of four 'cats' (and three 'mice') can first 'tag' successfully four times?

11 *'Criss-cross cat and mouse'.*
Played in one half of the pitch with four 'mice' and one 'cat'. All players have a ball. The 'cat' must always 'tag' the 'mouse' who last crossed between him and the 'mouse' trying to escape.

12 *'Breaking out of the cage'.*
Eight players (two teams of four) dribble a ball inside a 10-yard square that is marked out in the middle of the pitch. Each player has a personal opponent in the other team. When one team's name is called out, its players run as quickly as possible to one of the side-lines or goal-lines of the full-size pitch in order to cross it before they are tackled by their opponent chasing them with the intention of bringing the ball back to the square. Every time a line is crossed, or every ball that is brought back to the square, scores one point for the team concerned. Players dribbling a ball should try to shake off their opponents with one or more sudden changes of direction.

13 *'Black or white'.*
On the half-way line, a maximum of six pairs stand opposite each other, each player with a ball. Each player's left shoulder points towards the goal he should attack, and his right shoulder points towards his partner. After one team's colour is called out, the players of that team should try to dribble their ball into the circle and score a goal, while the players of the other team must leave their balls and chase their opponents in order to win the ball and dribble it to the half-way line. Instead of calling out a colour immediately, the coach can also give a running commentary in which words are used that have some association with the colours black and white, e.g. snow, ski-ing, coal, bride . . . death!

14 *Dribbling the ball in a triangle.*
The ball runs along the lines of an isosceles triangle in front of a player's body. The baseline of the triangle runs between each player's feet, one yard in front of his body. For each side of the triangle, which is almost one yard, the ball can only be touched once with the stick. The feet may be moved.

15 *Triangle dribbling with break-out.*
The ball moves as in the previous exercise with few touches inside the triangle, until it is suddenly dribbled out of the triangle, forwards, backwards or sideways, with a sudden change of pace, initiated by pushing off from the

outstretched foot. As a variation, the break-out can also be made when a visual or aural signal is given.

16 *'V-shape'.*
A player draws with the ball a 'V' on the ground starting from the intersection of the two lines, first forwards to the left, then backwards, and finally diagonally to the right and back again to the intersection. When he arrives at the end of a line at the top of the 'V', he pulls the ball back with a quick turn of the body, pushing off his outstretched foot. The ball should be touched at the top of the 'V' with reverse (left line) or with forehand (right line) only once and should again be controlled in the intersection. The player, by keeping his centre of gravity low and by bending his legs sharply at the knees, should not stop the ball as he turns, but should play the moving ball by pushing it suddenly in the opposite direction, so as to achieve surprise.

17 *Efficiency test (speed, dexterity, muscular endurance, and skills).*
From the intersection of two 3-yard lines, a player runs to the end of one line, turns after he has reached the end of the line, dribbles as quickly as possible round the intersection to the end of the other line, and without stepping into the area inside the right angle, returns to the intersection (fig. 13). Each 3-yard dribble from the intersection to the end of a line or vice versa scores one point. How many points can the best player score in thirty seconds?

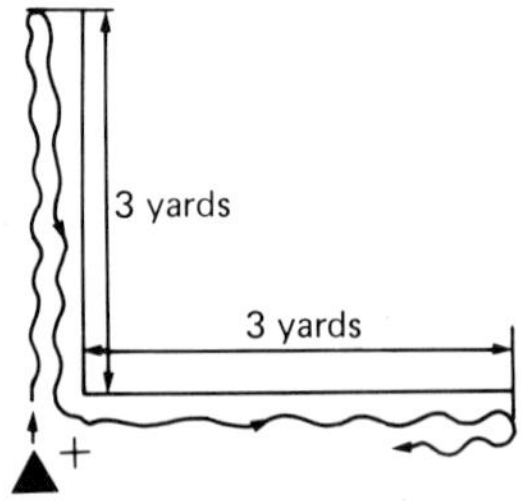

Figure 13

18 *Changing directions.*
Each player has a ball which he dribbles forwards in a straight line until an agreed signal, 'right' or 'left', is given. He then immediately turns from his straight course through approximately 45 degrees to one side and pulls the ball backwards (as in the 'V-shape' exercise) when he receives the second signal.

19 *Beating a passive defender by means of a sudden change of direction.*
A passive defender stands in the middle of a flag-post goal 20 yards wide. When an attacker breaks from his straight run and tries to dribble through the goal between the defender and one flag-post, the defender attempts to close the gap by taking a few steps to the right or to the left. Then, with

the defender taken to one side, the attacker suddenly draws the ball in the opposite direction, and runs past his opponent through the goal without coming within tackling range.

20 *Beating a semi-active defender by means of a sudden change of direction.* A semi-active defender stands in a 10 yards wide goal beside the right- (or left-) hand post with a forward 10 yards in front of the left- (or right-) hand post. The forward dribbles at top speed straight at the goal, in order to cross the goal-line before the defender can tackle. Dependent upon the position of the defender, the forward either dribbles into space across the goal-line, or keeps out of the defender's range with a sudden change of direction into the space previously covered (fig. 14). Should his first change of direction not have been successful, the attacker should try to change his direction a second time in order to shake off the defender.

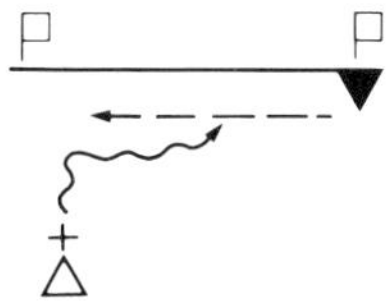

Figure 14

21 *Beating an active defender between the 25-yard and half-way line by by means of a sudden change of direction.*
An attacker starts a solo run from the half-way line towards a defender blocking his path 5 or 10 yards in front of him. Instead of running directly at the defender, the forward suddenly runs into space using the width of the full-sized pitch. If the forward, despite his speed, cannot gain any advantage because the defender is close, he must suddenly change the direction of his dribble, stop abruptly, and with a sudden burst of speed sprint in the opposite direction. If stopping and changing direction are properly executed, the defender will lose 0.1 or 0.2 of a second in reacting to the forward's movements. Should his first change of direction not have been successful, then the attacker must try a second sudden change of direction with the ball, in order to cross the 25-yard line unimpeded. A forward's most common mistake when running with the ball is to get too close to a defender.

22 *Beating active defenders by means of sudden changes of direction in a game of three against three.*
Played between the half-way line and the 25-yard line, using the width of the pitch. The opponents' line must be crossed with the ball at the end of the stick.

23 *Skilful running* (see Chapter 4 exercise 12, and *The Science of Hockey*, pp. 225-6 exercises 1 and 2).

Photo 18 Beating a defender by means of a sudden change of direction–preparatory phase (Germany vs Canada 4:3 in Buenos Aires).

Photo 19 Beating a defender by means of a sudden change of direction–final phase.

24 *Games for transferring pressure.*
(4:2, 5:3 and 4:3). (See page 82.)

25 *Three against three, with four goals 12 yards wide.*
Each team defends two goals opposite each other, and at the same time attacks the two goals defended by the opposition. The ball must be carried over the line at the end of the stick (fig. 15). Two players should defend one goal each, while the third member of each team acts as a midfield player assisting the defender whose goal is threatened. When possession is gained, the goal that is defended by only one defender should be attacked. By sudden changes of direction when dribbling, this one-at-one goal situation can easily be brought about.

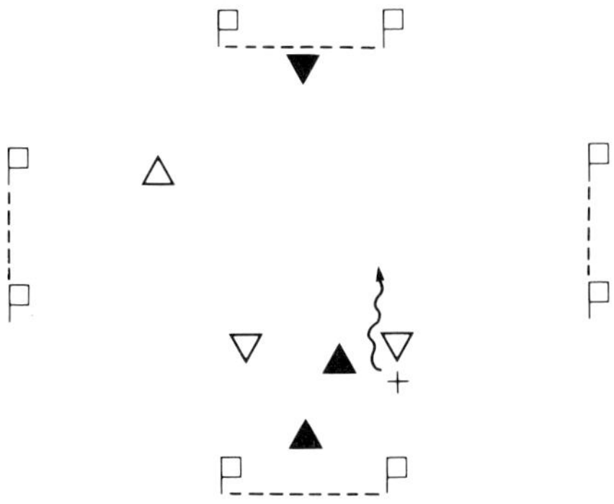

Figure 15

10 Scoring goals

Forwards are often found to be lacking when it comes to making the most of goal chances. In many cases, this can be traced back to the planning stage of a training programme that includes shooting practice. More often than not, shooting skills are still practised without any opposing outfield player and with only a goalkeeper to beat, a situation which helps neither the goalkeeper nor the player shooting at goal to improve his skills.

Shooting practice should always be carried out under conditions as close as possible to the real game situation, so that a player is not so unprepared when a chance to score suddenly presents itself, as is usually the case. A player should learn to recognise the build-up to a shot at the goal through regular practice under match conditions, and to score goals despite a hastily taken shot or the attentions of an opposing player. Shooting exercises should be organised so that forwards and defenders alike have no advance warning of a particular move's build-up and execution, but learn, in ever-changing match situations to make quick decisions.

All the following shooting exercises are based upon typical attacking moves that occur frequently in competitive matches. By practising these exercises regularly in training, attacking players will gain a wealth of practical and theoretical experience in a short space of time, which will help them to make better use of chances at goal in future games.

So that strikers learn to get their shot away even at top speed, all the exercises should first be mastered in their most simple form. An extra player (e.g. a sweeper) can then join in at a later stage to make it more difficult to shoot and score. It is up to the coach to observe closely each player's technical skills and tactical awareness as he practises so that he can give advice or make corrective comments if necessary. Comments should always be brief if an exercise is actually taking place, and any lengthy pieces of technical or tactical advice should be withheld until an attack has finished. The coach's observations can then be incorporated into the exercise and practised under less demanding conditions if necessary (for example, with defenders who are not fully committed in the tackle). A coach should not make too many comments, however, as this will inevitably lead to his players' attention straying from the task in hand and to a reduction in their willingness to listen to advice. This in turn will restrict the learning process and the acquisition of experience which can later be put to practical use.

EXERCISES INSIDE THE CIRCLE

1 *Shooting at goal without a defender.*

Three forwards have a competition to see who can score the most goals starting from the 25-yard line in the inside-forward and centre-forward positions. Each has four seconds to dribble into the circle (but no further

Photo 20 Ties Kruize scores the Netherland's first goal in a 1974 test against Belgium.

than 2 yards inside) and shoot past the goalkeeper. Each forward should follow up his shot if the goalkeeper makes a save, while the goalie must try to kick, hit, or flick the ball out of the circle parallel to the goal-line.

An attack is finished when the four-second time limit expires, or if the ball is played out of the circle by the goalkeeper. The attackers have four extra seconds to score if the first shot is saved and they should change starting positions when each has attacked once. Which forward can score three goals first?

2 *Shooting at goal after beating a defending player.*
The defender starts the game by hitting the ball from the penalty-corner mark on the goal-line through posts 11 yards apart on the 25-yard line. An opposing forward has to try to stop the ball crossing the line, dribble into the circle and score a goal within six seconds in spite of the defending player's attempts to tackle (see fig. 16).

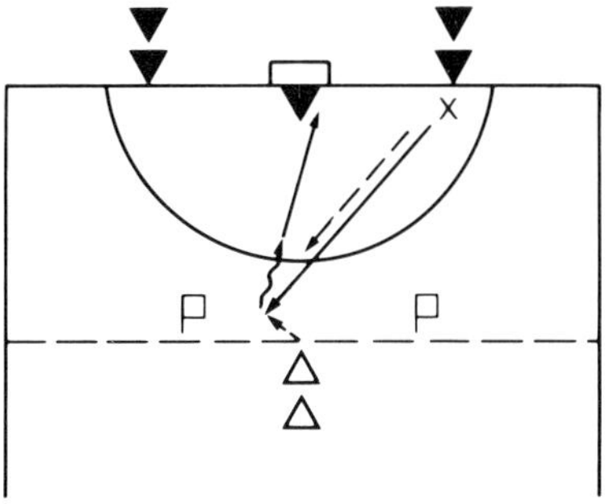

Figure 16

The goalkeeper and defender should aim to clear the ball out of the circle. The defender's initial hit should be hard, flat along the ground, and aimed just inside the goal posts on the 25-yard line. Whenever the forward fails to stop the ball, loses it to the defender who clears it out of the circle, or misses the goal with his shot, the two players should change places. Which player is the first to score three times?

3 *Two attackers against one defender and the goalkeeper, with a time limit.*
The two forwards start their attack from the 25-yard line with the defender standing at the top of the circle. By using any combination of passes (e.g. square ball with the defender drawn in the opposite direction, dummy square pass, scissors movement followed by a square pass to the other forward running into the first player's starting position as in fig. 17) the forwards have six seconds to beat the defender, dribble into the circle and shoot at the goal. Both players should follow up until either a goal is scored or the ball is cleared out of the circle. The game is played with the off-side rule. Which is the most effective attacking pair? Possible variations: (a) A forward who loses the ball or shoots wide immediately takes over as defender; (b) As long as the forwards can get their shot away within the six-second time-limit, they keep their attacking role whether a goal is scored or not; or, (c) No hitting of the ball is allowed in this exercise. A goal earns the two attacking players one point each. Which of the three players is the first to score six points?

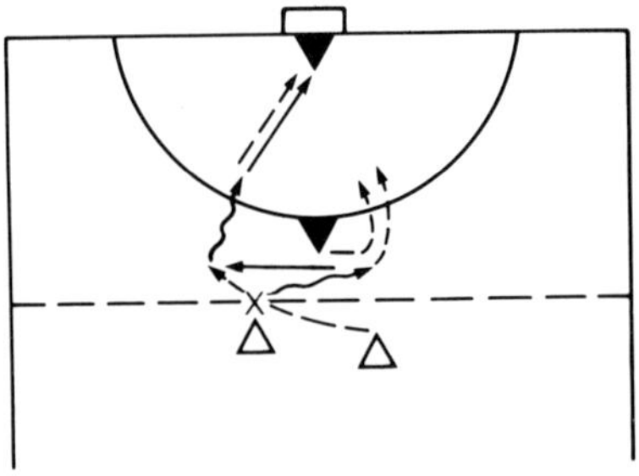

Figure 17

4 *Four attackers against two defenders and a goalkeeper, with a time-limit.*
The forwards again start from the 25-yard line, with the defenders standing at the top of the circle. The forwards have eight seconds to finish their attack. What is the most effective attacking movement? The game is played according to the offside rules.

5 *Three attackers against two defenders and the goalkeeper, with a time-limit.*
This exercise limits the defenders to the area of the circle, making it easier

for the three forwards to build up their attack. Once again, the offside rules are to be followed. One possible variation on this is that the defenders are no longer restricted to the circle. How many goals can the three forwards score in ten attacks?

6 *'Change and change about'* (4:3).
Four attackers take on three defenders and the goalkeeper. The four forwards lose their turn to attack if the ball crosses the goal-line, side-lines or 25-yard line from a forward's stick. If they fail to get a shot at goal within twenty seconds, they again lose their turn to attack. When this occurs, three of the attackers should change places with the defenders, while the fourth forward remains in attack.

To begin with, the defenders should allow the four forwards to build up their attack by not setting foot outside the circle (fig. 18). If they win possession, they should aim to pass the ball to the coach who watches proceedings from the 25-yard line. One possible variation is that the defenders are allowed to tackle wherever they like. The game is again played with the offside rule.

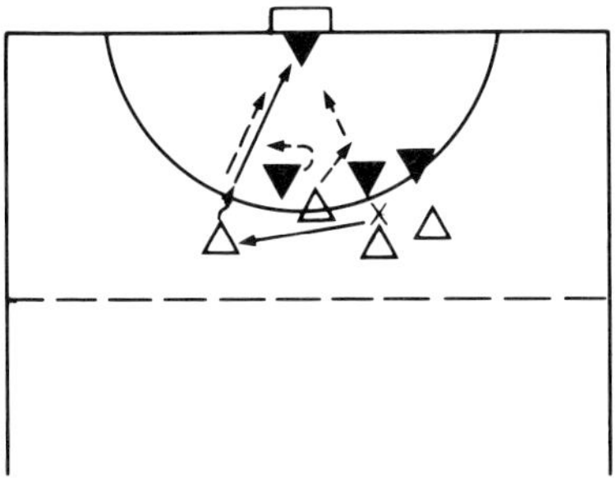

Figure 18

7 *'Change and change about'.*
Three against three and the goalkeeper. This game is played according to the rules given in exercise 6, beginning with a free hit on the 25-yard line, but with one exception. So as not to lose their turn to attack, the forwards have twenty seconds to shoot at the goal or at least force a short corner. Instead of actually conceding a short corner, any defender's mistake results in his not being allowed to defend during the next twenty-second attack.

A possible variation on this is that if the defenders succeed in winning the ball and keeping possession for a minimum of two passes, it becomes their turn to attack.

8 *Attacks with neutral wingers, four against two (five against three or five against four) in one half of the pitch* (see also exercises 1 to 5 in Chapter 12).
Two inside-forwards and two neutral wingers attack a goal guarded by two defenders and a neutral goalkeeper. After a goal is scored or a shot is saved,

the two defenders should try to dribble the ball over the half-way line with the help of the two neutral wingers, despite the tackling of the two inside-forwards who take up defensive duties on losing the ball (see fig. 19). Once the players are well acquainted with this exercise and the various tactics involved, attacks should be carried out with time-limits imposed. If it takes the forwards more than ten seconds to work a shot at goal, then they must give the ball to the defenders who attack with the help of the two wingers. One point is awarded to each defender who succeeds in dribbling over the half-way line and to any forward who is able to force his way into the circle. Two points are awarded for a goal, as long as no player is in an offside position!

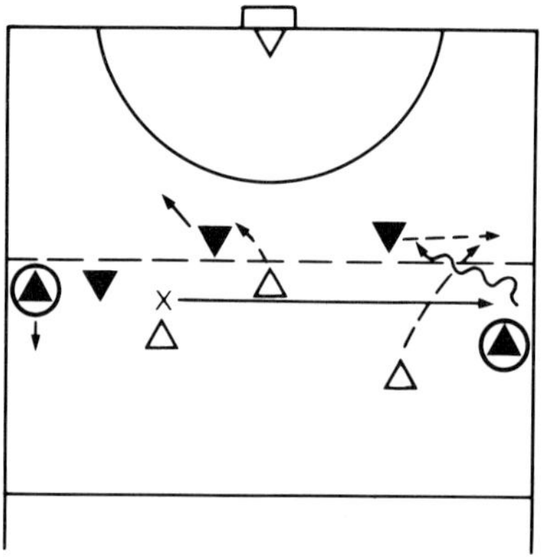

Figure 19

9 *Attacks involving the wing-halves.*
Three teams of three players each compete in one half of the pitch. The three forwards of team A are marked man-to-man by the defenders of team B. In addition, team A has three players in the midfield: one in possession of the ball and 2 wing-halves (see fig. 20). As soon as the player with the ball makes a successful pass of at least 11 yards to one of his forwards, the nearest wing-half should sprint upfield along the side-line. The attacking team now has a numerical advantage and must aim to enter the circle and score. At the same time, the other two players in the midfield stay back in defence to cover in case possession is lost.

A possible variation: the game can be played with only two forwards and two defenders. This reduction in the number of players makes the forwards' task easier and makes greater demands on the defenders, who change from man-to-man marking to zonal marking once a forward gets in possession of the ball.

10 *Attacks involving a midfield player.*
This game is played in one half of the field with a goalkeeper defending the

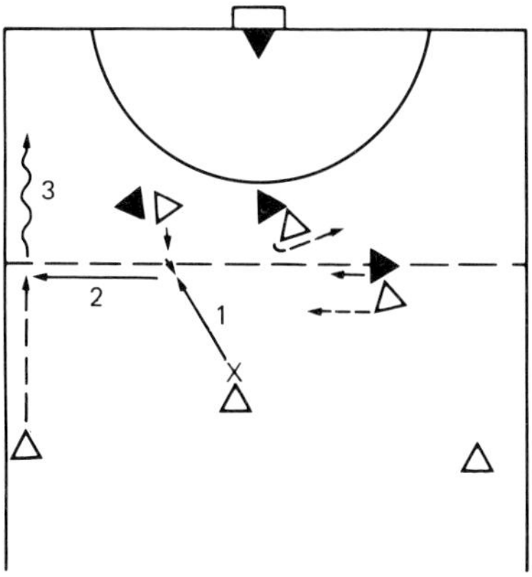

Figure 20

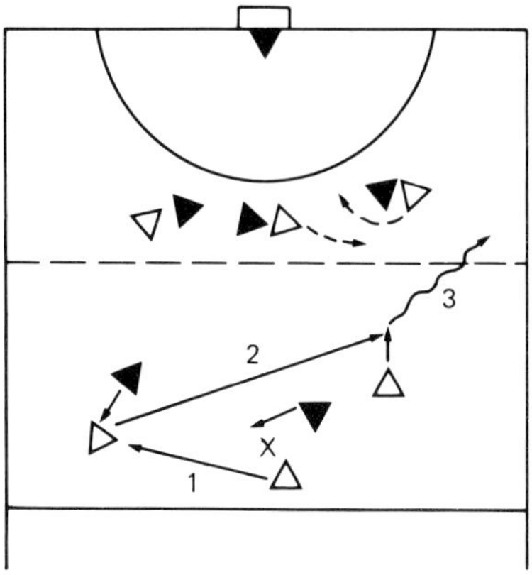

Figure 21

goal. Three midfield players have to beat two defenders between the half-way line and 25-yard line in such a way that one of them is able to dribble into the 25 or pass the ball over more than 11 yards straight to one of three marked team-mates running into space (fig. 21). The ratio of midfield players to defenders between the half-way line and the 25 can be increased to four to two, or four to three according to the players' standard. Another alternative is instead of only one midfield player being allowed to cross the 25-yard line, two midfield players and one defender may do so.

11 *Counter-attacking with four against three (or five against four).*
Two teams of 6 players are engaged in one half of the pitch with a single goal defended by the goalkeeper. On the half-way line and on the 25-yard line, there are three pairs of players with one of each pair from either team (see fig. 22). Between the two lines is a seventh (neutral) player in possession of the ball. Without making his intention obvious, he passes the ball towards the half-way line and as he does so, the nearest pair sprint away from the

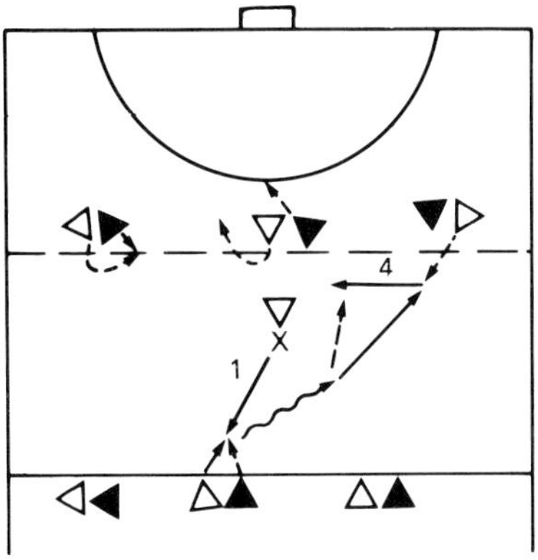

Figure 22

line. Whoever reaches (touches) the ball first is on the attack (whilst his personal opponent has to stay inactive) and his team-mates should then attempt to shake off their markers in order to be available for a pass or to make space for another team-mate to run into. It is up to the forwards to score a goal by virtue of having one man extra, while the defenders should try to regain possession and pass the ball back to the player who originally lost the ball on the half-way line.

One variation: it is recommended that this exercise is first played with only 4 men in each team. It then becomes easier for the players to start their move and they are involved in the action for greater periods of time.

Another variation: the player originally not touching the ball on the half-way line can tackle back until the move is completed. One of his team-mates should leave the half-way line to give him support as the attack develops.

Photo 21 Juan-luis Coghen (Spain) misses a great chance to put his team 3:0 in front against Australia in the Champions Trophy 1980 (Spain vs Australia 2:2).

11 The methodical development of the wall-pass and first-time pass

GAMES AND EXERCISES

1 *Wall-pass game with a partner standing opposite.*
When making a first-time or wall-pass, make sure that the upper part of the body is over the ball, that the right hand is gripping the stick lower down the handle than usual, and that the stick is as vertical as possible, to avoid the ball bouncing over the head of the stick.

2 *Wall-pass combination with a partner, 10 yards apart.*
This is practised from goal-line to goal-line. How many mistakes occur in dribbling to the end of the pitch and back, or how much time does the best pair take for one length of the pitch? The ball should be passed at least four times between the goal-line and the 25-yard line, and between the 25-yard line and the half-way line. If the ball is controlled before playing or not properly stopped, then the attack does not count, and the players must repeat the exercise. The ball should always be played towards the left-hand player's back leg, since he can only make a wall-pass if the ball is somewhat behind his body. On the other hand, the ball should be passed into the path of the right-hand player just in front of him. In order to make the players look up from the ball while running and passing, the exercise should be started from both goal-lines simultaneously.

3 a *Three players standing in a triangle pass the ball first-time between them without stopping the ball; the distance of the players from each other should be less than 6 yards.*
How many first-time passes can be made clockwise or anti-clockwise without a mistake? Which team of three has the best record in three minutes?

b As in 3a, but players are not allowed to stay on the same spot for more than three seconds, and should make themselves available for a return pass immediately after passing by setting off into space.

c Ditto, but playing in one specific direction followed by a shot at goal from inside the circle.

4 a *Three against one on a pitch of reduced size.*
According to the situation, the player receiving the ball must decide whether to risk a first-time pass (wall-pass) or stop the ball first. While each first-time pass (wall-pass) to a team-mate counts one point, a pass

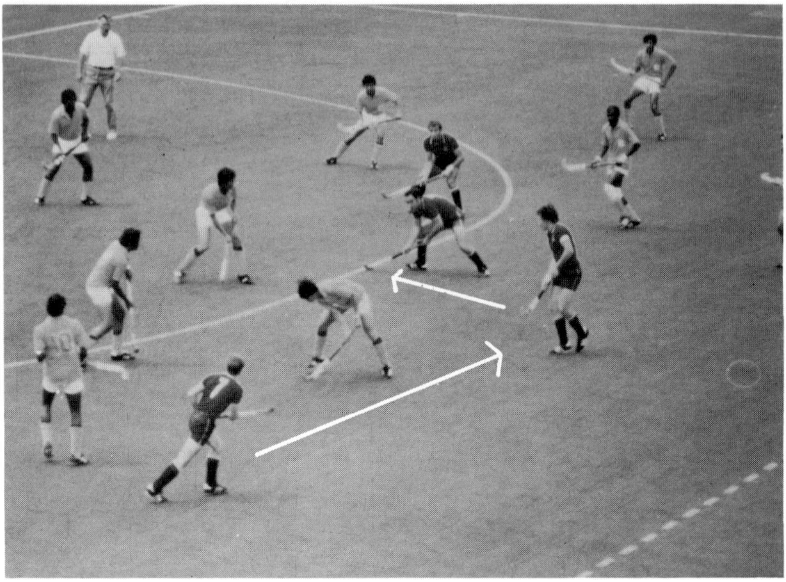

Photo 22 Spain employs the first-time pass to beat the defence of Malaysia in the 1976 Olympic Games (Spain vs Malaysia 2:1).

that is first stopped scores nothing. The next first-time pass (wall-pass) against scores a point. When the ball is touched by the defender, the player who made the mistake must defend in the middle. Which team of three can achieve the highest number of points?

b As 4a, but played in one specific direction. The three attackers must try to beat a defender standing behind the 25-yard line by means of at least two first-time passes in his immediate vicinity between the 25-yard line and the circle, and score a goal.

c As in 4b, but with one extra defender between the half-way line and the 25-yard line. Both defenders are only allowed to tackle in their own area, and must be beaten in succession by the three attackers, using first-time passes as they move in the direction of the circle.

5 *Four against two, or five against three on a pitch of reduced size between the half-way line and the 25-yard line.*
The intention is simply to keep possession.

6 *A midfield player is to take a free hit in front of the circle.*
As soon as the striker standing diagonally to his right sprints towards him (and away from his marker), the midfield player plays the free-hit onto his stick. The striker plays the ball directly back to the midfield player, who must try to score a goal with the help of the striker.

7 *Wall-pass game with three teams.*
On a pitch marked out 25 yards square, two teams A and B (with three players each) fight for possession. Each first-time pass within a team or using the three players of team C, who are off the pitch but available on the sidelines for a pass, scores one point. Which team is the first to score ten points? Each team should play once off and twice on the pitch in order to make a true comparison between the three teams possible.

8 *Two against two with a neutral player in a limited field.*
Each first-time pass counts one point for the team in possession whilst a pass played after controlling the ball first, doesn't count. The player using the first-time pass leaves to run free immediately after playing the ball.

9 *Two against two with two neutral players in a limited field.*
Whilst one neutral player should stay close to the ball, the other is offering himself for long passes further away.

10 *One against one on two wide goals with a neutral player.*
The neutral player should be used a few times, and when doing so mainly for playing the wall-pass.

12 Games for transferring pressure

One tactical requirement important for successful hockey is the ability to find space or areas which are not well covered by the opposition systematically and then to exploit this decisively by fast attacking moves. Attacks built up in areas of the pitch that are defended in depth by the opposition hold little hope of success, because there is insufficient time and space for the strikers to carry out their technical and tactical moves; more promising are individual or group attacking moves set up in the less densely marked spaces, usually found on the side of the pitch away from the position of the ball.

1 *Wing play, four against two.*

a Between the half-way line and the goal-line of a full-size pitch, the two wing forwards are to combine with their two insides so that, despite the challenge of two opposing defenders, one of the four attackers can dribble the ball over the opponents' goal-line (fig. 19). If the four attackers lose the ball to the defenders, then the defenders become inside-forwards and support the two wingers (who remain on the attack), while the previous two insides take up defensive duties until the next 'goal' is scored or until they regain the ball. Which attacking formation can first score ten goals?

b Ditto, but with a time limit. By the time fifteen (or ten) seconds have elapsed after winning the ball, an attack must have been successfully conducted by dribbling over the opposite goal-line. If the time set for the attack runs out, then the defence automatically receive the ball to try to score a goal within the time limit. Two neutral wingers help the attack.

c Ditto, but without time limit. Instead of dribbling over the goal-line, the attackers have to enter the circle and score a goal (as a variation, this can also be played with a goalkeeper). While the team first in possession always attacks the goal, the defending team, if they win the ball, must try to carry the ball over the half-way line with the help of the two wingers. Half-time is reached after ten attacks, and sides are changed.

d Ditto, but with time limit (fifteen or ten seconds).

2 *Wing play, five against three* (see 1a to d).

3 *Wing play, four against three.*

The game is played as in the basic exercise and variations 1a to d above, except that now, one neutral player is introduced, who always assists the team that is not in possession of the ball. This neutral player should play as the central defender.

4 *Wing play, five against four.*
This game is played as in 3 except with offside rules.

5 *Wing play, five against five or six against six.*
Dribble over the opposition goal-line as in Rugby or score as in a normal game (see Chapter 24).

6 *Transferring pressure in the depth of the field.*
There are three teams of three players in three separate zones each at least 25 yards wide. The three players of one outside zone must hit (or flick) the ball through the middle zone to the opposite team. Before transferring pressure in the depth of the field a maximum of three passes within their ranks is allowed, without one of the 'middle team' intercepting the pass (fig. 23). Should the 'middle team' gain the ball, then it is given to the team who were ready to receive the ball. If a pass between the two outer teams is not controlled (i.e. not properly stopped), then a pass that successfully crossed the middle zone does not count. Both outside teams play against the middle team up to ten.

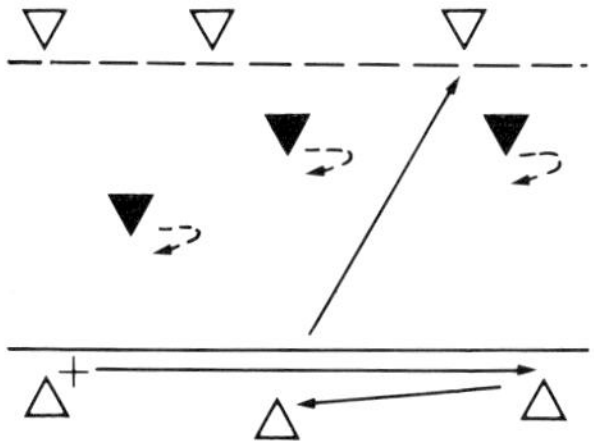

Figure 23

If less skilful players are involved, it is recommended that the game is played with only two players in the middle zone, until the players of the outside teams have learnt how to build up a good position for the pass across midfield (by means of up to three passes). The middle team initially takes up its position between the half-way line and 25-yard line, while with top players, the size of the zone can be extended to 35 yards. If an opponent's zone is entered, the pass does not count.

7 *Free-hits from the 25-yard line into the opposite half, where there are three team-mates and two (or three) opposing defenders.*
While the attackers must try to control the ball and then score a goal, the defenders' aim is to pass the ball back to the hit-taker if possession is won. Variation: four attackers against three defenders in the opposite half of the field.

8 *Five against four (six against five) in one half of the field, followed by a pass to one of two attackers (marked by one player) in the other half.*
No player is allowed to leave his half of the pitch. The game is started with a hit-out from the circle. How long do the five defenders need to pass to one of their two attackers in the other half of the field?

9 *Attacking three goals (three against three or four against four).*
Three flag-post goals are erected, five yards wide and fifteen yards apart, on the half-way line or on the 25-yard line. The player with the ball has to try to pass it to a team-mate through one of the goals, so that the latter can collect the ball before an opponent. All members of one team must run to find space, while their opponents must seek to prevent a successful pass through one of the goals (fig. 24).

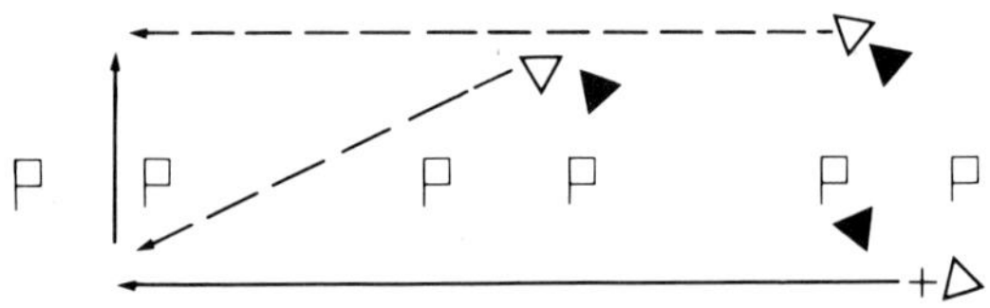

Figure 24

13 The development of tactical thinking and behaviour

In the coaching of hockey players today, the situation remains that too little use is made of the knowledge gained from sources that are important for the development of proficiency in our sport. Although in recent years some of the problems relating to the improvement of the processes of teaching and coaching skills and fitness have been solved with the help of sports science, too many coaches still carry on according to intuition or coaching principles which have long since become outdated.

The game of hockey is a complex activity whose character is determined by numerous performance factors and not simply by skill and physical fitness. A training schedule that contains both these factors almost exclusively (unfortunately still the case in many clubs) can have no satisfactory end product. The results and also the course that international matches have taken between leading Asian countries and the best European teams in recent years have clearly shown how players' tactical ability has become more and more decisive in performance. But tactics can solve complex situations in competition and in training only when physical and technical factors are otherwise equal. Teaching tactical skill is still neglected too often in coaching juniors and seniors both in Europe and overseas. Spontaneous tactical instructions mostly given only spasmodically, are simply not enough to raise the standard of the sport to a higher level. But in order to reach the required standard of hockey, tactical awareness must be embarked upon with beginners. Since thinking develops automatically with the motor-senses and action develops with thinking, tactical instruction should also be considered when teaching beginners the skills in order to optimise the children's talents.

It is well known that simple experimentation, practice and observation give a child experience. Now if this experience is captured by the child's mind, it will lead to correct behaviour in numerous daily situations. But if a child was to come to terms with his experiences alone, he would scarcely reach a high level of mental or physical activity: an adult's experience, by means of word and example, is required for this. This is not only true of the varied situations in a child's daily affairs (e.g. at school or at home) but also in the sphere of tactical thinking in hockey.

As soon as his technical skill allows, a young player should be given the opportunity in training to acquire tactical experience and knowledge by relying on his own thoughts and actions. The more that knowledge is gained by his own observations, thoughts and experiments, the more firmly will it be rooted. But subjective match experience alone is not enough. The acquisition of tactical knowledge does not come about simply by means of conscious action during a game, but often arises only in conjunction with a directed method of teaching. The important task falls to the coach of making the young player conscious of the tactics he himself has actively acquired by means of outside information, explaining them by careful detailed demonstration and systemising them with his superior awareness. Only a thorough and precise introduction and demonstration by the coach, together with sufficient repetition of the tactical move concerned in the same match situation, and by finally transferring the resultant conclusion to the problem in similar situations by slight changes in the exercise or game, can tactical foundations be laid. Tactical awareness can be particularly developed with the help of technical and tactical games (for example, three against one, two against one or three against two) since here players can clearly choose between many possible solutions. From game to game or from exercise to exercise basic tactical awareness is gradually developed to the point where the player's experience is wide enough for him to be acquainted with and understand the numerous solutions to a given match situation and use them in accordance with the particular position he is playing. Whether the correct tactics he uses in a match arise automatically from a move practised in training or whether they spring from the young player's creative ability in making tactically correct decisions remains unimportant as long as the most effective tactic is found and carried out successfully.

The ability to vary a tactical method once acquired, both quickly and properly, can only be attained if a systematic development of tactical awareness is undertaken from the beginners' stage through to competition training. Such development through games and exercises is a fundamental ingredient for raising the standard of hockey.

THE MOST IMPORTANT TACTICAL CONCEPTS

Before coming to the games and exercises that coach tactical awareness, the most important basic concepts which the average player needs to be acquainted with and master, in both attack and defence, should be enumerated.

In Attack

1 In general, running into a space that is not covered by an opponent so that a team-mate can pass the ball without risk of losing possession (see *The Science of Hockey*, pp 116 to 122). In particular, organised running into space in match situations with numerical superiority three against one, four against two, two against one, three against two and four against three with immediate running into space after a successful pass.

2 The ability to play an accurate and well-timed pass at the right moment to a team-mate, if necessary with a preceding (concealed) feint. How hard and in what direction the ball is to be played is determined by the player who is running into space and not by the player in possession (see *The Science of Hockey*, pp 132 to 136 and pp 147 to 150).

3 The ability to hold the ball at the right time instead of passing. The player in possession should dribble:

a If a pass to a team-mate is impossible due to insufficient running into space.

b In order to draw an opponent and thereby give a team-mate more space to receive the ball (see 'Methodical series of exercises for coaching organised running into space and passing in situations of numerical superiority').

c If a wide gap suddenly opens up in mid-field or near the opposition circle.

d If a forward has already run into an offside position.

4 The ability to give up dribbling in certain situations or at least limit its use:

a A dribble should not be instigated if a team-mate is free in a good position.

b Attacking play should not be delayed by dribbling the ball in mid-field. A hard pass takes up less time than the fastest dribble.

c No dribbling in one's own circle or as the last line of defence since if the ball is lost, it usually leads to a chance at goal for the opposition!

5 The ability to use sensibly dummy moves relevant to the match situation:

a Pretend to make one technical move in order to conceal the intended move (e.g. feinting as if to pass, but followed by continuing the dribble) and thereby confuse the opposition.

b In executing a dummy move, the distance between a player and an opponent must be greater (between 4 and 5 yards approximately) the faster the man in possession is sprinting.

c The feint must be executed quickly and clearly. However, the advantage gained by the feint is to be utilised even more rapidly.

d Feints should never be carried out without reason. They are particularly to be executed when there is no team-mate free or if the player concerned is under pressure.

e The dummy should be used only sparingly since an opponent can quickly adapt his play.

6 The ability to conclude an attack intelligently (see 'Exercises with a numerical advantage of two against one, three against one, three against two, four against two, four against three towards the goal defended by a goal-keeper') i.e.:

a Not shooting at goal if the shooting angle is too narrow. The ball should be passed instead to a better positioned team-mate who is unmarked or if no good pass is available try to force a penalty corner.

b In exploiting goal situations, show courage and determination (e.g. in the conversion of inaccurate crosses).

c In a situation where only the goalkeeper is blocking the way watch his position and reactions and do not be drawn to over-hasty action.

d Do not run too near the goalkeeper because the angle is then narrowed to the goalkeeper's advantage.

e Near the goal (up to 8 yards approximately) it is better to push rather than hit the ball. Pushing takes up less time, thereby allowing opposing defenders less chance to tackle and avoiding the possibility of 'sticks'.

f Shoot low and hard. Low shots are more difficult for the goalkeeper to save since reaction time when saving with the feet is approximately twice that with the hand or stick.

Photo 23 Samiullah (Pakistan) scores against Germany in the 1976 Olympic Games pool match (4:2).

In Defence

7 The ability to prevent an opponent running into space and receiving the ball unmarked by means of skilful, intelligent positional play and tackling (see 'Methodical series of exercises for coaching organised running into space and passing in situations of numerical superiority'):

a The defender must position himself between his own goal and an attacker such that he is on an imaginary line between the middle of the goal and that opponent.

b In doing so he must not only be aware of the position of both opponent and ball, but also the position of his fellow defenders in order to help them if necessary in sudden and unforeseen moves by the opposition.

c The defender must determine the distance of the ball from his own goal, his opponent's speed and technical skill, in order to decide how closely he should mark his opponent.

d An opposing forward should be marked so tightly that when he receives the ball he is already under pressure.

e Despite his assignment to mark an opponent tightly, the defender must not be independent of the other players in the defence, for a defender whose only concern is to block out his immediate opponent has not fulfilled his total role. He also has responsibilities to his team-mates.

f Giving up or losing the ball is to be seen in many players. Instead of standing still in disappointment, a player should immediately pressurise the opponent, so that the latter loses concentration and his actions become inaccurate because of a lack of time and space.

g The player in possession should not be tackled by running wildly at him or by standing still and waiting for him (see *The Science of Hockey*, pp 139 to 145).

h An attacker can be outwitted if he is offered one side on which to beat the defender while the latter particularly concentrates on his other side. There is an art in drawing an opponent to start a move or to make the first step. In this way he gives away his intention.

i A defender should try to force an opponent into a difficult position, e.g. by the side-line.

GAMES AND EXERCISES FOR DEVELOPING AND COACHING TACTICAL AWARENESS

In hockey, apart from the effectiveness of the corner routine, it is good teamwork involving the whole team that in the first place decides victory or defeat. But for successful hockey, not only should penalty corners and corners be practised, but also the typical moves that arise most frequently involving between two and four players of one team. This builds up a basis for mastering complicated systems and combinations.

Co-operative teamwork must be perfected in a long-term, systematic and progressive training schedule by employing one or more imaginary, passive or active opponents and by making conditions more difficult (rule changes, time limits, changes of the size of pitch or goal size etc).

For developing and coaching organised passing and running into space one should start with the numerical advantage 3:1, for this situation requires relatively less technical ability and tactical awareness.

In games of two against one, three against two, or four against three, besides additional tactical ability, greater technical skill (e.g. beating a man after a feint or by using a wall-pass) is required for success.

Three players against one rarely occurs in a match. However, the tactical awareness of individuals must be developed in training by means of this match situation since it prepares them for situations that arise more often: three against two, four against two, and four against three.

METHODICAL SERIES OF EXERCISES FOR COACHING ORGANISED PASSING AND RUNNING INTO SPACE WITH A NUMERICAL ADVANTAGE OF THREE AGAINST ONE.

In encountering a situation of three against one, players learn to recognise and master the following tactical points:

Notes for the player with the ball:

1 Before you pass, you must draw an opponent, in order to beat him by making a pass to a team-mate in a better position.

2 Try to make concealed passes or to feint before passing such that the player receiving the ball has more time for subsequent moves.

3 Do not carry the ball too near an opponent since by using his reach combined with a large step in your direction, he then has a good chance of intercepting your pass.

4 Do not stand idle after your pass but run into space again so that the player now with the ball finds himself in the middle and has two passes available.

Notes for team-mates of the player with the ball:

1 Running into space must take place so that the player with the ball has a team-mate available to both left and right.

2 Make yourselves square with the player in possession, or better still a little behind, for the square pass, otherwise you will force the player in possession to make a diagonal pass which a defender has more chance of intercepting.

3 Even the best combination play will fail if carried out too slowly. A defender should force errors from the three strikers by feinting and running sideways.

1 a *Square-pass combination in threes.*
All three forwards run in a line and pass the ball hard and square between them.

b *Square-pass combination in threes, changing positions.*
The players change positions continually so that the player with the ball is always in the middle (fig. 25).

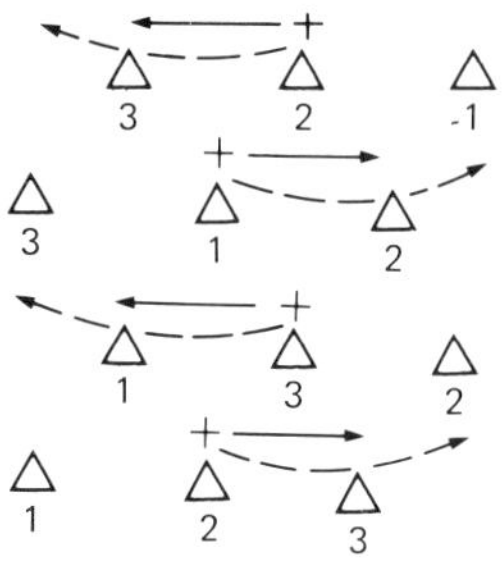

Figure 25

2 a *Three against one with wide-angle passing.*
So that the player with the ball has the opportunity to pass to either right or left, his two team-mates must run into positions to the right or left of the player in possession. The latter should help his team-mates, as they begin their runs, by stretching out an arm to either right or left and thus showing his partners which way they should run.

b *Ditto, on a pitch marked out 22 metres square (Photo 24).*
Which three attackers can hold the ball the longest without the ball being touched by the defender or crossing the lines? If either of these occur, one attacker starts counting out loud. After three (or five) attempts to get the best time possible, the defender becomes an attacker and one of the attackers becomes defender for three (or five) further attempts.

Photo 24 Khalid Mahmood tries to gain the ball from three Germans in a test in Munich 1970 (2:2).

c Ditto, but if the defender touches the ball, he changes places with the attacker whose pass was inaccurate, or who let the ball cross the line.

d *Three against one towards a small goal defended by a goalkeeper.* Played as 2a. Goals can be scored from both sides. The goalkeeper (who forms the defence with the one outfield defender) is not allowed to leave the goal-line.

3 a *Square-pass combination in threes, changing positions (see 1b) against one active defender who defends a goal 16 yards wide.*
The three attackers score a 'goal' when one of them succeeds in dribbling the ball over the line. The next attack is started from the other side of the flag-post goal in order to save time.

b *Ditto, but each team of three has ten attacks.*
After ten attacks, teams are changed. The defender goes into attack while one attacker becomes defender. Forty attacks are needed in all to establish the most successful attacking combination.

4 a *Three against one towards two large goals* (fig. 26).
A three-man team attacks two defences of one defender each. The attacking group is positioned in the middle of the pitch and attacks each of the two goals ten times. The three-man attack is beaten if the defender, who stands approximately 6 to 8 yards in front of his goal, can hold the ball for three seconds, but he should then quickly give the ball back to the attackers who continue by attacking the opposite goal.

b Variation: the trainer sets up an attacking team of the three best players in his opinion. This team should prove in ten attacks that they can score more goals than three weaker players.

c Variation: timed by the trainer, the attackers have two or three minutes to carry out as many attacks as possible at each of the goals. The number of attacks depends upon the stamina of the attacking players.

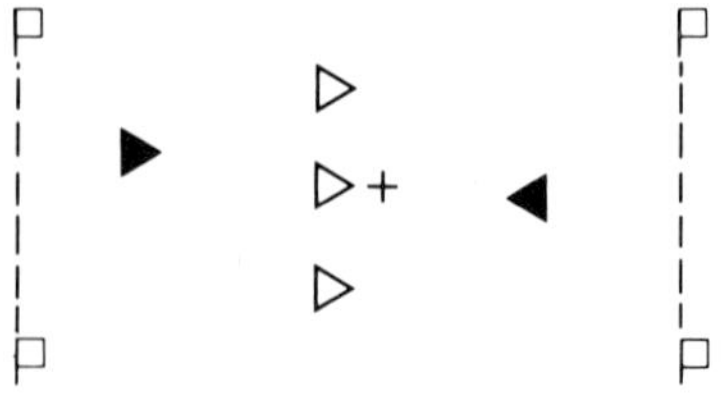

Figure 26

5 a *Three against one, alternating between three teams.*
A team of three players attacks two goals (4 yards wide), defended by three backs, on a pitch 25 yards long. If a defender or one of the two

'goalkeepers' (who are not allowed to leave the goal-line to clear the ball) succeeds in gaining the ball for three seconds, the defence gives up their defensive role and attack the opposite goal while the attacking team that lost possession now take up positions in front of (or in) the goal that they have just unsuccessfully attacked.

A goal can be scored from any distance except that the ball cannot be hit. When a goal is scored or missed, attack and defence change over as when a defender or the goalkeeper gains possession and holds the ball for three seconds. If the ball rolls behind the open flag-post goal, the new attacking team should play on with a reserve ball which is ready by one goal post. In the meantime, the previous attacking team should retrieve the ball that has rolled behind the goal. Which team scores the most goals in ten minutes? Distinguishing the three teams by different coloured shirts is to be recommended.

b Variation: the game is made more difficult if only six or eight seconds are allowed for the strikers to conclude their attack. If they fail to score before the time-limit expires, then the defending team automatically receives the ball and the chance to attack.

6 a *Game of three against one towards a flag-post goal 15 yards wide on the edge of the circle followed by a shot at the normal goal defended by a goalkeeper.*

Three strikers in combination start from the half-way line and try to work one player free so that the latter is able to carry the ball through the flag-post goal into the circle and immediately shoot at goal. This is to be played with offside rules (fig. 27).

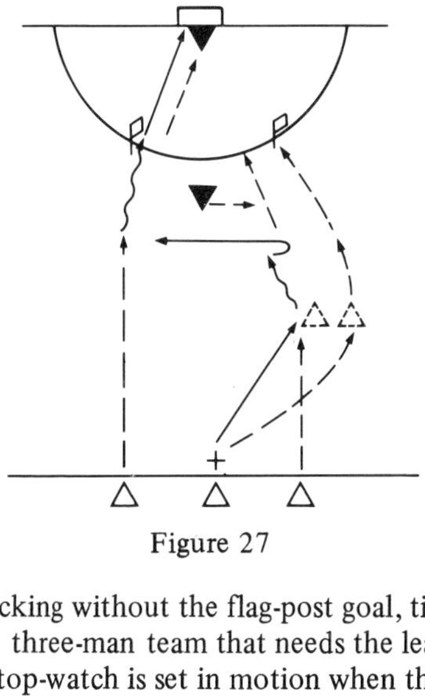

Figure 27

b Variation: attacking without the flag-post goal, timed by the trainer. The winner is the three-man team that needs the least time for a successful attack. The stop-watch is set in motion when the ball is first touched on the half-way line, and stopped when a shot at goal is made. Three 'penalty' seconds are to be added to the total time if no goal is scored. Each attacker must play the ball at least once.

c Variation: sprint-race with a halfback.
A defending halfback stands between 4 and 6 yards behind the three-man attack. He has already been beaten and sets off at the same time as the attackers who must try to conclude their attack as quickly as possible so that the halfback is not able to help out in defence. If the halfback succeeds in getting back to his team-mates and is able to help in successfully clearing the ball, he scores one point. If the attackers score a goal then they score one point. Which team is the first to score three points?

METHODICAL SERIES OF EXERCISES FOR COACHING TACTICAL AWARENESS WITH A NUMERICAL ADVANTAGE OF TWO AGAINST ONE

Players learn to recognise and master the following tactical moves in carrying out the subsequent exercises and game situations of two against one.

Notes for the player not in possession:

1 In general: run into unmarked space in such a way that a pass to you from the player in possession involves no risk.

2 In particular: make yourself available square of the player in possession or a little behind him for a square pass, or behind a defender's back for a diagonal through-pass. Sometimes, keep well back behind the ball and thus allow the player in possession to carry the ball into your position while you take up his position (scissors movement).

Notes for the player with the ball:

1 While carrying the ball, raise your eyes from the ball as often as possible in order to be able to see and analyse team-mates' and opposing defenders' intended moves.

2 Before you pass, draw the defender and then beat him with a hard, accurate pass to a team-mate in space.

3 Do not carry the ball too close to the defender however, since he then has a good chance of intercepting your pass by using his reach.

4 Any one against one situation has a chance of failure. Do not look for an opponent, but avoid him by using hard, safe passes.

5 Conceal your intentions by feinting as if to make a move that you do not in fact execute but carry out a completely different technical or tactical move instead. The success of a dummy-move not only depends on the perfect execution of the feint, but also on a balanced use of the various types of feint.

6 Do not remain inactive after a successful pass, but make yourself immediately available for another pass into space.

Photo 25 Instead of making the pass between the forwards impossible, the German defender Fritz Schmidt, because of the wrong position of his stick, allows the attackers from New Zealand in the second World Cup match to combine (Germany vs New Zealand 2:1).

Notes for the defender:

1 In defence, never stand still but keep moving either backwards or sideways.

2 First and foremost, concentrate on intercepting a pass, for if the player in possession makes a solo run, you stand more chance of robbing him of the ball.

3 Often feint by taking a step either forwards or sideways in order to put the attacker off, and thus create more favourable defensive conditions. If you cover clearly one side of you with the stick, then you will often induce the player with the ball to move to the opposite side for which you should be well prepared. Try therefore to force the player with the ball to move as you want him to.

(For preparatory exercises see *The Science of Hockey*, pages 104 to 106, Exercises 1 to 8).

GAMES AND EXERCISES

1 a *Two against one towards one wide goal, 11 yards wide.*
The two attackers score when one of them is able to beat the defender, either by collecting a square pass followed by a short dribble, or by dribbling past him using feints, such that the ball can be carried over the goal-line 11 yards long. Since only one team-mate is available for a pass, the latter must keep trying to create opportunities for the player with the ball by being always available. The player on the ball must keep his eye on the defender so that he is able either to play a square-pass or reach the goal-line by dribbling. An immediate run into space after his pass makes the defender's task all the more difficult. Through passes are not allowed.

b *Ditto, but as a competition.*
Each pair of attackers carries out ten attacks and then the teams are changed. The defender goes into attack while one attacker becomes the defender. Thirty attacks are required to find the strongest player.

c *Two against one without beating a man (the pitch is 16 yards wide).*
The two attackers should try to beat the defender between the 25-yard line and half-way line by a combination of square- and through-passes, and by dribbling the ball into the other position. Attempts at dribbling past the defender are to be avoided. The through-pass must be received before the line is reached such that the ball can then be dribbled over it.

d *Ditto, but as a competition (see b).*

e *Two against one on the right or left flank with one team-mate.*
The latter takes a free hit from his own 25-yard line to the IR (IL) or OR (OL) standing on the half-way line. How many seconds do the two attackers take to beat the opposing wing-half and run through the goal with the ball as far as the opposite 25-yard line? The player taking the free-hit passes the ball and then counts the time taken.

f *Two against one with no conditions or restrictions, playing towards one wide goal as a competition.*
The game is played without offside (as in all previous exercises).

2 a *Two against one towards two wide goals.*
The attacking pair stand in the middle of the pitch and play alternately towards two 9 yard-wide goals, each defended by one player. The attack is beaten if the defender standing approximately 6 yards in front of the goal can win and hold the ball for three seconds. After three seconds, he must give the ball back to the attackers who then attack the goal opposite. Which pair of attackers is able to dribble over the opposition goal-line most often in ten attacks?

b Variation: the trainer allows his best players to form a team. The pair should prove that they can score more goals than the others.

c Variation, under pressure: the attacking pair have three minutes to carry out as many attacks as possible at both goals. Which pair scores the most goals in the three minutes?

3 a *Two against one, alternating between three teams.*
As in 5a of 'Games and exercises with a numerical advantage of three against one', except that two attackers play against one defender plus a goalkeeper. The length of the pitch is reduced to 25 yards.

b Ditto, but timed by the coach. Only six (or eight) seconds are allowed for the attacking team to complete their attack.

4 *Two against one towards two small goals, each 1 yard wide.*
On a pitch 25 yards long, one player takes on a team of two. While the single player can score a goal from anywhere in his opponents' half, one of the pair can shoot at goal only if he is less than 5 yards from the goal. After two and a half minutes the teams are changed, followed by one minute's rest and then the defender joins up with one of the attackers, while the second attacker plays against them on his own. Which player comes out best after three games?

5 *One against one towards two small goals (1 yard wide) with one neutral player.*
The neutral player always assists the player in possession. If he or his present team-mate loses the ball to the opposing player, then he changes teams and plays alongside the latter.

6 *Two against two towards two wide goals (11 yards wide).*
The two players with the ball have to build up a suitable position (by means of skilful combination play) from which it is possible to dribble the ball over the opponents' goal-line. The team that scores the most goals in three periods of three and a half minutes, with one minute break between each is the winner.

7 a *Two against one on the edge of the circle followed by a shot at goal (defended by a goalkeeper with pads). See Chapter 10, exercise 3.*
Two attackers start on the 25-yard line aiming to score a goal against one defender and the goalkeeper (see photo). This is played with offside rules. A goal should be scored within six (eight) seconds. Both players should be urged to follow up the shot while the defender's task is to try to win and hit the ball out of the circle over a sideline, or over the 25-yard line. Which is the most effective combination?

b Ditto, but timed by the coach. Which pair of attackers takes the least time to attack from the half-way line and shoot at goal?

c Ditto, but as a sprint-race with a half-back. For the format of this, see exercise 6c of 'Games and exercises with a numerical advantage of three against one'.

Photo 26 Two Spanish forwards about to score their third goal against Poland in the third World Cup match in Malaysia.

8 *Two against two in one half of the pitch, followed by a shot at goal* (fig. 28).
Two attackers start on the half-way line and try first to beat one defender who may only tackle between the half-way line and the 25-yard line, and secondly another defender inside the 25, such that they are able to enter the circle and shoot at goal without being tackled. Which pair of attackers scores the most goals in ten attacks?

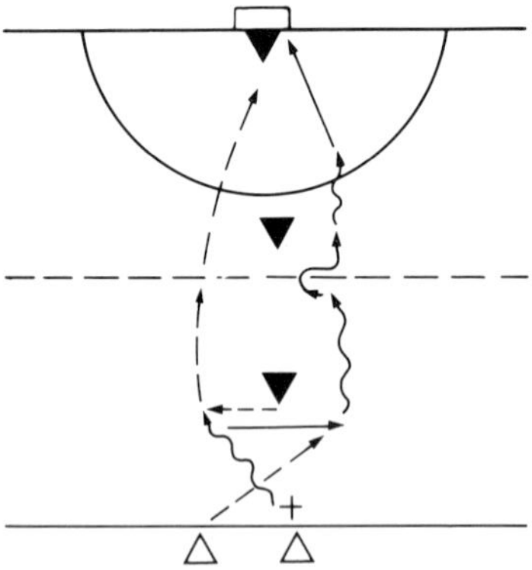

Figure 28

METHODICAL SERIES OF EXERCISES FOR COACHING ORGANISED PASSING AND RUNNING INTO SPACE WITH A NUMERICAL ADVANTAGE OF FOUR AGAINST TWO

Tactical play of individual players in both attack and defence:
The attacking team must always work towards the most effective combination for them i.e. a T-shape. Thus the player with the ball should always

take up Position 1 since he then gives himself three possible passes in three different directions, while the direction in which the attackers not in possession move depends upon where player 1 passes the ball.

a Player no. 1 passes the ball to player no. 3 (fig. 29).

b Player no. 1 passes the ball to player no. 2 (fig. 30).

c Player no. 1 passes the ball to player no. 4 (fig. 31).

If the three attackers respectively move into their most effective positions immediately after passing (figs. 30 to 31) then they make it easier for the player in possession to pass the ball to the best positioned team-mate. Along with the possibilities of passing right or left as laid out in the games for coaching a numerical advantage of three against one, the player with the ball soon learns to recognise a chance to pass the ball through the gap.

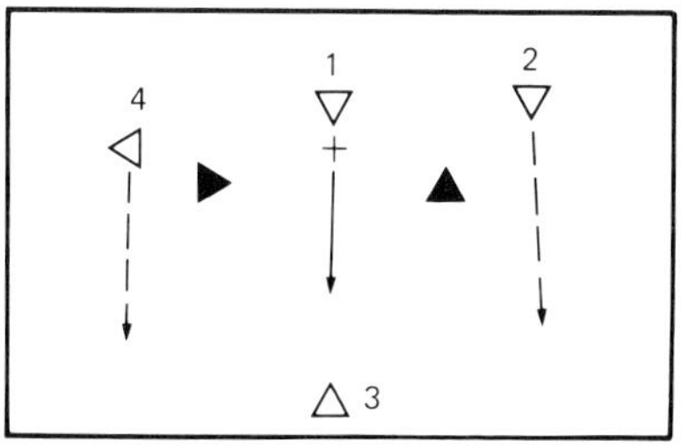

Figure 29

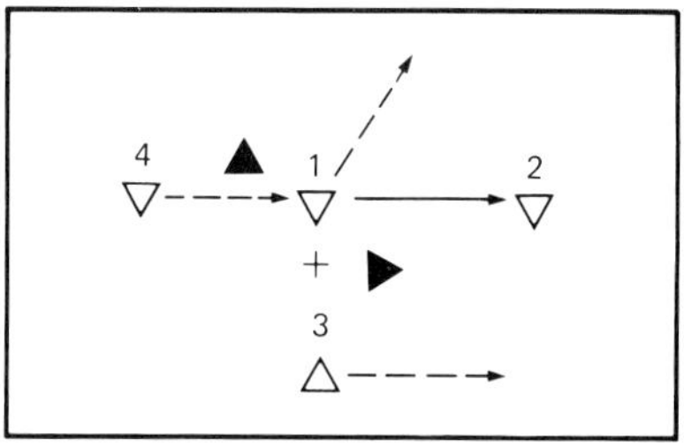

Figure 30

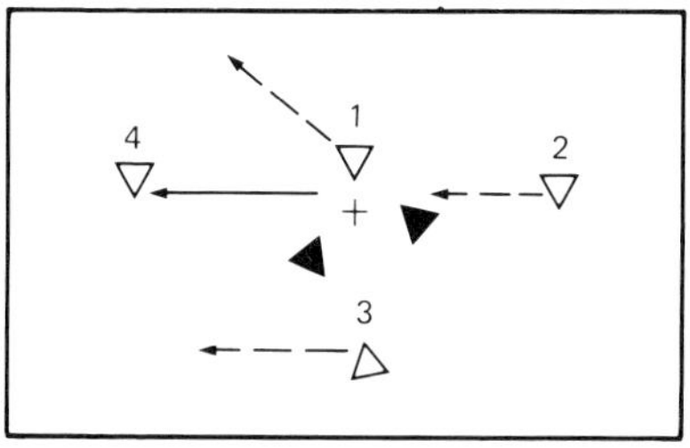

Figure 31

How are the two defenders to play in order to successfully defend against the four attackers? Only good co-operation between the defenders will give them a chance of winning the ball. A defender should not challenge the player with the ball by facing him, but side-on so that one of the players wide of him (nos 2 or 4) cannot be passed to. At the same time, he should be aware of a possible pass through the gap to no. 3. The nearer he can get to the attacker (and thus put him under greater pressure), the narrower the angle becomes, and therefore the greater the defender's chances of intercepting the ball. A defender should not challenge the player in possession too quickly since he can then be easily beaten by a skilful feint. But if he hesitates too long in tackling, he will give the player with the ball and his team-mates sufficient time to think out carefully a move. It is critical for the other defenders to be aware of how his team-mate is challenging the man with the ball, i.e. which of the three possible passes is cut off by the challenge. The second defender can usually cover the other two attackers with skilful zonal marking by staying in the gap between the player in possession (no. 1) and the other two attackers, (no. 3 and either no. 2 or 4). In this respect he should particularly watch for the through-pass to no. 3. By means of body-feints and dummy lunges, the two defenders should try as much as possible to harrass the attackers and thus make it difficult for them to keep possession of the ball.

EXERCISES AND GAMES

1 a *Four against two on a pitch marked out 25 yards square* (figs. 30 to 31).

b Ditto. Which four players are able to hold the ball for the longest time? Each team of four players has five 'record attempts' against the same pair of defenders before the teams are changed.

c Ditto. If a defender touches the ball (or holds it for three seconds) then he changes places with the attacker who made an inaccurate pass or allowed the ball to roll out of play.

2 a *Four against two towards a normal size hockey goal.*
The four attackers start on the half-way line and the two defenders are allowed to challenge just from in front of the 25-yard line. The four attackers should learn to combine effectively until they achieve a shot at goal (defended by a goalkeeper). A goal counts as two points. At first to be played without, and later with offside as the game develops.

b Each team of attackers has ten attempts. After ten attacks the two defenders change into attack and two attackers become defenders. Thirty attacks are sufficient to ascertain the most successful attacking combination.

c Ditto, but timed by the trainer. Which four strikers take the shortest time to attack from the half-way line and score a goal? Through-passes and fast dribbling speed up the attack while square passes slow it down.

d Ditto, but as a sprint-race with one half-back.
For the format of this, see exercise 6c of 'Games and exercises with a numerical advantage of three against one' (page 94).

3 a *Four against two towards two side goals* (fig. 32).
The attacking team starts in the middle of the pitch (33 yards long) and

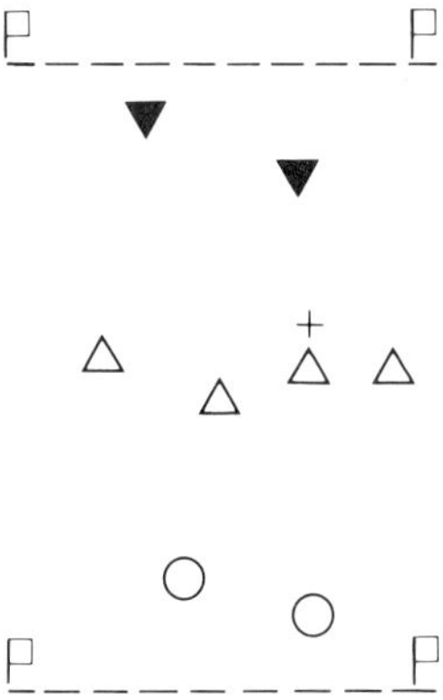

Figure 32

attacks the two goals alternately each defended by two defenders. The ball is cleared when the defenders, who take up positions approximately 9 yards in front of the goal, are able to hold the ball for three seconds. After three seconds have elapsed, the ball must be returned quickly to the attackers who must then try to dribble the ball over the opposite goal-line.

b *Variation: timed by the coach.*
The attackers have three minutes to carry out as many attacks as possible at the two goals. Which four attackers score the most goals in three minutes?

4 a *Four against two towards an open flag-post goal, 4 yards wide, which is defended by two goalkeepers without pads.*
The defenders remain in defence with the goalkeepers for two minutes. After this time, attack and defence change places. Which team scores the most goals in twelve minutes? Goals can be scored from both sides of the goal. Hitting is not allowed! If play switches to behind the goal, then defenders may change places with the goalkeepers. However two defenders must always be standing on the goal-line. If the defenders win possession, they must give the ball back after three seconds to the attacking team (who are not to be less than 13 yards away).

b *Variation: sides are changed when the defenders succeed in passing the ball twice between them, without being touched by an attacker.*
After possession is gained, the two 'goalkeepers' are allowed to leave the goal-line.

c *Variation: played with one goalkeeper (without pads).*
If an attacker loses the ball to a defender, he changes places with him. Each goal gives the four attackers one point. Which player has been involved in scoring the most goals after ten minutes' playing time?
Before the game begins, draw lots to see who defends first.

5 a *Four against two alternating between three teams.*
Three teams play across the pitch from sideline to sideline. Between the 25-yard line and the half-way line, the sidelines of the normal pitch form the goal-lines which are to be dribbled over with the ball at the end of the stick. Two teams each of two players defend these goal-lines while a third team (of four players) starts in the middle of the pitch and attacks for three (two or one) minutes. After the ball is cleared or after a goal is scored by dribbling over the goal-line, the attacking team regain the ball and turn around.

b *Variation: four against two, alternating between three teams.*
For the format of this small game see exercise 5a of 'Games and exercises with a numerical advantage of three against one' (page 92).

c *Variation: four against two, alternating between three teams, timed by the coach.*
The attackers have only twelve seconds to carry out an attack. If they fail to score a goal within this time, then the defending team automatically receives the ball and thus the chance to attack.

METHODICAL SERIES OF EXERCISES FOR COACHING TACTICAL AWARENESS WITH A NUMERICAL ADVANTAGE OF THREE AGAINST TWO

The basic tactical moves established in the exercises with a numerical advantage of three against one, two against one, and four against two, must now be extended to the match situation of three against two.

Tactical notes for the attacking team:
1 The player dribbling the ball must be able to review the whole situation by looking up from the ball. He must firstly be able to recognise team-mates' positions whether they are available for a pass or not. According to an opposing defender's reactions, he must either carry the ball or, if the defender comes in to tackle, immediately pass to a free team-mate, but he must also be able to deceive an opponent with a dummy pass to a team-mate, and then beat him by a quick burst of speed. An attempt to beat the man is only advisable however, when the defender seems too concerned with a possible pass or if a team-mate has run into a bad position. If the player with the ball goes on to make a successful pass, he must immediately run into space in order to be available for a return pass from his team-mate now in possession.

2 The players in the attacking team who are not in possession must make themselves available to both right and left, and run into space so that the angle between them and their team-mate is as large as possible. The further the other two attackers can spread out from the player making the pass, the more difficult is the defender's task. But if the two attackers without

the ball make themselves available close to the player with the ball (between 2 and 4 yards), they offer him no chance to run between the two defenders following a dummy pass.

Tactical notes for the defending team:
The defenders can most easily fulfil their role if one of them challenges the player with the ball side-on, while the second player tries to cover space.

1 Tackling the player with the ball should be a considered and restrained action carried out side-on, but such that in so doing the outside attacker who is no longer tightly marked should not be disregarded. The defender must not put himself in danger of being beaten because of an unrestrained and over-hasty challenge. He should rather try to force his opponent with body-feints and stick-dummies into a move for which he himself is prepared already.

2 The second defender has to try to make the tackling defender's task easier by covering the third attacker. But he should always be ready to tackle if the two attackers should beat his team-mate.

EXERCISES AND GAMES

1 a *Three against two on a pitch marked out 25 yards square.*
The two attackers without the ball must try by means of continuous running into space to give the player in possession a safe opening for a pass. The player with the ball should only then pass, once he has drawn one of the two defenders. After giving the ball he must then make himself immediately available for a return pass. Which three attackers are able to hold the ball the longest inside the marked-out pitch, without the ball being won by the defenders or crossing the boundary lines? If this happens a previously determined attacker must start counting out loud. After five successive attempts at achieving as good a time as possible, the two defenders become attackers and two of the attackers go into defence for five further attempts at holding the ball for the longest time.

b Ditto, but if a defender is able to hold the ball for three seconds, he changes places with the attacker whose pass was inaccurate or who allowed the ball to roll out of play.

c Ditto. Ask the defenders how a pass to a team-mate can best be prevented (by man-to-man marking).

d Ditto. How many successive passes can the attackers make?

2 a *Three against two towards a wide goal 22 yards apart.*
The three attackers score by one of them running over the opposite goal-line with the ball at the end of his stick.

b Ditto, but each team of three has ten attacks. After these ten attempts, teams are changed round: the defenders now attack with a third, neutral forward and two of the attackers make up the defence. Which of the two sets of attackers had greater success? The game is played without offside.

3 a *Three against two, towards two goals 22 yards apart.*
The attacking team starts in the middle of the pitch and attacks the two wide goals alternately, each of which is defended by two players. The ball is cleared when the defenders win possession and can pass the ball between them. After ten attempts a new team is established, composed of the two defenders and a third, neutral attacker. Which team was most often able to carry the ball over the opposite goal-line in ten attacks?

b Variation: the trainer selects the three best players (in his opinion) from the attacking team. They should prove that they can score more points than the other attacking teams with whom they are competing.

c Variation: the three attackers have three (two) minutes to carry out as many attacks as possible alternating between the two wide goals. Which team scores the most goals in three (two) minutes? The three-man attack is broken down if one of the two defenders can win and hold the ball for three seconds. Then, however, he must return the ball directly to the attackers who then attack the opposite goal.

4 a *Three against two, towards a small goal (3 yards wide) defended by goalkeeper without pads.*
After each period of two minutes, the two defenders and the goalkeeper change places with the three attackers. Which team has scored most goals after twelve minutes? Goals can be scored from both sides of the open flag-post goal except that hitting is not allowed.

b Variation: if play suddenly switches to the other side of the goal, one of the defenders may change places with the goalkeeper (fig. 33), but then one of the defenders must always stay back on the goal-line. If the defenders gain possession of the ball, they must pass it back after three seconds to the attacking team (who are not to be less than 13 yards away).

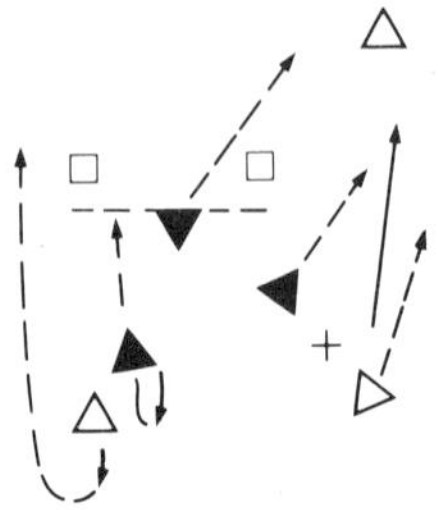

Figure 33

c Variation: a change between attack and defence is made if the defenders (along with the goalkeeper) can pass the ball between them twice in succession. While the defenders and goalkeeper are to run into space on winning the ball, the attackers, immediately after losing the ball, must try to prevent the two passes within the defending team by man-to-man marking. If they succeed in this, then they can continue to attack and one defender must again position himself in the goal.

d *Variation: with a 'fixed' goalkeeper with pads.*
If an attacker loses the ball to either of the two defenders (who must hold it for a minimum of three seconds), then he changes places with that defender. For each goal scored (hitting is not allowed), the three attackers are awarded one point. Which of the five outfield players has the most points after ten minutes play? Before the game starts, draw lots as to who is to start in defence. Somewhat weaker players may also be given a points advantage.

5 a *Three against two alternating between three teams.*
For the format of this small game see exercise 5a of 'Games and exercises with a numerical advantage of four against three'.

b *Ditto, timed by the coach.*
The three attackers have only ten (or twelve) seconds to carry out an attack. The length of the pitch should be between 38 and 43 yards with goals 22 yards across.

6 Two against two towards two narrow (or wide) goals with a neutral player who always assists the team in possession.

7 Players are divided into teams of five and each team is further divided into two groups (three attackers and two defenders). The game is played on a full-sized pitch, between the two 25-yard lines, divided into two equal halves by the half-way lines. Each team has a defending and an attacking half. Only the three attackers and the opposing two defenders are allowed in the attacking half; and in the defending half only the two defenders and the opposing three attackers. If attackers or defenders cross the half-way line a free hit at the open goal is awarded against their team on the half-way line.

8 *Three against three towards two narrow (or wide) goals.*
Although this is not a three against two advantage, occasions often arise in which three attackers are set against three defenders.

9 a *Three against two on the edge of the circle followed by a shot at goal defended by a goalkeeper (with pads).*
Three attackers begin their attack on the 25-yard line with the aim of

Photo 27 Three forwards from Spain on the way to beat two defenders from New Zealand in Malaysia 1975 (New Zealand vs Spain 2:1).

beating two defenders and entering the circle to shoot at goal without being tackled. This game is played with offside rules.

b *Ditto, timed by the coach.*
Which three attackers take the least time to attack from the half-way line and shoot at goal? The stop-watch is set in motion after the first touch of the ball on the half-way line, and stopped when the shot at goal is made. If the shot does not lead to a goal, then the attackers have three 'penalty' seconds added to their time.

c *Ditto, but as a sprint competition with a half-back.*
Between 9 and 11 yards behind the three-man attack stands a defending halfback who is already beaten. He sets off at the same time as the attackers, who must try to finish their attack before the halfback can come to the assistance of his defence. If the half-back can regain his ground and assist his team-mates, then the defensive team scores one point, as it does by means of a successful clearance. However, if the attackers score a goal, this counts two points.

METHODICAL SERIES OF EXERCISES FOR COACHING TACTICAL AWARENESS WITH A NUMERICAL ADVANTAGE OF FOUR AGAINST THREE

All the exercises laid out in the methods for coaching tactical awareness with a numerical advantage of three against two also help to develop and improve tactical awareness with an advantage of four against three. All games then, are carried out with one extra player in both attack and defence.

In all the exercises and games illustrated, coaches must watch for an improvement in players' co-ordination under conditions of fatigue as the frequency of errors increase with tiredness.

THE THEORY OF TACTICAL HOCKEY COACHING

Every tactical move (e.g. the exploitation of a two against one advantage which was taken as an example in Chapter 2) gives rise to three consecutive and connected phases.

1 *Perception and analysis of a match situation* must be considered one phase from when a situation is observed. Perception is thus clearly connected to analysis. ('We have a numerical advantage', 'My team-mate is running square and is unmarked', 'I've noticed how the defender is coming in to challenge and is obviously prepared for my solo run') it is, at the same time understood.

2 *The mental solution of a match situation* on the basis of evaluating the state of play. A mental solution leads to a conception of the way to physically resolve the problem in practice.

Since the defender in the example seems to be prepared solely for a dribble by the player with the ball, and his team-mate is in space, the player in possession should think to pass the ball square to that team-mate.

As a rule a beginner cannot judge correctly the advantages and disadvantages of the various possible solutions, nor has he sufficient experience to facilitate his choice. Thus he mostly attempts to solve a problem on the basis of any situation that has occured in training without first considering all the possibilities.

Only when he has collected sufficient tactical knowledge and experience, and when he has mastered the skills required to cover his tactical assignment is he ready to choose the most effective way of mentally solving his match assignment—by means of a critical evaluation of the various solutions possible.

3 *The physical solution of a match situation* e.g. by actually employing the square-pass. In the example described above, experience arises by an awareness of the result of a tactical move (in the previous example of a square-pass). If complicated thought-processes are required in both tactical training and in competition in order to solve a match situation of two against one, then (after frequent observations of the correct solution in matches and practice) the solution itself, in this case the square-pass, will eventually become associated with the perception of the specific match situation.

Immediately the situation concerned is observed therefore, the correct solution will be realised. By means of a broad consideration of tactics in training, a complex order of associations will be established which quickly facilitates a realisation of the moves necessary to solve various match situations as soon as they are perceived. This immediate association in solving simple tactical assignments is typical of top-class players and must therefore become one of the principal aims of tactical coaching. In the continuous and uniform coaching of all the players in a team (playing together over a long period with common theoretical and practical coaching) a 'blind understanding' almost exclusively on the basis of these associations is what is aimed at.

Tactical thinking therefore, only begins when it is of value to exploit the individual quirks of an opponent or of the situation. By means of tactical awareness, a player should always be in a position to either vary or reject the various associated solutions he has learnt to employ.

By correction and instructing the best way of resolving a given match situation, by means of encouragement etc., a coach should be able to advocate a direct tactical action, i.e. perception and analysis of a match situation and the mental and physical solution of that match situation so that the process of coaching tactical moves is accelerated and raised to a higher standard.

Whether a tactical move is successful or not in its execution depends upon various factors:

a **Perception or vision**:
Many tactical errors are to be explained by a player simply not seeing parts of the whole situation which are important for covering his tactical assignment. His field of vision might be too narrow then or his peripheral vision may not have been coached sufficiently (see *The Science of Hockey*, pp 27 to 30). An overall view of the situation is required for a player to get his bearings in free space and to act correctly as far as tactics are concerned. A correct analysis and also the solution of a match assignment often depends upon the breadth of perception.

b **Optical-physical assessment**:
In order to collect the ball safely and pass it accurately, it is not only faultless stopping, hitting, flicking or pushing that is required, but also a player's developing ability to locate the position of ball, team-mates and opponents on the field, as well as to correctly estimate their speed and distance away from him and convert this into relevant action. The skill of optical-physical assessment forms the basis of a good technical and tactical match performance. Each time the ball is passed or collected, or in fighting for a loose ball or when the goalkeeper kicks the ball clear, it is a case of synchronising optical calculations (which are conditioned by sensations in the eye-muscles and by experience) with kinetic perception. It can be observed again and again that an outfield player's first pass, or a

Photo 28 Manzoor Hussain (Pakistan).

goalkeeper's first defensive reactions, are usually worse than successive ones. The reason for incorrect action in a match lies in a faulty optical assessment or in a lack of kinetic perception when sporting activity begins. If a pass is thus made too softly, the next pass will be hit somewhat more powerfully; if it was too strong then the next pass will be better timed. Warming up before a match must, among other things, include the control and regulation of the system for optical-physical assessment. If two players with the same technical ability and the same physical fitness play to a different standard in a match (especially as regards passing), this is frequently due to the different condition of their respective optical-physical assessment systems. Practical experience in training and competitive matches, and in simplified training games (two against one, two against two, three against three, four against two, four against three) in close conjunction with a refinement of hockey skills helps to improve the ability to assess situations correctly. This will therefore lay the foundations for reaching a higher tactical level.

Players who are able to predict the movements of ball, team-mates and opponents, both spacially and temporally, usually reach a particularly high level of performance. Every top-class player should be able not only to grasp the present situation, but also to make a rapid mental picture as to how the situation might develop. An experienced defender can decide the move he is to make on the basis of his team-mates' positions, and of the way the player with the ball is moving and holding his stick, just as the goalkeeper can deduce from the position of the player and the movement of the stick, whether an attacker's shot will rise or not. The anticipation of a move becomes all the more difficult when normal conditions are changed–grass that is too long, very uneven, hard or muddy surface etc.–but a player's adaptation of a move can also be made difficult by conscious action. A concealed hit, a dummy-pass or a body feint can bring about a wrong reaction based on the mistaken anticipation of a move.

A first-class player should frequently employ all kinds of dummy moves (see *The Science of Hockey*, pp 96 to 101) in order to make an opponent's correct assessment of his movements more difficult, and to make him react wrongly. All ways of making anticipation difficult are involved in tactical play.

c **Tactical thinking**:
In spite of a correct solution to a match situation a tactical move can fail if skill is lacking or if the perception and analysis of a match situation were not correct. Thus in every match, frequent misunderstandings arise between players involved in a move, a clear sign of the different results of tactical thinking.

d **Knowledge and experience**:
Not only are field of vision and optical-physical assessment important for the perception and analysis of match situations, but also the ability to extract what is important from the general mass of observations in a match or action, which should be carried out in as short a time as possible. Increasing tactical knowledge and experience improve match perception. Match situations are then, for the most part, observed and analysed by players according to their tactical aspects, i.e. with regard to the most effective solution to a match situation. But even to find the mental solution to one match assignment, extensive tactical knowledge and experience are necessary. Every good player should have firmly fixed in his mind the knowledge and experience which he can use very quickly as his task continuously changes in a match, for there is usually no time to review the many possible solutions.

Tactical knowledge and experience can be acquired by theoretical coaching with various observational means (photographs, films, model pitch with figures or schematic drawings), but first and foremost by tactical exercises and simplified games. Each perception and analysis of a match situation leaves traces in the memory. Repeated observation leads to a reproduction of thoughts connected with it until a player, on seeing the same situation again, finally associates it in his mind with the same solution. In this way, tactical knowledge and experience are built up and become more established the more consciously that knowledge is acquired, and the more often it is reproduced.

If, however, the most effective method of solving an assignment is not known due to lack of sufficient knowledge and experience, then the most effective tactics cannot be employed. This is true of most players at junior level, and also of many adult teams, since tactical coaching has been largely neglected in training.

e **Speed of reactions:**
A technical or tactical move often fails, either because the correct answer to the problem was not found in the short time available, or because it was found too late since in the meantime the match situation has radically altered. A lack of reaction speed is the reason why many players, in spite of their acute perception in analysing the match situation and finding the correct mental and physical solution to their match assignment, still cannot best employ their tactical skill to the good of their team.

f **Features of movement:**
A high standard of basic characteristics of movement (speed, aerobic and anaerobic stamina, muscular endurance, speed, strength, flexibility and dexterity) is one prerequisite for successful tactical moves. Teams with greater fitness for example have much greater opportunity to vary their game tactically for tactical measures, e.g. such as fast counter-attacks and tight man-to-man marking can only be successfully mastered by players of outstanding physical fitness. Many individual tactical moves can only work by virtue of superior speed, dexterity or stamina. In preparing the tactics for a forthcoming match, an opponent's physical aptitude must be taken into consideration as the starting point of one's own tactical thinking. If an opponent is exhausted by a particularly fast match, he is neither in a position to use his powers of concentration to observe and analyse, nor to think correctly and adhere to the correct tactics as discussed beforehand. However, if his physical fitness regarding the various basic characteristics of movement is very good, their standard will have a positive effect on his perception and analysis of a given match situation, and on the mental and physical solution of his own assignment. Therefore, in training, tactical moves should be practised frequently under extreme conditions of stress so that players get used to playing properly even when suffering from exhaustion.

g **Skills:**
Even the most effective move cannot be carried out if a player has not mastered the necessary skills for the tactical move concerned, (e.g. a long overhead flick over the opposing defence). If too little attention is paid to the actual skills of flicking, hitting, pushing, stopping or dribbling, then a correct rapid solution can be made difficult or even prevented altogether.

The theoretical remarks above, concerning the tactical coaching of hockey players are principally to show that a player's tactical appreciation is not simply the result of his intellectual ability, but the result of all the factors concerned with his play, such as technical skills, his mastery of basic moves, and psychological and personal characteristics. A lack of concentration, or indeed over-concentration (e.g. hand-stopping at corners), inactivity, listlessness, anxiety, lack of self-control, indiscipline, obstinacy and over-excitedness in the heat of the moment, e.g. by dribbling too far, shooting at goal from a bad angle instead of passing back, can all be detrimental to the quality of physical actions.

Mistakes are, for the most part, due to one or more of the factors laid out above and it is clearly important to pay close attention to these factors not only in theory, but also in practice.

TACTICS IN ATTACK

Collective tactics

1 Tactical variety in the collective attack:
   a attack with centre forward
   b attack with two centre forwards
   c attack of pyramid system
   d attack with retreated centre forward
   e attack when opponent uses the offside trap
   f attack against packed defence.
2 Organisation of the positional attack (width and depth in attack).
3 Prepare, initiate and execute counter attacks.
4 Include with surprise for the opponent systematically a defender or a midfield player in the attack.
5 Tactical behaviour in the standard situations (penalty corner, corner, stroke, free hit, push-in, hit out etc).
6 Tactical behaviour in the standard combinations (2:1, 2:2, 3:2, 3:3, 4:3).

Individual tactics

1 Receiving the ball without obstructing.
2 Passing accurately at the right moment.
3 Pass and run free immediately.
4 Pass or dribble the ball?
5 Beating a man.
6 Variety in all individual plays.
7 Shooting and taking the rebound.

TACTICS IN DEFENCE

Individual tactics

1 Positional play.
2 Anticipation of opponents' play.
3 Use of man-to-man marking.
4 Application of different tackles following the actual game situation:
  a lunge
  b dummy lunge
  c tackling in retreat
  d 'jab'.
5 Variations in tackling.
6 Defence of standard situations 1:1 and 2:1.

Collective tactics

1 General tactics in defence (zonal marking, close marking, combined marking, width and depth in defence).
2 Cooperation in zonal marking, man-to-man marking and combined marking.
3 Defence of standard situations (penalty corner, corner, stroke, free hit, push-in, hit out etc).
4 Defence of standard combinations 2:2, 3:2, 3:3, 4:3.
5 Slow down counter attacks or attacks with equal or superior number of opponents.
6 Application of the off-side trap.
7 Defence against a deep lying centre forward.
8 Defence against attacks with continuous interchange of positions.

GENERAL TACTICS

1 Choice of system.
2 Balance between defence and attack in quantity and quality.
3 Balance in defence and in attack in quality.
4 Choice of offensive or defensive tactics.
5 Tactics of using fast breaks.
6 Tactics in certain phases of the game (substitution of players, change of rhythm offering the middle field etc).
7 Application of special measures after considering the characteristics of the opponent as well as the external conditions.
8 Application of special measures after considering the characteristics of the umpires.
9 Mutual understanding through eye-to-eye contact.

14 The importance of man-to-man marking in children's hockey

Hockey as played today by good teams has little in common with the 'traditional' hockey of thirty years ago, but this old-fashioned game is still, to some extent, in evidence. Since the middle 60s, when tactical ideas first transformed hockey in Europe, those skills have established themselves as common knowledge. If coaches and players here remain equally keen to experiment and are open to new ideas, then Europe need have no more worries about its future in international hockey. However, the future of hockey will be in danger if we fail to apply what we have learnt from the experience of top players when training our youngsters.

Serious mistakes are made in school and club coaching programmes for children, which can delay, or even prevent, young people reaching the top (see Chapter 25). Observations of and conversations with schoolboy international players have shown that success is gained in many schools and clubs by means of systematic skills training alone, and the systematic development of tactical awareness, which allows further development of the players' skills, is unheard of in such training.

A consistent mistake, not only in Europe but also in Africa, Asia and Australia, is to teach children zonal marking, either first, or to the exclusion of man-to-man marking. This mistake ought to be remedied even if our models in terms of hockey technique, the Indians and Pakistanis, have as yet given it no thought. The importance of man-to-man marking for fourteen and sixteen year-olds is discussed here.

THE PHYSICAL ADVANTAGES

With man-to-man marking, each defender has one, quite definite, attacker to mark. He is to follow him continuously in his own half, remaining on the goal side of his man in order to prevent a goal. Tight marking demands of the players concerned, both defenders and attackers, concentration and attention, the ability to move fast, stop suddenly, change direction, quickly execute dummy moves, and above all the ability to be able to change from one finely co-ordinated activity to another, according to the changing game situations. In contrast to zonal marking, man-to-man marking therefore develops particularly the skills of movement–dexterity, speed, stamina, and strength.

One essential requirement of a top player, dexterity, can be coached and improved in games under match conditions through man-to-man marking, as can reaction skills. Not only, in man-to-man marking, does the defender learn to react quickly to every movement an opponent makes, but the attacker too learns to make decisions rapidly. Man-to-man marking requires individuals to run more, and therefore training has a more intensive effect than in the more relaxed zonal marking. By this greater workload of running, stopping suddenly, changing direction and speed—activities that do not occur so frequently or intensively in zonal marking—muscular endurance in the legs improves. A dedicated attempt to follow an opponent's movements for just one minute will convince any player of the strengthening effect of man-to-man marking on the leg muscles. In comparison, such development is poor for both attackers and defenders in zonal marking, so the disregard of man-to-man marking in schoolboy hockey is difficult to understand.

THE TECHNICAL ADVANTAGES

If a methodical development and consolidation of technical moves takes no account of man-to-man marking, then the technical skills cannot be coached or learnt to a competitive level.

If a defender brings man-to-man marking tactics into play, attackers are forced to execute the moves they have learnt more quickly, and they have to minimise risk by keeping the ball close to their bodies. If, on the other hand, zonal marking is employed, the player with the ball usually has more space and more time to carry out moves; this freedom is usually allowed only in midfield in the modern game. If man-to-man marking is practised in the games and exercises given to young players, they become more technically efficient.

Teams employing man-to-man marking systems have an enhanced chance of success against other teams who are equal in terms of skill, fitness and conversion of corners, if they play in a disciplined fashion. Zonal marking allows the opposition to settle down in a way that man-to-man marking prevents, and thus demands of defenders the widespread use of one of the most difficult techniques of hockey—tackling in retreat in order to gain the ball from an opponent. This defensive tactic is mastered by only a few top players. Harassing an opponent as he receives the ball (which occurs when man-to-man marking is employed) is, by contrast, much easier and more successful, not least by the fact that the defender is given a great advantage with the obstruction rules.

THE TACTICAL ADVANTAGES

Man-to-man marking is preferred to zonal marking for physical, technical, and tactical reasons. A game with man-to-man marking is more variable, and makes greater demands on a player's flair because situations change far more quickly. A player has to look up from the ball more often than with zonal marking, so as to locate the positions of team-mates, their markers, and his own marker. He has to be able to assess the distance, speed and direction of the ball more quickly, in order to act effectively.

Photo 29 Man-to-man marking was used by Spain in the replay for second place in the pool in the Olympic Games 1976 (New Zealand won 1:0 at second extra time).

All these skills are prime requirements for good co-ordination, so young players must be coached methodically and systematically in man-to-man marking (see *The Science of Hockey* on pages 146 to 150).

THE PSYCHOLOGICAL ADVANTAGES

Man-to-man marking offers a greater scope for building up determination in young players; the effect of training is thus greater. Each player is personally responsible for one opponent. The competitive enthusiasm of a young player is heightened if he is given the task of finding his specific opponent immediately the ball is lost. The better his personal opponent, the greater the will-power required by the defender to fulfil his defensive assingment successfully. Even if he is exhausted, demands are made on his sense of responsibility, and on his will-power: he will try his utmost so that his opponent is prevented from having an easy game. Determination in adhering to his defensive task, decisiveness in tackling, and persistence, even when mistakes are made or exhaustion comes on, are important characteristics. They are developed in a man-to-man system. Further, players acquire the ability to control better their feelings and actions, even when excited, in a state of dejection or worried by unexpected events. Such control is not always easy for young and often impulsive players.

Young players gain strong motivation not only from the success of the whole team, but also from winning a personal victory over an opponent.

After a game employing man-to-man marking, a player can judge his own defensive performance in the light of his opponent's success or failure; all this is important in the psychology of learning. So, apart from its tactical advantages, man-to-man marking is an outstanding method of coaching determination in hockey players (see Chapter 6).

SUMMARY

Should man-to-man or zonal marking be used in schoolboy hockey? Which will develop a team best? In man-to-man marking, the details of movement are developed, technical and tactical skill is improved, and qualities of determination are better acquired. Man-to-man marking makes far greater demands of the motor-functions of both attackers and defenders, so that players acquire a wider experience in the different kinds of movement. Man-to-man marking in schoolboy hockey is the basis of a high standard of performance from those young players when they are older.

GAMES PROVIDING THE BASIS FOR MAN-TO-MAN MARKING

Since repetition exercises easily become monotonous and unattractive, it is best to fall back on suitable basic games, varying them according to the needs of man-to-man marking. These can be both the physical and mental preparation for man-to-man marking, and also the consolidation of movement skills which are characteristic in this type of marking. At first, without stick and ball, the player should learn to recognise, understand and use the necessary movement skills required.

1 *Tag.*
In a limited area (e.g. the circle) one player has to try, as quickly as possible, to tag one of three players four consecutive times, but without holding him. Each tag is counted out loud. After the fourth tag, the player caught becomes catcher, while the first catcher has a short rest. Repeated tagging of the same player requires keeping with the man as long as possible, and following him closely.

2 *Tag with touchpost.*
There are now two catchers, both of whom must try to tag one of the four escaping players four consecutive times (as in game number 1). A flagpost on the penalty spot serves as a touchpost for one of the runners. If holding on to or standing by the touchpost, a player cannot be tagged, but he cannot remain there for more than five seconds. It is recommended that players escaping and catchers are clearly distinguished from each other with different coloured shirts.

3 *Tag with target-switching.*
In an area approximately 20 yards square, there are three players escaping and one catcher. The three trying to avoid being caught must form a team to try to prevent the catcher from tagging a player for as long as possible. This is achieved by running across the catcher's path as he chases a player: the catcher can only chase the player who last crossed his path.

Rapid change to the pursuit of a different player is vital for the catcher if he is to succeed, as is the anticipation by the other players of their own or others' movements, and keeping a clear view of the situation as a whole.

4 *'Hen and chicks'.*
A catcher must try to tag one escaper in a limited area. His task is rendered difficult by a third player, a guard who tries to be always between catcher and escaper. If the catcher tags the escaper in close proximity to the guard, then the guard becomes catcher and the tagged player takes over the role of guard. Holding is not allowed.

An easier game for the catcher involves the addition of further players, who stand in a line with their hands on their hips behind the guard. If the chain is broken, the player responsible takes over the catcher's role, as when a player is tagged.

5 *Running past a defender without being touched.*
Two players stand opposite each other in an area 16 yards square. One player has to reach the opposite base-line by using speed and skilful dummy moves, while the defender must get as near to the man as possible in order to tag him before he crosses the line. After each attempt at running past, the roles are reversed. Who is the first to succeed four times?

If the catcher is no longer allowed into the square and can only tag on the base-line, then less effort is required from the runner. The runner thus learns how to conceal his intentions with dummy moves, sudden changes of speed, and running into space instead of towards a man, and also how to remain out of an opponent's reach to avoid being tagged—all actions and skills he must later use in beating an opponent. The catcher learns how to stay close to a player and how to prevent himself being shaken off by dummy moves; he will also acquire powers of observation and anticipation of the runner's movements.

A graduated series of exercises designed to practise tight marking is given in *The Science of Hockey*, pages 146 to 150.

15 The development from zonal and man-to-man marking to combined marking

When the author moved away from zonal marking, towards agressive man-to-man marking, he was met with surprise and criticism. Zonal marking had been employed for a long time, and the move was a revolutionary change in the 1965-6 season. Up to this time, each defender had had his own defensive zone, in which he had to tackle any opponent who penetrated that area. But when, thanks to a combination of improved skills and physical fitness, play became more accurate and more variable, the strikers, with improved physique and technique, gained a definite advantage over defenders who used the old scheme. Man-to-man marking was introduced, at first only in a few top German clubs, as the most promising tactic for defending. Each defender, with the exception of the sweeper, was allocated an opponent whom he was to follow everywhere in his half of the field in order to prevent him receiving the ball, or at least forcing him to obstruct.

Now continuously following an opponent, each marking defender's range became much wider, so that the demands on his fitness became greater, and responsibility to the team more pronounced, since each player was forced to rely on others. Defensive play by the full-backs and half-backs became more consistent and aggressive, and they learnt to play more offensively and to score goals; they became all-round players (see Chapter 20).

The first great tactical move towards breaking the Asians' superiority was half-backs' defensive play and full-backs' offensive play, introduced in 1963 by H. Budinger. The introduction of tight man-to-man marking in 1966 (introduced by the author in his club-team and later on in the German National Hockey Team) was the second. Without the more offensive tactics of man-to-man marking, the resultant physical fitness and tactical discipline, the great successes of German teams since 1967 would not have been possible.

MAN-TO-MAN MARKING IS NOT ALWAYS SUCCESSFUL

With man-to-man marking accepted and used everywhere in Europe by the top teams, new systems have emerged based on these tactics (firstly the 4:2:3:1, then the 3:3:3:1 system). Nowadays, tactics of close man-to-man marking require an examination as critical as that of zonal marking in 1965-6. It must be ascertained whether they are still equal to modern tactics in attack. To anticipate the answer, a new direction is necessary in defensive tactics, as was the case some years ago.

Photo 30a Zonal marking in front of the goal demonstrated by New Zealand against Spain in the Olympic replay match 1976.

Photo 30b Zonal marking in the midfield demonstrated by New Zealand.

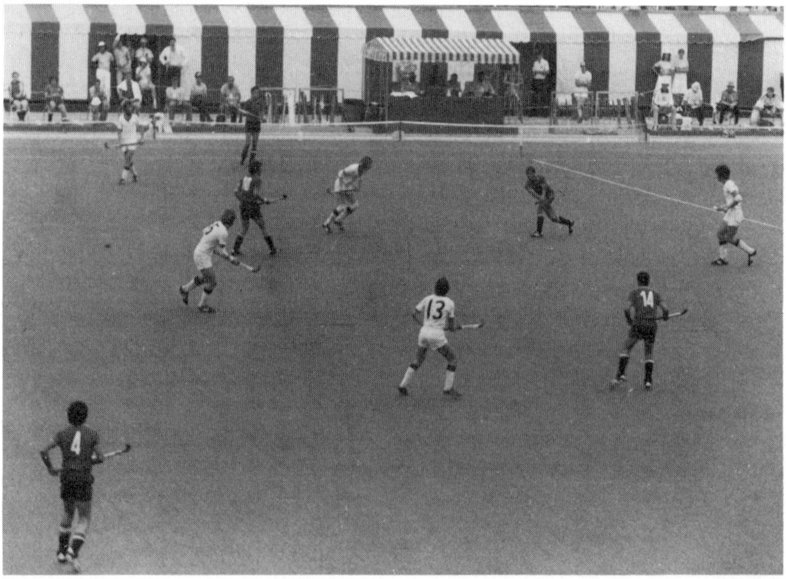

By man-to-man marking we generally mean the close marking of a particular opponent by a particular defender who shadows him everywhere. Although it is impossible to think of modern hockey without man-to-man marking, facilitated by the obstruction rule, this tactic should, in the author's opinion, no longer be exclusively employed. Many clubs which consider it the best defensive method should think again, since the same method can be disadvantageous against tactically very clever and physically very hard opponents.

FIRST REACTION OF ATTACKERS TO MAN-TO-MAN MARKING

In the early years (1967-73), a consistently tight man-to-man marking system was very uncomfortable for attackers. They felt inhibited by the tight 'clinches', and thus out of the game. If attackers had held the upper hand a few years before in the heyday of zonal marking, defenders suddenly had a clear advantage by using man-to-man marking. The attackers' first reaction came at the end of the 60s, with quick positional changes in the forward ranks being used to free themselves from this restrictive system. At first experts were not all in agreement. Should the defender go with his man when a positional change occurs, or not? Extremely fit defences finally adhered to a continued marking of particular opponents even if positions were changed and thereby forced attackers, after running in vain, to give up their increased efforts to get free and return to their preferred regular position.

Defence had thus achieved its aim, and maintained its superiority over attack. Problems that arose when the attack had numerical advantage or equal numbers were solved by continuous match practice. Defenders learnt to recognise certain situations quickly, and provide a solution by short-term reversion to zonal marking combined with tackling in retreat. Defence's superiority was once more established and the strikers' first attack beaten off.

THE ADVANTAGES OF MAN-TO-MAN MARKING BECAME DISADVANTAGES

In the European Championships of 1974 something happened that almost always happens when an intrinsically correct theory is overdone. Almost unnoticed, previous advantages became disadvantages, when the players of top teams played against each other, both employing man-to-man tactics. Intelligent strikers used rigid man-to-man marking that was so uncomfortable for them, to their own advantage. By skilful manoeuvering and changing positions, they were able to draw their markers away from the circle, so as to make space for defenders, who arrived quickly in support. Defenders however, continued to react to these deep positional changes with continued man-to-man marking. They chased around the field whenever it pleased the attacker, (this was evident in the final in Madrid, West Germany versus Spain). Order and cohesion in the defence were destroyed, and gaps in front of the goal opened up. The central defender was involved somewhere on the pitch with the opposing centre forward; the left-half suddenly found himself playing alongside the right-half while there was nobody to defend in his zone at left-half.

Apart from using systematic positional changes in both the width and depth of the field, man-to-man marking was broken down by not taking up positions in attack, in combination with sudden long square passes which transfer pressure. An attack on the left-side involving right attacks from the flank, created unmarked space on the right flank for team-mates suddenly sprinting forward from behind.

Modern attacking play, where positions are consistently changed in the width as well as in the depth of the field, is still in its development, but is the great answer to man-to-man marking. Since all top players can nowadays play in any position, and can change positions according to the situation, such a flexible method of play must upset the exclusive use of close man-to-man marking.

Photo 31 Passing the ball to a marked player often results in a free-hit for the opponent because the forward did not make himself free from the marker (Malaysia vs Canada 1:0 in Montreal).

A SYNTHESIS OF THE TWO MARKING SYSTEMS IS REQUIRED

Surprised by the effect of modern attacking play on man-to-man marking, many clubs considered in the mid 70s a return to the old zonal marking. But this step was not ultimately taken because man-to-man marking did bring success in matches against less clever teams with unimaginative attacking ploys. An attempt to play with zonal marking, however, would have had no such success against the generally increased standard of play, since the numbers of defenders would have to be further raised, so that individual defensive zones would become smaller and easier to control. This defensive system, comparable to a 'wall' that is difficult to break even for an attack switching positions frequently, would have been a retrograde step in the development of defensive play however. After the zonal defence that was prevalent in West Germany until 1966 and man-to-man marking practised from then on, we found ourselves after 1974 in a synthesis, a combination of the two which seeks to combine what is effective and useful in both forms of marking, but which tries to avoid their mistakes and shortcomings, including their exclusivity.

COMBINED MARKING

Combined marking is the defensive tactic which adapts successfully to flexible modern attacking play with continuously changing positions in the forward line. It was used successfully by Spain in the 1974 European Championships, the 1976 Olympic Games and the 1978 World Cup. As with zonal defence, each defender is given a zone to mark, but also an opponent who is in that zone. In contrast to zonal defence, the defender stays close to the opposition player in his zone. In principle, man-to-man marking is adhered to, but is not limited to one particular player. Rather, defenders 'swap' the opponents assigned to them without basically changing their own field of action; and thus order and cohesion in defence are maintained. Taking over an opponent who is changing positions is an important characteristic of combined marking. If one player completes the take-over by closely marking an opponent, then a team-mate must clearly mark a different opponent. This take-over, however, can safely be carried out only approximately between the half-way line and the 25-yard line. Near to one's own circle, the change becomes a danger, since handing or taking over the marking of an attacker means that he is unmarked for a second–a situation which might lead to a goal, and for which reason all ten outfield players must play a tight man-to-man marking system, especially at free-hits in front of the circle.

Once his team has lost the ball, each defender must move into his own zone where he marks an opponent closely. If no opponent is in his zone, he may possibly pick up an unmarked man in the next zone, but he must not ignore his own marking area. Defenders in combined marking should be coached in both zonal and man-to-man marking. If, during an opposition attack, there is an equal number of attackers as defenders, or even numerical advantage in favour of the attack, then the zonal defence must be adopted both individually and as collective defensive measures. Zonal marking aims to hold off an opponent and slow down an attack; attackers furthest from the ball are not marked at all, or only at some distance away; attackers close to the ball are more tightly marked. The change from the zonal marking of an opponent at some distance away to tight man-to-man marking in each defender's zone is to be effected when numbers are again balanced.

A prior study of an opponent's team will show whether combined marking (in the case of forwards who continually switch positions) or close man-to-man marking must be employed.

16 The free hit near the opponents' circle

Victory or defeat in hockey is decided in the space between one's own or the opponent's goal-line and the nearest 25-yard line. The greater number of players assembled in this part of the field inevitably leads to the occurence of most breaches of the rules (fouls, obstruction, 'kick' or 'sticks'), most of which result in a free hit or penalty corner. The Fourth World Championships in Buenos Aires 1978 showed, as did the 1980 Champion's Trophy, that very few free hits close to the circle lead to a shot or a corner for the attacking team. Attackers fail to run into spaces; frequently the hit is taken too slowly; misunderstandings occur between players (occasioned by the lack of proper training) of skilfully executed free-hit combinations, taking no account of the obvious numerical superiority of the defenders; these are all basic causes of errors which facilitate defence for the opposing team.

Photo 32 Free-hit for Argentina in the fourth World Cup pool match against Spain (0:0).

Speed of execution, the effect of surprise and a consideration of dummy manoeuvres combined with attackers' runs, involving quick changes of direction, are all factors which make for success. Speed is expressed most clearly in the way in which the player taking the hit carries it out immediately he puts the ball down. Surprise lies in the sudden change between apparently taking one's time in preparing for the hit and its rapid execution.

At a free hit in front of the circle, insofar as it is not taken immediately, several players must work together in a pre-planned way. Planned co-ordination must not, however, lead to a stereotyped hit. Any good team will naturally have practised and mastered in training several possible variations of the free-hit in front of the circle, so that taking the hit is not merely carried out according to a single previously made plan.

The following are some rarely used variations of the free-hit near the opponents' circle, which strikers should practise until they are fully mastered and can be quickly taken.

1 A simple dummy move can be carried out: the first player who finds himself on the ball suddenly runs away from it and a second player, arriving quickly from the right-hand side or from defence, takes the hit, and passes it either to the first player or to another player running into space.

2 The player taking the free hit receives the ball back from a team-mate who has made a sudden run towards him (thus freeing himself from his marker) to play a wall-pass, (see Chapter 11).

3 Players nos. 1, 2 and 3 carry out a dual dummy-move as follows: nos. 2 and 3 position themselves diagonally behind no. 1 who has the ball. Both remain in these positions passively and inconspicuously at first. Suddenly no. 1 runs away from the ball to the right-hand side, no. 2 (who was standing to his left) runs to the ball and takes the free-hit with a dummy to the left to no. 3, who, at the same time as no. 2 left his position, running behind no. 2 to the left. Only two seconds should elapse between no. 1's feint to take the free-hit and no. 3's actually receiving the ball. At the same time as no. 1 feints to hit the ball, the fellow players in the central and inside-left positions should create space for no. 3 to receive the pass from no. 2. Attention must be given to the rules. There must be 5 yards between the player taking the hit and any other player.

4 An attacker stands about 5 yards in front of and to the left of the player taking the hit and lets himself be tightly marked by an opposing defender. If the defender is marking at arm's length, then the attacker should go to his right hand side. The free hit is taken such that the ball is played into space to a spot approximately 2 yards from the left-hand side of the defender as he stands facing the hitter. While the defender tries to stop the ball on the reverse, the attacker follows up on his right hand side and tries to tackle on his open side, or force an obstruction winning a short corner.

5 An attacker positions himself a few yards inside the circle, just onside in the IL position, since from this position, a pass can be hit at goal most quickly and easily first time. An opponent will try either to mark him

tightly, or to put him in an offside position. If the IL is marked by an opposing defender, then the IL should consciously keep close to him and at first, not try to shake him off. But as soon as a team-mate prepares to take the hit, the IL should sprint towards him. If he is able to shake off his marker, then he plays the ball to him. If, however, he is closly pursued,

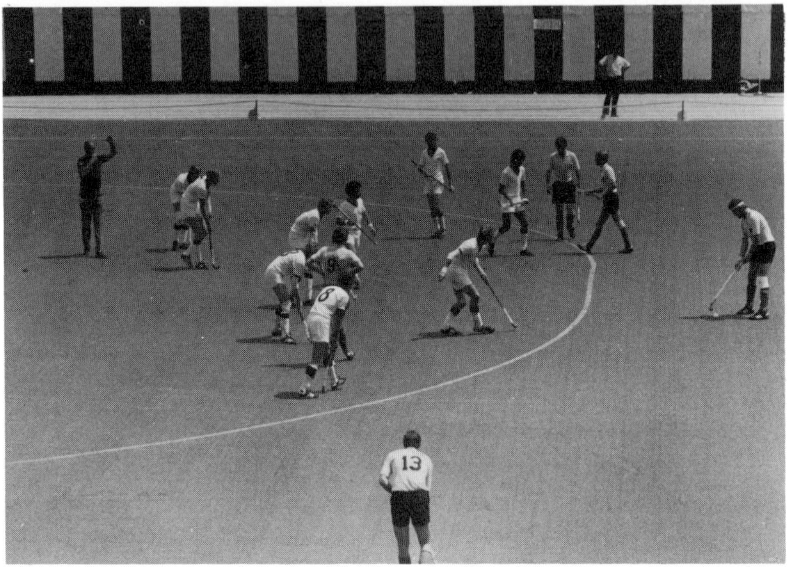

Photos 33a & b Belgium about to execute a free-hit against New Zealand in the Montreal Olympics (1:2).

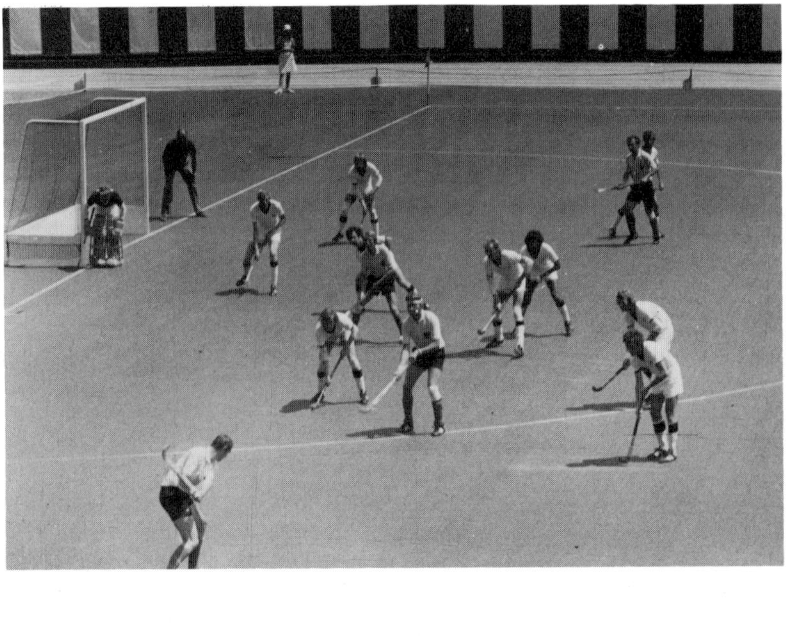

he slowly diverts out of the circle without receiving the ball in order to draw the defender out of his marking system. At this moment, a gap is created for another striker running behind him and the ball should be played into that gap. If the space in front of the forward involved is marked, however, then this free-hit variation is not possible.

6 An attacker stands approximately 2 yards to the right of the right-hand goal-post, and after sprinting suddenly towards the ball, receives a hard pass aimed at the goal-post on his open side, in order to deflect it first time into goal.

Developing the skills to carry out various different free-hits in front of the circle creatively and not just automatically requires a consideration of free-hit exercises in training, at first with passive, and later with active opposition. According to changing match conditions, attackers must learn, having mastered the various moves, to recognise the best solution to a given situation, and carry it out in practice.

17 How a new attack begins with the push-in

Weekend after weekend on pitches everywhere, players can be seen arguing about who is to take a push-in after the ball has gone out of play. But seeing what little advantage is gained from the push-in by the team in possession, the previous argument seems hardly worth it. Around forty per cent of all push-ins taken at the 1st International Cup in Rome did not reach a player of the team which took the push-in.

As with many other technical and tactical 'trifles', too little attention is paid to the push-in. Since even the best teams often fail to utilise the advantage gained, a few comments and pieces of advice on the push-in seem appropriate.

A push-in requires understanding between players. This understanding cannot come about without previous discussion, and the move must be practised in training. The principle that the team with the ball is on the attack also holds true for the push-in; that is to say, a good team can use it to advantage by building an attack from it. An attack can best develop if understanding between the players, together with an awareness of the concealed push, is developed, and all the attackers run in as many different directions as possible, so that a wing-half has the choice of several possible passes. But there is no reason why an inside and a winger should not change places quickly at a push-in, as they would in their normal complex combination play. If the winger, who is usually a long way upfield, comes back for the push-in, then he often draws his defender with him out of defence so that space is made upfield for his inside forward to dart behind the defender's back. Equally, a long push-in, above all in combination with a dummy move, can surprise opponents. How helpless, for example, can a badly organised defence look if the ball is pushed in 20 or 30 yards to an unmarked player who suddenly sprints into space and collects the ball. The next occasion will certainly find the defence prepared for this long push. In this case, a short push followed by a cross can equally create havoc. If a half-back continually plays the same ball when pushing in, an opponent will see his intention and take steps accordingly. So, a half-back should know as many variations of push-in as possible, keep them up his sleeve, and bring them out when appropriate.

The right-half most often gives a short pass to his linkman running towards him. If there is no possibility of this or a push to another player in the middle of the field, then the right-half should pass the ball backwards. The left-half should always take into consideration that pushing the ball along the side-line, gives the opponent, who expects the ball with his open side, at least the same chances to control it as his team-mate. New Zealand exploited this fact in Montreal in 1976, by frequently hitting the ball over

Photo 34 Where should the push-in go? Observe also the unnecessary preparation of the young goalkeeper although the ball is far away.

the right side-line in line with the opposing circle. For this reason, the left-half should, as far as possible, dispense with a long push-in along the side-line unless an apparently passive player suddenly sets off behind an opponent and is unmarked in space. More often than the right-half therefore, the left-half should play the ball diagonally, disguising his intention, back to a defender. Such a move does not gain ground, but the receiver can safely collect the ball and set up a new attack for his team.

If the push-in is to be taken level with the opposition circle, then the wing-half or winger concerned should, on natural grass, take the opportunity of pushing the ball hard into the circle. Basically, when the ball goes off the pitch, it should be retrieved quickly by the half-back. Then the push-in can be taken before the opposition has had time to mark up. If, however, the player loses so much time in retrieving the ball that the opposition is already in position, he should wait until one of his team-mates had made himself available for a pass.

Using a variety of push-ins, including dummy passes, and taking them quickly, greatly increases the chances of the ball reaching a team-mate, compared with time-consuming push-ins which allow the opposition to mark tightly.

These few remarks, though by no means exhaustive, lead to the conclusion that the push-in is a basic constituent of successful play. Therefore, sufficient attention should be paid to it in training, and especially to the push-in near the circle. A skilful push-in, or a bad one, exploited by the opposition, can lead to a goal chance.

18 Half-time coaching

Coaching can be considered as the tactical and psychological measures taken by a coach to keep his players' standard constant, or to modify it according to circumstances. On the basis of a critical analysis of what is actually happening, coaching can be seen as one form of rapidly imparting information both during the game itself and at half-time.

Photo 35 The author at half-time of the European Cup final 1974 with Juan Amet, Agustin Churruca and 'Pepe' Borrell from Spain.

Most hockey coaches only discuss mistakes in the five or ten minutes half-time break and criticise the performance of individual players or the team as a whole in argumentative fashion. The consequences of a too great emphasis on errors may be:

1 That the player spoken to at half-time will want to show the rest of his team, the coach and the spectators that he is able to overcome the mistakes he made in the first half. In such cases, over-hasty, irrational and ill-considered action is often the result. Moves come to nothing.

2 That the player or group of players concerned ignore their guiltiness, become lazy, no longer feel responsible to the team and give up.

Although modern psychological coaching methods dictate that encouragement can lead to greater effort, but that censure can hamper performances, the half-time break is still used by many coaches for censure and for running over mistakes. Valuable time is thus lost, time which could better be used for developing a strategy for the second half.

Instead of censuring players (or groups of players) publicly, factual criticism should be coupled with new tasks to be accomplished so that when a player's role for the second half is explained to him, his mind is not concentrating on mistakes but on the new task in hand. The coach's implied criticism of his first half performance is thus accepted by the player but is concealed within the new task to be accomplished. Criticism must always be tied to facts. There will be plenty of time after the game and during later training sessions to discuss and improve upon mistakes made in a match. Match observations and a statistical analysis are useful in this respect, though a video-tape recording is obviously the key solution (see Chapter 27).

19 Movement in hockey

THE PHYSICAL NATURE OF INDIVIDUAL MOVEMENTS IN HOCKEY

Movements specific to hockey have a characteristic articulation, which is usually visible to the eye. The use of three phases is characteristic of all single movements such as hitting, pushing, flicking, beating a man etc. For example, in hitting: a slight change of balance onto the back foot together with the raising of both arms and stick, is the preparatory phase of the movement; the follow-through until the stick meets the ball is the main movement and the stick stopping together with the recovery of the body's balance is the end-movement.

Photo 36 Andre Bolhuis (Netherlands) demonstrates perfectly how to hit the ball on the run off the right foot in a test match against Spain (2:2) in Utrecht 1976. On the right is Jaime Arbos.

In the *preparatory phase*, the player is concerned with creating the best conditions possible for the subsequent main phase in order to maximise power transfer to the ball. The greater the backswing, the longer the muscles can perform their job of acceleration in the main phase. This is particularly evident in a comparison of hitting and pushing. Hitting is significantly more powerful because the ball's acceleration can be increased by a higher backlift. With a run-up, the preparatory phase can be made even more effective.

Leaving the run-up out of consideration, it is characteristic of all preparatory phases of movements that they occur in the opposite direction to movements in the main phase. A main movement forward is preceded by a backward preparatory movement: a main movement diagonally forward and upward, as with the flick, is coupled to a preparatory movement diagonally backwards and downwards, and so on. Top players are able to suppress partially the preparatory movement, for tactical advantage (especially in flicking). Slow motion, however, shows that there is always a preparatory movement, since it is part of the basic structure of pushing, flicking, beating a player, or whatever. A high backswing gives away the direction of the ball to a defender or goalkeeper, and as a result of the delay, gives an opponent more time to tackle than if the preparatory phase is suppressed. But such suppression has disadvantages, since it generally impairs the quality of the main phase–for example a flick could be less long or less accurate.

In the *main phase*, the emphasis lies in co-ordination of movement, making the individual components of the main movement into one smooth action. The *final phase* is a retardation; it is also often a transition stage for the start of a new movement (e.g. stopping and hitting; or pushing and running into space). There is reciprocal dependence between the individual phases of movement, for if a phase is altered, the effect is not limited to the phase concerned, but affects subsequent phases too.

From what has already been said, the following conclusions for learning and coaching can be drawn:

1 The phase structure of the movements to be learnt should be well worked out in training, because otherwise, for example, a beginner might flick without proper lean-back, and separate that lean-back from the main action with a pause.

2 The preparation phase should correspond to the distance, power and speed of the main action. Therefore, for example, too great a step to one side in feinting with the ball can prevent a player beating an opponent, or excessive speed of the run-up when hitting the ball can mean that the actual backswing cannot be properly executed.

EFFICIENCY CHARACTERISTICS OF MOVEMENT COMBINATIONS

In the game of hockey, it is not individual movements, but combinations of movements which provide solutions to match problems. In order to succeed, the two basic characteristics that belong to a perfectly executed movement or combination of movements must be present: accuracy of movement and anticipation. Each is vital for teaching and coaching movement properly; the rhythm, flow and flexibility of movements are not of such great importance in hockey as in most other Olympic sports. Nevertheless, only all these characteristics together can determine the level of co-ordination of movement reached.

The *rhythm of movement* observed in top-class players is only vital in one aspect of hockey, since that rhythm achieves the most economical use of strength, in beating a man, defending, flicking, hitting, etc. The change between tension and relaxation is the change between using up energy and restoring it. Without this rhythm, which is lacking in beginners, the point of exhaustion in a match is reached far sooner, and since tension increases rapidly because of cramp or a lack of technical skill, movements flow less economically, and too much strength is unnecessarily used up in unco-ordinated movements.

As part of coaching difficult technical skills, the rhythm and flow of hockey movements is only of minor importance, compared to hand ball or volleyball. Whilst rhythmical movements are an essential requirement for top-class performance in the high-jump, shot-putt, swimming or rowing, they can be positively disadvantageous for a hockey player, considered tactically. Especially if opponents are well acquainted with a player, a distinct rhythm of movement can make defence easier for the opposition.

According to Fetz, *accuracy of movement* is a very complex phenomenon (related to the motor-senses) which comprises, and is influenced by, a great many constituent parts (accuracy of observation, estimation of distances, controlled expenditure of energy, speed of reaction, ability to concentrate, directional instinct, intelligence, etc.). The exact, precise movements of top players, which are not only accurately directed but also exact in execution, give them self-confidence and belief in their own ability; every inaccuracy makes a player unsure of himself and explains disappointing performances on some days. The success of the three players involved in a corner routine, therefore, is in direct relation to the accuracy and exactness of their movements.

A lack of accuracy in movement is immediately self-evident in hockey. A shot at goal goes wide, a pass is not stopped, and a tackle fails to win the ball. The reason for lack of accuracy in movement might be one of the following:

1 The phase structure involved in carrying out movements has not been sufficiently considered (most frequently it is the preparatory phase which is not thought about sufficiently).

2 Because of nervousness, tension and relaxation are insufficiently rhythmical.

3 The development of physical qualities has not been sufficient.

4 The player's ability to control his own movements is insufficiently developed.

5 The player is over-affected by an opponent or the state of the pitch.

Anticipation of movement is a psychological process that happens before random actions are carried out. The anticipation of one's own or others' movements is one decisive characteristic of the quality of a movement or combination of movements, and forms one prerequisite for flow and rhythm in action. It occurs more or less distinctly in all connected movements in hockey, for in every movement's preparatory phase, anticipation of the main phase already exists (anticipation of one's own movements). But anticipation of one's own movements is also involved if, in the course of the final phase of a movement's execution, as a part of a combination of movements (e.g. stopping the ball), the following move is preconceived (such as a pass to a team-mate). This anticipatory process can be observed in watching closely the two component movements, which melt into one harmonious combination when a player anticipates his movements. That the following movement is preconceived is evident in the position of the feet, the direction of movement, and the direction of vision. While with beginners and more advanced players who have had little practice, a little pause occurs after stopping the ball before moving on to the second phase of passing it, anticipation of the pass is evident in the final phase of the preceding movement in top-class players. The motor-system of top players functions with greater fluidity, harmony and elegance.

Even in daily life, people constantly anticipate their own movements. The movements involved in picking up an object are planned, on the basis of experience, before the object is actually grasped. The size and weight of that object are anticipated and allowed for. (This explains why even experienced players need some time to adjust to a hockey stick that is different in weight, stiffness or length.)

As well as anticipating his own movements, a hockey player must anticipate the movements of the ball, of one or more team-mates and of opponents. This anticipation of external movements is a distinct skill. All players try to anticipate the direction and the speed of the ball, the positions and movements, both spatially and temporally, of opponents and team-mates. The goalkeeper can anticipate a shot at goal from the way an opponent is moving, as well as from his team-mates' defensive actions. An attacker anticipates the defensive moves of an opponent, the goalkeeper's position, and opponents' strengths and weaknesses. A defender can anticipate the movements of the player he has to mark from the defensive actions and positions of his colleagues.

The correct anticipation of external movements is a skill acquired only through experience of the real conditions. In hockey, as in daily life, widely varied experience is necessary to allow one to adapt one's own movements to those of others. An inexperienced hockey-player will, for example, frequently play the ball too far in front of his team-mate, or will not be able to anticipate an opponent's pass because he cannot interpret an opponent's position, the direction in which he is looking and the backswing of his stick.

With increasing practice and experience, however, he is more accurately able to differentiate between, and anticipate, external movements. The anticipation of team-mates' and opponents' movements is considerably more difficult than anticipation of the path and speed of the ball, since once the ball is moving, it is subject only to the laws of physics. Nevertheless, an uneven surface or a very strong spin can bring about a wrong anticipation of the ball's movement.

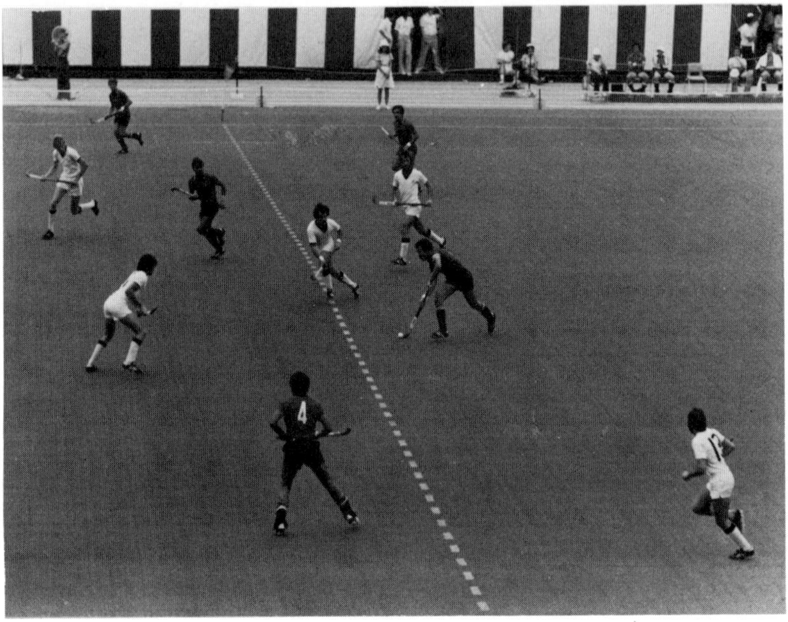

Photo 37 Two New Zealanders about to anticipate a possible pass from Jorge Fabregas (Spain) to Juan Arbos (4) in the Montreal Olympic Games.

More difficult than anticipating a team-mate's movements is anticipating an opponent's, particularly if the latter is trying to conceal his moves, or deceiving a player of the opposing team by a dummy move or switching to a totally different move. His feint can succeed if only the backswing is made (the preparatory phase of a move) and the main and final phases are not carried through, or if the dummy move is broken off during the main phase (e.g. in the case of a dummy pass with body and stick feints). Instead of carrying out the move as originally suggested, a different move ensues which an opponent cannot anticipate. The opposing player can thus no longer react quickly enough to reach the ball or player.

Good players employ dummy-moves of all kinds time and again in order to make anticipation by an opponent difficult (e.g. at a free-hit). Experienced players who, besides an exact knowledge of the peculiarities of the player carrying out a dummy, have at their disposal a good eye, can quickly analyse the game situation, and are even able to anticipate an opponent's dummy, rendering it useless, until a player finds a new way of disguising his movements.

PRACTICAL CONCLUSIONS FOR COACHING

On the grounds of its great importance in improving skills and tactics in the game of hockey, anticipation must be properly considered in coaching. In coaching the anticipation of one's own movements, it must be borne in mind that anticipating too soon can be as disadvantageous for following moves as anticipating too late. For example, anticipating a hit too soon at stick-stopped corners often means that the ball is not properly controlled. The anticipation of external movements should be systematically developed over a long period, with regular competition with team-mates and opposition in exercises and small games, in training matches, and, finally, in competition.

20 Comparison of players' range of action in Pyramid and 4:2:3:1 formation

A physically fit team, tactically prepared, should always aim to have as many players as possible in either defence or attack, as the game situation requires. One requirement for realising this basic tactical premise, besides outstanding physical fitness in all players, is that each player must be able to play not only in his own preferred position, but also be adept at playing the roles of other defenders or attackers.

This tactical premise doubtless led to the dissolution of the traditional system that had dominated for decades, with five attackers, three half-backs, two full-backs and a goalkeeper. Since 1966 when, for the first time, a system was practised in West Germany, with four strikers, two link-men, three backs, one sweeper and a goalkeeper, the game of hockey has become more varied and more dynamic.

Key to diagram:

(1) Receives the ball and passes immediately.
(2) Receives the ball, dribbles a short distance (up to 2 seconds).
(3) Receives the ball, dribbles over 5 yards (more than 3 seconds).
(4) Free-hit or bully.

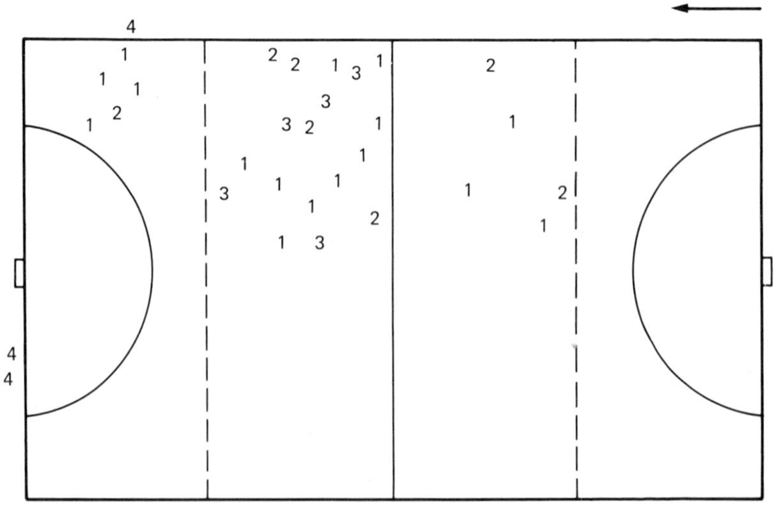

Figure 34
Inside-right in the pyramid formation: Nagaya (Japan).
Second half: Netherlands v Japan.

In particular, the ability to drive forward and vary an attack by frequently changing positions without neglecting the notion of 'defensive safety first' brought about the change whereby an individual player's effective zone no longer remained restricted to one limited area of the pitch, as was previously the case.

The increased effective radius of a player's duties both in defence and in the build up of an attack is the result of the greater demands of stamina and technical and tactical ability made on an individual player by a 4:2:3:1 system. In the old system, each player had his own particular limited zone (see figs. 34 and 35) which he only rarely left. There were thus more rest periods, and players had to master fewer technical and tactical moves—only those which were directly related to their own positions and which recurred time and again.

Observations of men's and women's national teams between 1967 and 1971 were to prove these findings, and determined answers to questions such as these:

1 How often and in what part of the field does a player gain possession of the ball?
The effective radius of each position could thus be established. Several observations were made of each position, and those that showed the most typical features were finally considered to be characteristic. The effective radius is increased negligibly by runs made by a player who then fails to gain possession of the ball.

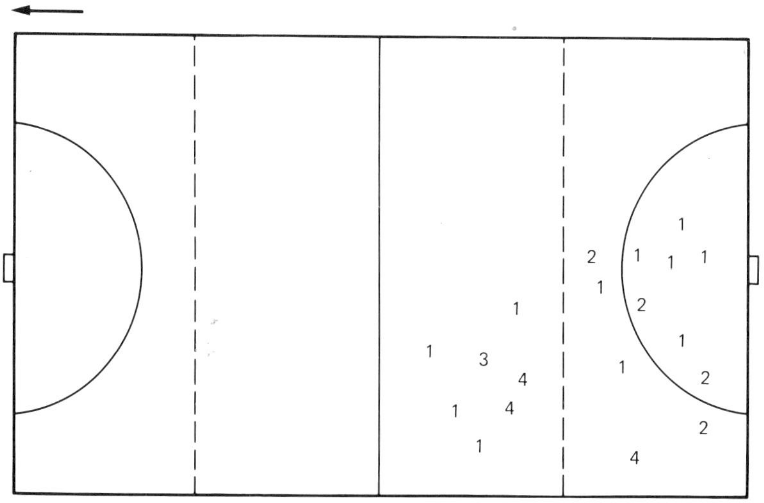

Figure 35
Left-back in the pyramid-system: Hannelore Blumenberg (W. Germany). First half: West Germany v. U.S.A.

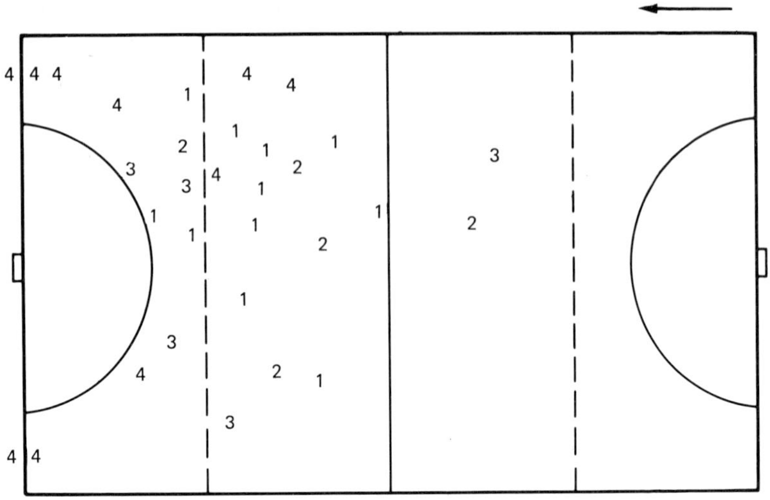

Figure 36
Inside-right in a 4:2:3:1 system: Detlef Kittstein (W. Germany).
First-half: W. Germany v. Rhodesia.

2 How long is the player in possession?
For collecting the ball and passing it on immediately by hitting, flicking or pushing, two seconds were thought accurate (no. 1 in the key), four seconds for a short dribble (no. 2), six seconds for a longer dribble or more than 5 yards (no.3), and two seconds each for taking a free-hit or a corner, hand-stopping, pushing-in and taking the bully (no. 4). The frequency of the various moves results in the time (out of thirty-five minutes) that the player was in possession of the ball (see Chapter 28).

Through an analysis of numerous observations, the result emerged that midfield players have the greatest effective radius of all players. It is greater than that of an inside-forward in the pyramid system, since midfield players play not only deep in the centre, but also on the wings (figs. 36 and 37).

The four attacking positions in the 4:2:3:1 system are more variable regarding the use of the length and width of the pitch, than the attacking positions in the pyramid system, the characteristic of which is the strict retention of positions in channels up and down the pitch. The wingers likewise show different tendencies. While almost all wingers in the pyramid system, and many wingers in a 4:2:3:1 system, keep mainly to their own positions, other wing-forwards in a 4:2:3:1 system prefer to wander occasionally across the entire width of the pitch. But in these cases, the tactical instructions of the coach must come into play along with the player's individual characteristics and the opposing team's tactics.

It is difficult to make a general statement about the centre-back's effective radius in the 4:2:3:1 system, in comparison to the centre-half in the pyramid system, since the centre-back's effective radius in the 4:2:3:1 system is

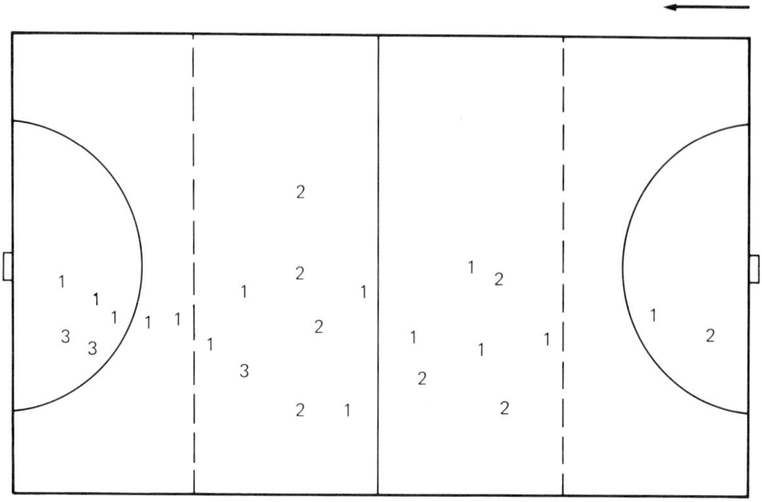

Figure 37
Left-link in a 4:2:3:1 system: Ulrich Vos (W. Germany).
Second-half: W. Germany v. Rhodesia.

greatly dependant upon the danger that the opposing centre-forward constitutes, and how often the latter switches from the centre channel in order to attack down the wings. If the opposing centre-forward is a strong player, but one who rarely switches to the wings, then the effective range of the centre-back is restricted and does not correspond to the centre-half's range in the pyramid system. But if the opposing centre-forward attempts to evade the centre-back's close marking by frequent moves to the wing, then the radius of the centre-back (who generally plays defensively in the 4:2:3:1 system) is almost equal to that of an attacking centre-half in the pyramid system. His range extends over his own circle, the entire midfield and deep into the opposing half. In this last area of the pitch however, a centre-half in the pyramid system generally appears more frequently.

Wing-halves' play, which was tactically very limited, especially in West Germany between 1960 and 1969, slowly began to develop a larger effective radius, and thus also more complex technical and tactical moves in attack and defence. By safeguarding defence with a 'sweeper', it is now possible for wing-halves, whose role was previously defensive, to become more often involved in attacking moves without taking excessive risks, and thus help to take pressure off midfield players. The effective range of a wing-half generally covers a channel approximately 15 yards wide near one side-line between his own goal-line and the opposition 25-yard line. In setting up an attack, he is not generally to be seen using the whole width of the pitch, as in the case of the strikers and occasionally the midfield players, but rather a channel of space approximately 15 yards wide, which a winger cutting inside leaves free.

Photo 38 Germany's young wing half E. Schmidt drives his way through into the 'Indian circle' (Germany vs India 4:3 in Karachi 1980).

The 'sweeper' has the smallest effective radius. His play is determined by the need to safeguard the goal and cover his team-mates. But his effective range is still greater than that of a left or right-back in the pyramid system. The better understanding a defender shows in the 4:2:3:1 system, the more often his 'sweeper' can suddenly move forward into attack if a suitable situation arises, whereby his effective range increases to nearly that of the other players.

If the effective range of each of the ten outfield players in the pyramid system is compared with that of the ten outfield players in the 4:2:3:1 system, then the effective areas of individual players clearly emerge as larger in the 4:2:3:1 system, with one area overlapping others. Furthermore, the amount of running required of individual players in the 4:2:3:1 system is less variable than in the pyramid system. The level of match intensity can be much higher in a 4:2:3:1 formation with man-to-man marking combined with frequent positional changes over the length and width of the field. Strict positional play, as is still demonstrated in 1980 by the Indians and Malaysians, results in many highly trained players showing no obvious sign of fatigue after seventy minutes' play. In the pyramid system, less demanding of fitness, therefore the fitness of players (nowadays better trained than previously) is not utilised to its full potential. This is another argument for the pyramid system being considered outdated.

21 Team tactics for the 3:3:3:1 formation

Together with general individual tactics (e.g. running into space, marking closely or within a zone, passing, dribbling) which set out the basic format of each individual's play, and general team tactics (e.g. using more defensive or attacking tactics, or changing rhythm), group tactics must also be considered. Group tactics are largely defined by the choice of system of play.

Group tactics, as a part of an overall tactical plan, embrace all the effective moves that groups of players (also the group wing, wing-half and left or right link) make in both attack and defence, including the perfect co-ordination of two players (as such the smallest team unit) within a group of players. While individual tactics and team tactics have altered little in the last decade, the basic tactical rules for groups of players have been subjected to great change, all over Europe, following a successful conversion to modern systems, and alterations in the off-side rules.

1 The sweeper

Like all players, has a variety of tasks to perform, particularly so as both attack and defence. For example:

- the organisation of defence;
- covering the foremost player by means of zonal marking;
- cover defence, using feints if there is no numerical advantage over the opposition;
- temporary marking of an opponent man-to-man if a team-mate takes over the role of sweeper for a few moments;
- the intelligent, varied build-up of counter-attacks using long passes to take pressure off the defence, or, when appropriate, short passes;
- occasionally attacking as far as the opposition circle, at suitable and well-considered moments;
- forcing an offside position in co-operation with his fellow defenders.

2 The wing-halves and the centre-half (centre-back)

These mark their opposing players. If opposing attackers continually change positions, then they can 'swap' their opponents who must also be tightly marked. By moving into attack, the wing-halves can support their forwards with surprise breaks from defence, i.e. along with their specific defensive skills, these players ought also to possess an understanding of attacking moves.

If an attacker is tackled on the opposite side of the pitch, the players of this group must make themselves available for a square-pass switch, and then dribble along the side-line in the direction of the goal after collecting the ball. In this case, the winger should run inside, thus making space available on the wing. In more defensive tactics, the winger in front of the corresponding wing-half can also retreat, in order to support his defender, whereby a change of position deep in midfield becomes possible. Attacks by the half-backs should be concluded by safe passes, accurate crosses, or even by shots at goal. A dribble into a numerically superior defence (carrying the ball quickly into space is not to be included in this) runs the risk of losing the ball, with the chance of a dangerous counter-attack by the opposing team.

In defence, when the opposition is attacking on the opposite side of the pitch, a wing-half should cut inside in support. If the ball is passed 40 yards to his unmarked winger, he will still have sufficient time to prevent him crossing the ball or dribbling into the circle.

The centre-back should control the centre of the field in front of the sweeper, with whom he should be in continuous cooperation. He should move occasionally into attack, avoid any dangerous dribbling near his circle, and generally serve his midfield players with hard push-passes.

The midfield players

These are the link between defence and attack and vice-versa. They cover the length and width of the field. One of the three midfield players is usually given the task of tightly marking the key player of the opposition, while the two others should pick up their opponents in a zonal marking system in front of their own 25-yard line, but put the opposition under pressure by tight man-to-man marking between the 25 and their own goal-line. One of their most important duties is to keep their strikers in the game with accurate passing, and, with sudden long dribbles out of defence into space, to disturb the teamwork and numerical superiority of the opposition.

All three midfield players thus need outstanding physical fitness and good qualities of foresight, so that they can exploit opponents' weaknesses, and vary the speed and rhythm of the game to suit the situations and the opposition. In this respect, they are supported primarily by the sweeper.

The three strikers

These should be able to dribble at speed, shoot from all positions, use the wall-pass, and be able to change positions in order to create gaps for a team-mate's passes, distract an opponent's attention, and draw defenders into positions in which they are unsure of themselves.

Since the strikers are often unsupported, they must be able to force a

Photo 39 Two of Europe's most successful midfield players in the 70s: Francisco Fabregas (Spain) and Ron Steens (Netherlands) playing together in 1975 in the European All Star Team 'Los Caracoles'.

way through even a numerically superior defence, or at least be able to hold the ball until support arrives from midfield or defence. In the opposition half of the field, they are also the first line of defence, i.e. they are to tackle the opposition in their own half in order to disturb the planned build-up of counter-attacks.

Systematic wing play should attempt to draw the opposing defence (especially the sweeper) away from the goal, so that the other strikers and midfield players have more space to score. Before crossing the ball accurately, the winger will often need to outrun his marker up to the 25-yard line (or beat him in combination with a team-mate), and then head towards goal by the quickest route. Before the sweeper can narrow the angle, the winger should give an accurate and well-timed centre. The centre-forward (or any player finding himself in that position) should consider heading often towards the sweeper, as long as the ball is not in immediate playing distance. In doing so, he commits two opponents to a relatively confined space, thus creating gaps for his team mates.

A precise system, or simply overall tactics?

In a system, the distribution of players on the pitch is stipulated. This distribution is usually obvious only at the beginning of play, since the rigidity of positions is relaxed as every player tries to fulfil the more general defensive or attacking duties ascribed to him by the system. A system can in no way define an individual player's role in every detail, because first the opposition and its system is an unknown quantity, and secondly, the individual qualities of each individual player are very different. These two areas are the realm of tactics. Tactics concern technical ability, and individual players' physical, mental and psychological attributes. A system is therefore the base upon which tactics are established. It is basically a consistent form that does not alter throughout the entire season—in contrast to tactics.

Features of a good system

1 It should be simple, intelligible and easy to carry out in practice. It should not make too heavy demands on a player's attention, since if it does he will unnecessarily tire mentally.

2 It should assist both attack and defence to the same extent: it must be balanced. For example, a system that principally requires players to attack can lead to failure against a team of equal ability if it takes too little account of the opposition's attacks.

3 It should distribute the players evenly on the pitch, and should, as far as possible, make equal demands on the running of individual players. In addition, it must take note of any part of the field of play where particular pressure is to be applied.

4 The system should be flexible (i.e. adaptable to any opposition), without requiring changes which depart from the well-drilled basis of the system.

5 The system should facilitate a smooth transition from defence to attack and vice-versa.

Only relevant tactics can lead to success with a system. The fact that some of the world's best teams have not yet started the transition from the pyramid system via 4:2:3:1 to the 3:3:3:1 system is due to a failure to subject their tactics to critical scrutiny. An understanding of the necessity to mark several players of an opposing team man-to-man was the principle reason for changing the traditional system in 1965-5. Tactics can thus lead to new systems if they are employed over a longer period, but a new system can often facilitate the successful use of new tactical measures.

22 The growth and development of sporting performance according to age

The mastery of technical moves is a decisive factor on the road to peak performance, and because the road to a solid mastery of a technical move and its use in a match is often very long, teaching a hockey player his skills should be started at an early age.

The Pakistanis were found to hold this view, when, during the PIA Champions Trophy Tournament in 1980, they were asked about the Pakistanis' technical superiority: 'The West European national hockey teams all play excellent hockey, and we are impressed above all by their physical fitness, but they will probably not (in the next four years) come anywhere near our level of skill–which does not fade at top speed–because, seen as a whole, they begin playing hockey too late. Most of our successful Olympic players started to dribble at the age of six or eight and today, after twenty years of repeated practice, they have reached a standard of dribbling that Europeans, who mostly start at the late age of fourteen, will find it hard to achieve. Of course, there are other reasons to be put forward for our technical superiority–for example, our superior agility and dexterity. But in the last resort, it is that early acquaintance with stick and ball which makes the difference.'

As players grow up to be world-class only according to their experience, there is an urgent need to introduce hockey to our youngsters earlier than has previously been the case. Talent must be discovered and fostered at an early age.

BASIC TRAINING SHOULD START AT THE LATEST AT TEN OR ELEVEN YEARS OF AGE

At the very latest, children should begin to play hockey when they are ten or eleven years old, but without neglecting active exercise in other sports. All children go through a phase when they are between eight and eleven, of being particularly dexterous. At this skilful age, the very coordination of difficult movements is easily learnt, so that hockey skills are quickly acquired, and many technical elements are provisionally mastered straight away.

The adolescent child (according to Neumann) is thus endowed with almost all the requirements for learning sporting movements: a balanced development of height and weight and tremendous drive and curiosity.

The unknown game of hockey is especially attractive to the inquisitive child of this age who is alive to everything. From stick and ball come a great impulse to participate. Once his initial inquisitivieness and curiosity have been channelled, the child progresses to master some more difficult technical moves and begins to understand the problems of free space, then he will have 'bought' the game. It is up to the coach concerned to utilise this 'optimal learning time', between the ages of eight and eleven, to the full. Whatever coach and child neglect at this stage cannot be fully regained later on.

Just as fast as he learns, the child will forget again if the technical moves are not 'fixed' by repeated exercise. The coach ought not to proceed too quickly through his exercise programme, but does need to vary it sufficiently within the framework of the basic notion; the child at this age can only concentrate for a short time on the move he is engaged upon, due to his high level of response to the world about him. His desire to carry out the exercise correctly lasts only a short time. A little variation in the form of the game or exercise, however, usually re-arouses his interest, and this renews his will power and activity.

On no account should a coach or ambitious parent make the mistake of having the child play hockey exclusively at this stage. He should rather be urged to play many forms of sport up to the age of fifteen or so, in order —on the basis of a rich experience of sporting activity—to learn the complicated movements of hockey more easily and lastingly. The process of acquiring and using tactical skills runs more smoothly for the player who has not been taught hockey from an early age to the exclusion of all else.

Early specialisation (between ten and thirteen years old) often leads to the success desired of a child and young teenager. But, as the Russians Juschkow and Wolkow's investigations show, success in sport at this stage in a player's development does not always guarantee adult performances crowned with success. Although in the sixties it was recommended that exclusive swimming training should begin at the age of seven or eight, the majority of 'Masters' between 1960 and 1972 started swimming training after this age (with more than 2,000 examples from this sport in the U.S.S.R.). Among the Soviet swimmers who reached the finals of the Olympic Games up to 1972, not one, according to Wolkow, had begun swimming training before the age of ten.

Championships for eight-to-twelve year olds on a large scale at regional, provincial, or national level, are therefore to be discouraged despite the apparent attractions of single sport coaching, preparing children according to adult coaching principles.

Early specialisation and organising championships at national level can lead to:

a Over-stretching players, reaching peak performance by means of excessive demands on as yet not fully mature players, because those in charge want to win tournaments as much as do the children.

b Excessive determination, method and seriousness in training, which detracts from the enjoyment in playing, and allows no time for spontaneity or trial and error.

c One-track, monotonous training, brought about by imposing limitations on the game, aimed at developing certain moves deemed 'important' for results.

d Abandonment of growth in performance according to rate of physical development.

Competitive experience can be gained by young players at an appropriate scale in friendly matches, tournaments, and local league matches. If a child takes part in his first championship match at a higher level at about fifteen, it remains new and attractive. His interest and motivation will not stagnate but will reach a new high-spot which must be put to best use by means of planned and progressive training methods.

SPECIALISATION AT THE AGE OF FOURTEEN

Specialisation in one particular sporting discipline (e.g. hockey)—that is to say a planned systematic development through training—should take place at the age of fourteen with boys, and twelve with girls. In this respect the relationship of the twelve-to-fourteen year old boy or the eleven-to-twelve year old girl to their contemporaries is determined by the fact that they are competing with others of the same age group and form a picture of themselves from interaction with them. Each wants to be better than his or her contemporary. It is understandable that for this reason a child will now go for a sport in which his or her talents triumph over those of an opponent.

The conditions for successful hockey teaching at the ages of fourteen-to-sixteen for boys and twelve-to-fourteen for girls are none too advantageous at this stage, due to the physical development of the child. Only modest success in training will be observed at this stage, partly to be explained by the fact that boys and girls are often weak and weary, and tend towards listlessness if exercises do not suit them or are too difficult to carry out. Besides this listlessness, the situation is further complicated by feelings at the other extreme; sporadic desires to let off steam in acquiring technical skills. On the whole, children of this age usually run around in a game using up their strength very uneconomically, and to some extent very clumsily. The fact that little interest is generally shown in explaining individual moves is a further reason for the modest coaching successes in comparison with eight-to-twelve year old boys and seven-to-eleven year old girls. Greater headway is always made however, when the coach shows understanding of the children. The child usually shows little interest in a method of hitting or flicking which is technically correct. However, if flicking is undertaken—after a short introductory exercise ('Let's train first')—as a competition, then the egocentric child who wants to show off will at once accept each piece of technical advice from the coach in order to better his chances in the competition. For this reason competitive exercises should be uppermost in hockey training for this age group (fourteen-to-sixteen for boys, and thirteen-to-fourteen for girls), rather than repetitive practice.

COMPETITIVE TRAINING FROM THE AGE OF SIXTEEN

At the age of sixteen for boys and fourteen for girls, the requirements for serious competitive training are first appropriate. The scope of training is considerably broadened. The child's physique is once more 'in harmony' with his motor-functions. This physical balance becomes more evident year by year and is followed, in many cases, by an increasing desire to compete, and by tenacity in practice.

Photo 40 Especially in Pakistan young players of eighteen already play in the national team, in this case Azam in the 1978 World Cup.

HIGH-PERFORMANCE TRAINING FROM THE AGE OF EIGHTEEN

High-performance training, that may continue for the next fourteen years, has as its aim the development of the qualities that determine the level of performance up to peak capacity and the attainment of the highest standards. Peak performance for a hockey player is generally reached between the ages of twenty-four and twenty-seven.

The clear conclusion from these brief observations is that a hockey coach must not only have a full knowledge of the skills of hockey but must, in addition, be at home with the most important psychological characteristics of children in the various stages of their development. In this way he can show them greater understanding and sympathy which will simplify his task of developing skilful players.

23 Talent-spotting in hockey

Interest in talent-spotting in all sports has increased dramatically in recent years. Everyone has realised that truly outstanding sporting performances (even with the best coaching methods and optimal living and training conditions) can be achieved only by individuals with an extraordinary gift for following the disciplined schedules required. Especially talented sportsmen, in comparison with less gifted players, do have a greater chance of success, given the same amount of coaching. Talent selection up to and into the 1960s was based on personal experience and intuition; this has now been replaced in the foremost sporting countries by a more systematic search for sporting talent. Nowadays, especially in Eastern Europe, teams of sports scientists, working with the top coaches in the sport concerned, single out the basic physical characteristics (body size, weight, proportions and constitution) and psychological qualities which, for the sport concerned, might be the performance-limiting factors. It is necessary then to find individuals with these attributes and characteristics, using a series of simple tests at schoolboy level, tests which have objectivity, reliability, and validity.

In hockey, as in most sports, it is the characteristic motor qualities that could particularly be used to discover sporting ability. After much personal experimentation, I tried to reduce the talent-spotting tests to five: accuracy and speed of reaction, speed-strength, general stamina, mobility, anticipation.

In order to obtain a quick, realistic idea of the value of these five tests for talent-spotting in hockey, the tests were tried out not with ten to twelve year-olds who had played no hockey, but with fifteen year-olds from a single club, who therefore came from the same social conditions and had the same demands made of them by the same training methods. Repeated observations of their performances in matches in 1977, along with an analysis of their sporting careers in the four years in between (the best nineteen year-olds were playing in the Junior National team while the weakest could only manage a place in their club's third XI) resulted in the following interesting conclusions, which might be considered in the search for future outstanding hockey players.

THE BEST WERE OFTEN NOT THE MOST GIFTED

The players that fared best in the specially classified aptitude tests were at that time considered the most gifted, since the standard of their motor skills, as well as of their anticipation, was higher than their contemporaries'. However, the children who fared best in the 1973 tests did not fulfil their promise, and the children of *average* standard in those basic physical qualities are today much better hockey players. Does this mean that the tests we devised are inappropriate? Or were the results confused by a separate factor not allowed for or recognised?

An exhaustive study of technical literature on the subject of talent-spotting supplied the answers and explanations. The problem is that the majority of coaches, selecting on the basis of results of a test taken only once, give preference to the best-placed and faster-developing children in their forecasts, and do not allow sufficiently for variations in the extent to which individuals of the same calendar age may vary in their physical development. Thus, some slow developers were judged to be of low actual ability when in fact their skills were to develop later, whilst the good performances of some players in the tests were not the result of their high innate sporting talents, but merely of their accelerated genetic maturity. According to W. N. Wolkow, young players who mature faster than their contemporaries have greater strength, speed, and aerobic stamina, which can often result in better performances in aptitude tests and matches. However, if their performances are compared with children who are at the same stage of development but of different ages, then the differences of physical attributes are negligible.

A concentration of interest on the faster developers of the top group was therefore not appropriate; indeed the gifts of children with a slow or retarded development were only to come to light later on (in 1976-77). While the faster developing children quickly reached a certain level and then improved little up to their nineteenth year, the slow developers showed a much greater increase in standard, and by their nineteenth year had generally reached a higher standard than the fast developers.

The acceleration of a player's development between the ages of ten and eighteen is therefore only a temporary factor which can improve performance, yet non-selection at this age can often bar the way into the national team for slow developers, thus giving them little chance of systematic assistance by the national Association. Selection for under-sixteen national teams, in both boys and girls, should not be taken as an automatic indicator of the players' value for the preparation of future top players.

NO PROGNOSIS IS POSSIBLE AFTER ONE SINGLE TEST

An aptitude test that is carried out only once, on children of the same calendar age, (as was the case in 1973) is not suited to talent-spotting, because the standard of the basic motor characteristics established by the test may have little or no relevance to a young sportsman's future development, but may simply record his ability at that moment.

A direct statement of this can be found in the experimental work of H. J. Bulgakowa, V. M. Zaciorsky and N. M. Kremljova. These Russian sports scientists argue that an assessment of a child's swimming ability must not be made according to his performance in a one-off test, and still less must weaker swimmers be sifted out on the basis of their performance in that test. If this practice were to become widespread then, in their view, many talented children would be lost to the sport of swimming and indeed, the final results of a test taken after the second year of training did prove that quite a large proportion of the children that had received low marks in the first test had reached a similar or higher level of performance than the others. After two years of coaching, the order established in the first test had been completely upset.

TALENT-SPOTTING CAN BE CARRIED OUT IN PHASES

According to Siris, tests can lead to a fairly reliable prognosis of a young athlete's potential only if both peak performance level in the test and the rate of increase of that performance over the following eighteen months are taken into account. This, however, requires a training schedule lasting eighteen months for all the children involved in the test under the same conditions, in addition to at least one repetition of the first aptitude test at the end of that time. The faster the rate of development of a child's physical qualities in the first eighteen months, of training, according to P. M. Gaidarska, the more easily the young player can be coached. If we were therefore to adhere to the advice of these Russian sports scientists, we would carry out talent-spotting in hockey in several stages, and not select with an aptitude test that is taken only once.

SELECTION BEFORE PUBERTY WITH CHILDREN AT THE SAME STAGE OF PHYSICAL DEVELOPMENT

In order that good performances in the tests due solely to faster physical development do not lead to false prognoses of children's potential, school children should no longer be selected according to calendar age, but according to their biological age. Alternatively, according to Ulbrich, an aptitude test should be carried out at a calendar age of eleven or twelve years, in which case a prognosis is fairly reliable, unlike tests carried out at ages approaching puberty (thirteen-sixteen years old). The age of eleven or twelve is also the best time for talent-spotting for another reason, since this age is often when children turn towards sports training for the first time.

To coach a beginner up to international level takes, on average, twelve to fourteen years. Peak performance in hockey is generally reached between the ages of twenty-four and twenty-seven. This long time-span also requires that talent-spotting should start with children prior to puberty. But a system of talent-spotting which covered all these factors, and saw hundreds of children of the same biological age for a period of eighteen months, tested them, coached them under the same conditions, tested them again, and finally judged their sporting potential, would be on too large a scale for the funds and personnel that hockey has available in most countries. And even if these requirements could all be met, the results and effectiveness of this aptitude test would have to be valued against the great expense of time and organisation.

Further, even when the tests are extended over eighteen months, some children might still be too near the age of puberty at the time of the final test, or might have gone through a period of physical development within the eighteen months which is greater than that of the other children of similar biological age. So even an eighteen-month test may produce distorted results. There are other points to be considered in organising and carrying out talent-spotting in hockey.

Photo 41 Both aged twenty-seven, Jorge Fabregas (with the ball), and Frans Spits, were captains of Spain and the Netherlands in the 1974 European Cup semi-final (1:0), and both showed peak performances.

DOUBTS AS TO THE RELEVANCE OF THE RESULTS GAINED FROM TESTING MOTOR QUALITIES

In the complex game of hockey, with its twenty-two players continuously changing the state of the game, and its infinite number of possible individual moves and combinations, it is unrealistic to try to expand the innumerable performance factors into a group of aptitude tests. Even the very best test exercises could only partly correspond to the technical and tactical moves in hockey and would, furthermore, exclude numerous factors that play a decisive role in the successful execution of a move (e.g. perception and analysis of a situation in a match, considering varying pitch conditions, including artificial turf, ability to concentrate, willingness to play hard, tactical discipline, anticipation, etc.). Thus, even these aptitude tests which look at the rate of and speed of development over eighteen months are of little value to hockey compared with similar tests in swimming or athletics.

A group of tests which examined the most important characteristic motor skills for canoeing is listed in *Specific and general performance testing of top canoeists in the D.K.V.* (German Canoe Federation) by M. Letzelter and M. Glaser. The two authors showed that of three specific canoeing tests (250 metres, 350 metres and 2000 metres) and four general motor tests (4-minute run, and 10 km run, in addition to bench-press and bench-lift with 40 kg weight for 45 seconds), all of which were used by the German Canoe Federation to test their canoeists, only the specific test of 350 metres canoeing had a statistically valid relation to competitive performance. All the other tests were not reflected in competitive performance. Transfer this conclusion to the complex sport of hockey, and one would expect that any significant relation between test results and match performances would exist only if the structure of the aptitude test were very closely related to match situations (see 'Natural' selection of talent below).

Taking all these experiences into account, we cannot assume that even the best group of tests for talent-spotting in hockey would be able to give any reliable results, but only that, at best, it would provide limited information about future hockey talent. Time and again, players who have been considered ungifted and not worth encouraging suddenly burst to the top after their twentieth birthday, and become regulars in the national team. Control of sociological and psychological factors in particular have made the achievement of a very high level of performance possible on the basis of merely average physical endowment. On the other hand, highly gifted and intelligent players who seem set for a great career in club or international hockey fail to progress because they do not show the necessary willingness to play, sufficient willpower, or enough discipline in carrying out a tactical assignment in training. Getting the best results in a test are ultimately of no use if a young sportsman is insufficiently motivated!

In the author's opinion, aptitude tests should not be used primarily for prediction of ultimate skills, but rather as a stimulus to better performances in coaching. Since there remains no objective criteria which define talent in hockey, nor will there be in the foreseeable future, it remains the expert's experienced eye that recognises and selects talent from a group of children. But this brings us to the next problem: how can a child's hockey skill be recognised if he has never played, or never ever heard of, this Olympic sport?

'NATURAL' SELECTION OF TALENT

Even if such tests were to exist, hockey aptitude tests would not lead to better prediction than a 'natural' selection of talent based on two sporting disciplines that are well known to most school-children—football and either handball or basket ball.

Test No. 1

For approximately five minutes, six children of the same age should play football in two teams of three players, on a pitch 25 yards long (without side-lines) and with goals (no goalkeepers) 8 feet wide. As well as observing technical skill, the experienced coach conducting the test should watch for information about such important performance-determining factors as overall coordination, mobility, speed (speed of reaction, speed off the mark, and agility in various situations), toughness, stamina, tactical appreciation, positive play, etc. The result of a complex analysis of all these factors is scored: three (talented), two (limited talents) and one (ungifted).

Test No. 2

Eight children of the same age should play handball or basketball in two teams of four on a normal-size pitch. Each youngster must first, according to his ability, name which of the two sports he will take for Test No. 2. His performance is judged as in Test No. 1 on points (one to three), whereby the specific skills of handball or basketball which the youngsters have already been able to master, should not colour the judgement of their later potential as hockey players.

To avoid unnecessary frustration or discouragement from failure, selection should take place at the end of the test: all youngsters who scored less than four points as a combined total are eliminated from further plans. If doubt remains in classifying some of them, either the test should be carried out again under the same conditions, or the children concerned should be allowed to be part of a group in which hockey talent can be recognised, so that children who have, after all, an aptitude, are not lost to the game.

Test No. 3

Measure the maximum oxygen intake, so that the cardio-pulmonary system's performance can be determined. Finding a maximum oxygen intake is one of the most important parts of talent-spotting. The difference between a top-class sportsman in endurance sports and an untrained person can be as much as one hundred per cent, and the value varies by fifteen or twenty percent in the individual, according to how often he or she trains. Only if a youngster achieves a good result in this test too can we consider him to have outstanding potential.

If a club is looking for talented youngsters, another limited kind of talent-spotting can be employed, first used by the author in 1963. If a club member visits a school near to the club, schoolboys can be acquainted with the game of hockey in a games lesson. Those who are sufficiently interested by the game and who want to, can spend two months attached to the club, without cost and with borrowed hockey sticks. They are invited to a special training session twice a week. According to the number of those interested, up to three groups of twenty-five schoolboys per trainer should be established. After each coaching session, the coach should record, alongside the schoolboy's attendance, important observations in physical and psychological matters. After two months' coaching, the children are released for the summer holidays and told that they may hear from the club again at the end of the holidays. However, only those the coach sees to have talent do finally receive an invitation. He selects schoolboys who demonstrate real potential in their motor skills, in the ability to acquire technical and tactical hockey skills rapidly, and in their intellectual attitude to the sport.

24 'Bambino-hockey' for 8 to 12 year-olds

Many mistakes are still made everywhere in the world in the organisation and teaching of the game of hockey. The match itself, focal point of all practice and training, is wrongly organised, from both pedagogical and psychological viewpoints, for children.

A competitive game of hockey, with its complicated and difficult rules, and with the technical and practical demands it makes, exceeds the mental powers of eight to twelve year-olds. They are not acquainted, for example, with the distribution of assignments in the game. If a ball is thrown into play, they will all run after it; they will all try to do the same thing. This is not simply due to a lack of vision, and to impulsive movement, but also because children of this age-group are egocentric. Each boy or girl wants to make a better impression than the other. Now if children are given simple tactical assignments (e.g. 'you are an attacker' and 'you are a defender'), they will immediately feel hampered in their game. In a match, a child will not willingly keep to the trainer's instructions, if they impose restrictions upon him and prevent him running around!

The frequent bunching near the ball of eight to twelve year-old players leads to bad distribution of players, and to dangerous tactical situations which do not increase the attraction of the sport. This packing together of players means that moves, so carefully worked out in training, are neglected (e.g. beating a man), and the general result is a haphazard and dangerous clearance hit in the direction of the opposing goal. The coach is disappointed not only because what he has taught in training has not been put to use in a match, but also because he frequently fails to keep the children in their positions despite his great vocal efforts. Neither are the players happy, especially the wing-halves and wingers, since the coach may have put them in positions where they cannot play the ball as often as, say, the players in the middle of the pitch.

Until recently, the relationships between players' age-groups, their technical and tactical standards, the number of players in a team and the size of the pitch, and all these factors which combine to make for good play, were not considered. The author finally concluded, however, that the hockey-playing child under the age of twelve cannot advance his skills with weekend matches or coaching sessions followed by practice matches, if there are eleven players in a team; thus he or she cannot be effectively given enthusiasm for the full-scale game of hockey. When playing with more than seven eight to twelve year-old players in each team, the game soon reaches its critical level. The greater the number of players, the more the quality of play falls, until, with ten or eleven players, the game breaks down. The

Photo 42

modest standard of an eleven-a-side match, as already shown in various examples, emerges in the physical sphere, but even more so in the technical and tactical sphere. The principal performance-limiting factor is not really the standard of coaching of the young players or their lack of talent, but rather the size of the field of play or the greater number of players in a team. For eight to twelve year-olds, the best game of hockey is 'bambino-hockey', played on a pitch 100 yards by 60. It is best played with a 'mini-ball' approximately 100gm in weight, and of the same circumference as an adult ball.

THE ADVANTAGES OF 'BAMBINO-HOCKEY'

'Bambino-hockey', with only six outfield players and one goalkeeper, played on a full-size pitch allows the children to play hockey 'like grown-ups' without the disadvantages of the eleven-man game. Players bunching together, and the resultant dangers are all now more easily avoided, and the game spreads out. Children come into contact with the ball much more often in 'bambino-hockey', and since they are now continually involved in the game, and have little time to stand idly around, stubborn and selfish play is soon eliminated, and more and more combination play appears. However, during the first five minutes, teamwork is rarely evident, because individual players still see only themselves, the ball and the goal, forgetting their five team-mates entirely. But since the game lasts two halves of twenty-five minutes (with five minutes for half-time), and involves much more physical exertion than the eleven-man game, each child soon learns to consider his team-mates, a fact that, especially in the second half, leads to combination play. Even if a team-mate is considerably weaker, he will still receive passes relatively often (which is hardly ever the case in eleven-a-side), for with a smaller number of players, the other players of the team are constantly forced to depend upon him. Thus in 'bambino-hockey', even the weaker players can perform an important service towards the success of the team as a whole.

Along with increased running and more frequent contact with the ball, 'bambino-hockey' has one other advantage, in that it allows the young beginner more time and twice as much space for technical and tactical moves than does the game with eleven players. Moves that have become automatic as a result of coaching can thus first be tested tentatively in 'bambino-hockey' and after the first successful attempts, more regularly and confidently.

Even the tactical ability of children can be developed more easily in 'bambino-hockey' than in the careless and often wild play of eleven-man teams. Gradually, individual and team experience of tactics will develop, since in 'bambino-hockey', certain match situations recur more often due to the reduced number of players. This experience will later facilitate a child's integration into an eleven-man team. Thus, for example, children no longer play by themselves as time goes by, but call upon assistance from team-mates more and more. Dribbling, which uses up a lot of energy, is reduced in favour of more economical passing. Players soon learn not to carry the ball too near to an opposing defender, but to pass it beyond his reach, or begin a combination move to beat him.

Furthermore, children will learn to consider attacking the opponent's goal and defending their own equally. Just as they should always leave a fast striker in attack when under siege, so they can soon learn that play that is too offensive allows the opposition the chance to counter-attack and thus score. But it is not enough to make simply these and many other general and specific tactical observations. The coach must point them out to the children, explain them and demonstrate them. Only by precise instruction and demonstration by the coach, with sufficient repetition of tactical situations in practice, will the tactical foundations be laid on which the further specific development of a child's tactical play can be built. (see Chapter 13).

25 Is our way of teaching hockey to children still up to date?

Coaches constantly gain new experience and knowledge from teaching children, and from contact with competitive sport. They should apply this to examine critically the teaching methods used in hockey coaching.

Children, their way of life, and their expectations have without doubt changed greatly in recent years. What was valid only a few years ago has frequently already been overtaken, or is no longer relevant. Even the predominant method of analytical coaching in hockey, where the answer to one technical element of play, or to one tactical move, is found by analysing the overall course of the move is no longer attractive enough in the opinion of a growing child. In such a scheme, that single move is then practised in isolation, with a few variations of the exercise, so as to mimic the game's requirements.

The youth of today certainly has the desire to compete but it is soon satiated if persistent repetition is involved in practice, as is the case with the analytical coaching method. Long and persistent analytical practice makes training uninteresting and boring for children. Exercises offered in the name of hockey mostly dispense with the drama of the game, and with its wealth of variety. These are the characteristics which make the sport so attractive and interesting. Children can hardly believe that 'real' hockey players do analytical practice as they are often forced to. Often the coach has limited them to a few exercises (e.g. hitting and stopping, or simply dribbling) because he is determined that he should first create the necessary basic skills for the game before moving on. The analytical method is very easy to manage, too, as he moves from one technical element to the next, using many exercises, and only at the end letting the children play hockey. In this training, it is not then the trainee that has become the focal point, as it should be, but the content of coaching.

If the child's expectations are not fulfilled (and what he wants is experience and enjoyment from playing), then his readiness to practise will slowly diminish. A weariness in practice emerges from suppressed instinctive play. If the coach detects such weariness or listlessness in practice, he must try to spur the children on or awaken their interest till the end of practice, till the beginning of the game to follow, or till the match at the weekend, by consciously using refined methods of motivation. However, this will succeed only a few times. If training continues to be uninteresting and boring from the players' point of view, because it does not correspond to their desires, then children will draw their own conclusions. Children, especially around the age of fourteen, where they become very critical, will suddenly have no further interest in hockey. They stay away from training

Photo 43 Ties Kruize teaching boys and girls from Hillside junior school (Salisbury) as a special mission during the 'Los Caracoles' tour 1975.

because they can see no sense in preparatory exercises, and they have no understanding of the need for practice for a future target, nor the willingness to do it.

Willingness to train with application is usually to be expected only at the age of seventeen or eighteen. In order to awaken the willingness to train systematically in younger players, children should be shown, in practice games, that for good play, they still lack mastery of some particular technical skill or tactical element. Only if a player has experienced failure will he recognise the need for practice and work willingly to improve the move or movement concerned. His training should thus be motivated. It should not originate in the coach's authoritarian attitude (he should now abandon the role of coach and become a helper or counsellor) but in his own willpower.

Coaching that does not correspond to the needs and wishes of children, lacking sufficient actual play, and simply requiring exercise after exercise, will fail to motivate players, and must of necessity fail in its aims. Hilmer is also of this opinion, and he states in *Grundzüge einer Theorie der Spielerziehung* (*Fundamentals of the Theory of Games Teaching*) 'The specific practice of skills appears pedagogically meaningful and justified only at the stage in which children can show interest from within, and can view practice as relevant to the game.'

Coaching in which match play has the dominant role however, limiting exercises in favour of hockey matches, has equal problems, since it can hardly lead to a true improvement of standard. As early as 1902, Schleiermacher in his *Pädagogische Schriften* (*Pedagogical Writings*) stated that physical education without the practice of sufficient exercise becomes mere play. He was to consider match play as being 'purely in the present, the absolute negation of the future'–to be compared to an activity which does concern the future, i.e. practice.

If we organise the exercises that relate to the future so that they at the same time offer satisfaction in the present, then we have found a way of making practice attractive again from the viewpoint of a critical youngster. That is to say, practice will always be attractive to a youngster *if* it is related often enough to the basic situations of hockey. These basic situations are:

shooting at goal, and defence of the goal;

creating chances and blocking the circle; and

setting-up attacks in midfield and preventing the build-up of opponents' attacks.

Only in these situations do youngsters really feel that they are hockey-players. It matters little whether they are in attack or defence; they are then whole-heartedly involved. Due to the fact that situations change continuously, they can play 'properly' and thus gain experience of the basic situations of the game.

A new method of teaching hockey, one which takes the youngsters' wishes into account, should put the young hockey-player regularly in one or more of the match situations above. By accepting the single basic forms of the game, it is possible to let boys and girls play actual hockey in their first hockey lessons; in the conventional analytical procedure they would still be busy with systematic practice. By simple practice alone, the youngsters cannot capture the spirit of the game and experience its true character. If we offer more games in teaching hockey, then we should be able to attract the youngster to hockey for good.

It is important to develop games from this important theoretical basis which are valuable as exercise because of the learning patterns they involve, and which can be accepted by children as 'the real game'.

GAMES INVOLVING SHOOTING AT GOAL AND DEFENDING THE GOAL (SHOOTING GAMES).

1 Hitting the ball to a partner through a set of flagposts (2 yards wide), either from a stationary position or whilst running, or after dribbling the ball. The players are to stand 10 yards from the posts when hitting the ball, and 6-8 yards away when pushing. Who is the first to score ten goals?

2 a Two small goals (2 yards wide) are set up 20 yards apart, using four

flagposts. In doing so, care should be taken that all four posts are in a straight line (fig. 38). Two players (outside-right 1 and 2) should stand eleven yards behind one goal, the first of whom is in possession of the ball. He dribbles it at full speed parallel to the goal-line as far as the second goal, when he hits the ball through the goal to a third player (3). This player continues similarly. After a player has hit the ball through the goal, he must always follow the ball in order to wait for the next cross, approximately 10 yards behind the goal.

b Hitting on the run can also be practised from left to right with the players taking up positions as in fig. 39.

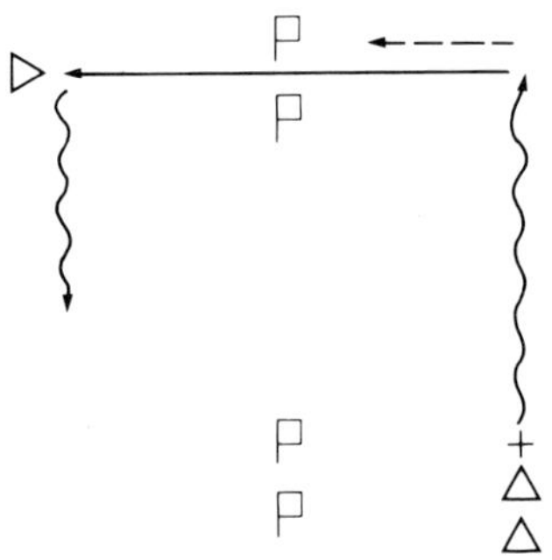

Figure 38

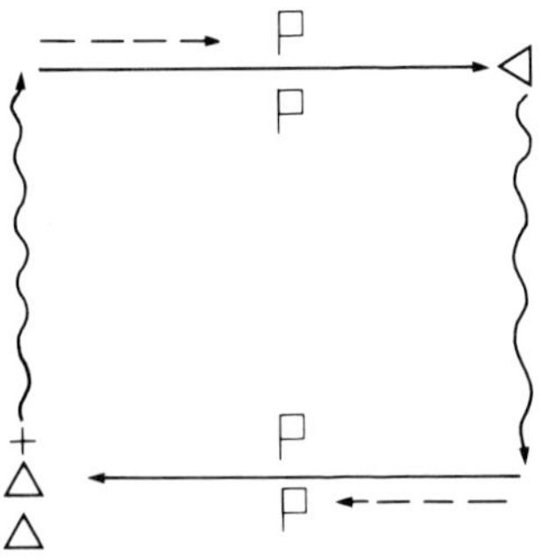

Figure 39

3 Two goals (15 yards wide) are set up opposite each other at a distance of about 35 yards–more or less according to the standard of the players involved. One player stands on the line in each goal. Each player has to hit the ball at his opponent's goal, or try to stop the ball on the line. Having stopped the ball, it must be hit back at the opposite goal within three seconds. Who is the first to score ten goals? All shots above knee height automatically give possession to the other player. Pay attention to 'sticks' in more advanced players.

4 Hitting the ball from a stationary position or whilst on the move, or dribbling, through a goal of flagposts 4 yards apart defended by a goal-keeper (without pads). Distance from the goal is approximately 12 yards. Whoever scores a goal becomes goalkeeper. The player who has been goal-keeper most times within five minutes is the winner. Minimum of three players.

5 Penalty-corner striking, with a neutral goalkeeper (with pads). Whoever has scored the most goals after five (or ten) shots is 'corner-king'. If the ball rebounds from the goalkeeper's pads, following-up is allowed, with a second shot at goal.

6 Corner-king (or 'penalty-king') without a neutral goalkeeper. Between three and six players hit (or flick) at goal from the edge of the circle (or the penalty spot) in strict rotation. Each player begins with ten points. Whoever lets in a goal, as goalkeeper, loses one point, and every player failing to score becomes the goalkeeper. If a player fails to stop a shot as goalkeeper, he not only loses one point but has to stay in goal. A player who has no points left has to retire from the game.

7 The idea of this game is to hit the ball across the entire width of the pitch over the side-line in the area between the 25-yard and the half-way line. The trainer decides which team shall hit first, and the game begins with a hit 7 yards in front of that team's goal-line. Wherever the ball can be stopped dead by one team, the next hit can be made from that spot in the opposite direction. Both teams of two or three players should line up suitably across the length and width of the playing area, in order to stand a better chance of intercepting the ball. If the ball goes over the side-lines (i.e. the half-way line or the 25-yard line) then it is hit back by the opposing team from the point where it crossed the line. To ensure that all players can join in, no player may hit the ball twice in succession. The winner can be decided either by the number of points scored in a specified time, or by the game being played until a specific number of points is scored.

Although these seven shooting-games only comprise one part of a well-played hockey move (the first two exercises involve only shooting at an open goal) children do begin to feel like 'real' hockey-players. The simplicity of these seven games also makes it possible for the weakest players to experience playing hockey.

GAMES WHICH, BESIDES SHOOTING AT GOAL AND DEFENDING THE GOAL, INVOLVE CREATING CHANCES AND BLOCKING THE CIRCLE.

1 a Two against one (or three against two) towards one goal defended by the goal keeper.
A team comprising one (or two) defenders and a goalkeeper defends the goal until the two (or three) attackers have shot wide (or allowed the ball to roll out of play over the side-lines or 25-yard line).

b Ditto, but with a time limit, i.e. the attackers must shoot at goal within thirty seconds or else they lose their chance to attack.

2 a Two against one, alternating between three teams.
Three teams of two players each play on a pitch 25 yards long with two goals each 3 yards wide. If either the defender or the goalkeeper (who may not leave the goal-line) can gain the ball for three seconds, then they give up their defensive role and attack the opposite goal, while the

players who were previously on the attack must take up positions in front of, or in, the goal that they had just unsuccessfully attacked. A goal can be scored from any distance, but if the ball is hit, then the goal does not count. If the ball misses the goal, the attacking and defending teams change places, as when the defender or goalkeeper is able to hold the ball for three seconds. If the ball rolls behind the open set of posts, the team that is now on the attack should immediately play on with a reserve ball (kept ready beside one of the goalposts). In the meantime, the ball that has rolled behind the goal is retrieved by the team who were on the attack prior to loss of possession. Which team can score the most goals in ten minutes? It is advisable to distinguish the three teams by means of different coloured shirts.

b This game of two against one, alternating between three teams, is made more difficult if the attacking team has only eight seconds to score a goal. If they fail to score within this time, then the defending team automatically receives the ball and the chance to attack.

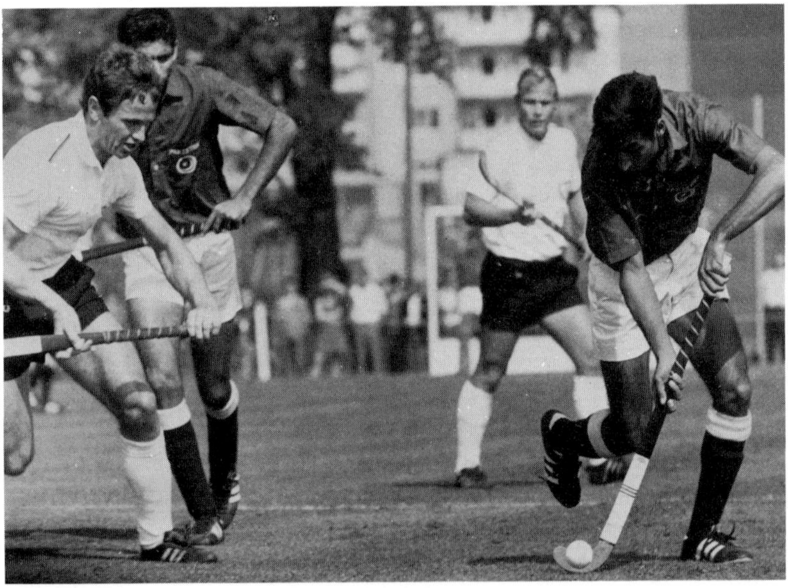

Photo 44 Two players of Pakistan (Laeq with perfect positioning in posession of the ball) about to beat Suhl (Germany).

3 'Ball over the line', with three teams.
Three teams play across the pitch from side-line to side-line. The goal-lines are formed between the half-way line and the 25-yard line by the side-lines of the normal pitch, and these must be dribbled over with the ball being controlled. Two teams of two players each defend their goal-line, while a third team of three or four players, positioned in the middle of the

pitch, attacks for two minutes. The number of attacks carried out in two minutes depends upon the stamina of the individual players concerned. After an attack is cleared, or after a goal is awarded by dribbling the ball over the goal-line, the attacking team are immediately given the ball back in order to build up a new attack towards the opposite goal-line. This is played without offside and without side-lines.

In approximately ten minutes, each team must have attacked for two minutes and defended for four minutes. After the three periods, the best team is the one which has scored most goals. There are two players to each team who are then strengthened by a third neutral player, when they get the chance to attack for two minutes. The work-load can be varied by lengthening or shortening the duration of the game or the size of the pitch.

Further exercises and games are to be found in Chapter 13 under the heading 'Games for coaching organised running into space and passing'.

To the basic task of scoring and preventing goals in these games further match functions were added—those of creating chances and blocking the goal. In all three games, the roles are only fixed for a certain length of time, and at the end of this time players are given a different function to perform—e.g. defending instead of attacking. There is, at this stage, no free play. One characteristic of these games is that the build-up of an attack is not yet hampered by opponents, since the latter are active only near the goal.

The games that follow represent the first step towards playing in a team of eleven players and demand of youngster that they can change their function to that of the goalkeeper, goal-minder, defender, attacker or link-man, according to the match situation.

GAMES INCLUDING ALL THREE BASIC SITUATIONS IN HOCKEY.

1 a 'Ball over the line', two against two (or three against three) with a neutral player who always assists the attacking team. The aim of the three (or four) players in the attacking team is to build up a situation, by means of skilful team-work, from which the ball can be dribbled over the opposite goal-line (the goal is 15 yards wide). After a goal, the neutral player changes to the team now in possession of the ball.

b 'Ball over the line', two against two (or three against three). Played according to the rules of 1a, but without the neutral player.

2 'Ball over the line', four against four, with and without neutral player, from side-line to side-line across the hockey-pitch. The goals are the side-lines between the half-way line and the 15-yard line. If played without the neutral player, the use of man-to-man marking over the length and breadth of the pitch is advisable, both on psychological and physical grounds.

3 'Ball over the line', five against five. If possession is lost, four players of each team must adopt tight man-to-man marking tactics over the whole field while the fifth man covers space behind the defensive line, and 'sweeps'.

4 Game towards four goals (see fig. 15).

5 Game towards three goals (see fig. 24).

If the exercises and simplified games illustrated here are adopted in coaching hockey to children, youngsters will move from one assignment to the next, readily taking roles of increasing variety, until they gradually evolve into a hockey-team. Furthermore, interest and enthusiasm will be awakened and maintained, an indispensable requirement for good play. Particularly valuable for the development of tactical awareness are the games on pages 165 to 167; they form the basis for any improvement in a player's standard, and are not to be underestimated.

6 Mini-hockey. Besides the exercises and games already illustrated, a six-a-side hockey league should be organised for young hockey players up to the age of twelve. This league should last throughout the whole season, interrupted only by special 'bambino days' when seven-a-side hockey tournaments are organised, with several matches for all the teams participating.

Rules for six-a-side hockey

a The game can be played on a pitch approximately 25 yards by 60 yards, on any smooth surface (grass, gravel or tarmac, indoors or outdoors). If a normal hockey pitch is to be used, then four pitches can be marked out (see fig. 40), with the side-lines acting as goal-lines. The goals marked by posts or flags must be full-size (4 yards wide) so that as many goals as possible can be scored.

b A team is made up of five or six players including a goalkeeper.

c The duration of a single game on any one day is sixty minutes maximum. In tournaments, two halves of fifteen minutes each, with a break of five minutes, are advisable.

d There are no long and short corners and no offside. Instead of a shooting circle, a 10-yard line is drawn parallel to the goal-line. A goal can be scored below the height of the goalkeeper's pads from anywhere inside the 10-yard line. The goalkeeper is allowed to kick the ball, or to stop it with his or her body between the 10-yard line and the goal-line.

e For a breach of the rules inside the 10-yard line by the defending team, a free hit is awarded to the opposing team from the 10-yard line. If the offence is deliberate, then a penalty hit is awarded 7 yards in front of the goal.

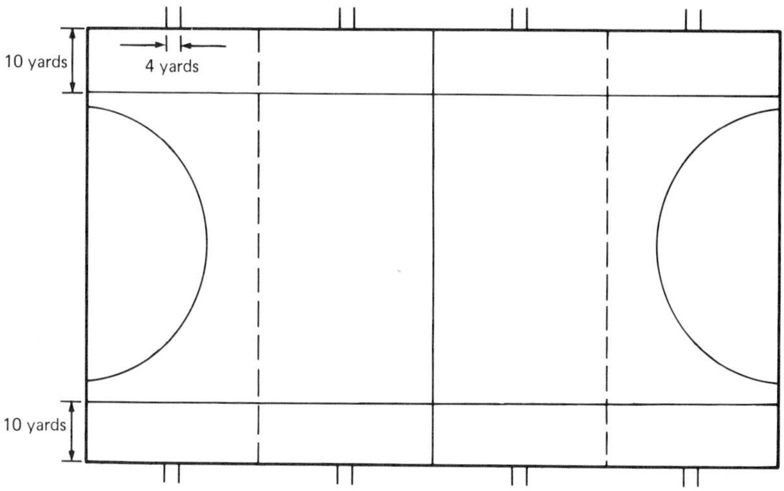

Figure 40

Photo 45 'Mini-hockey'.

f If the ball goes over the side-line, a push-in is taken. If the ball goes over the goal-line outside the goal, touched last by the attacking team, a free-hit is awarded to the defending team on the 10-yard line. If the defenders were the last to touch the ball, an indirect free-hit is awarded to the attacking team, on the 10-yard line, opposite the spot where the ball crossed the goal-line.

g All other rules are as the official international rules.

Note: The umpire should always explain his reasons for stopping the game. He or she should use the whistle sparingly in order to let the children play as much actual hockey as possible.

7 'Bambino-hockey' (see Chapter 24).

26 Organisation and methods of coaching in schools and clubs

While the didactic of hockey is concerned with *what* is to be coached and learnt, in order to give the game characteristic moves, and the competition a progressing improvement, the methods (i.e. the actual way in which the technique involved in the game is taught) are concerned with *how* best to coach the content of the training programme. However, the most suitable methods and organisation can only be established if the aims of coaching hockey in schools and clubs are clearly defined in advance. These aims must remain in the forefront of our minds whenever we consider what and how we should teach our sport.

Modern hockey-coaching in schools and clubs should seek to:

1 Coach ability in special movements (skills).

2 Develop and perfect the characteristics of movement (speed, aerobic and anaerobic stamina, strength, flexibility and dexterity).

3 Coach the ability to play hard, competitive hockey.

4 Develop these requirements through regular playing and training.

Note to 1. In *The Science of Hockey*, the chapter 'The methodical coaching of technical skills', gives the relevant comments and explanations.

Note to 2. Also in *The Science of Hockey* is a comprehensive discussion of the development and perfection of these characteristic movements. Amongst other things, the point emerges that developing skills and perfecting the characteristic movements are not to be carried out in isolation, but are to be seen as part of one unified process. While a technical move is learnt in its rough form, and then refined and made second nature, the teaching process should be so established that the coaching of the characteristic movements of hockey is guaranteed at the same time. But if the development of these movements is included in the programme, then exercises that have a definite effect on those technical moves or are related to them should be those used most.

There are three good reasons for this. Along with the time saved, it is, above all, the relevance of practice and training to the game itself that is important, since it is that very combination of characteristic movements and skills that should run throughout all the moves of the game. In addition, it is important to remember that coaching all the basic movements of hockey is a pre-requisite for the acquisition of more difficult skills. Certain technical moves are insufficiently mastered only because the corresponding basic move was insufficiently developed and perfected. Thus, for example, the weakness of many players in tackling in retreat or in beating an opponent by quickly changing direction, is explained by insufficient coaching of dexterity.

To be successful in hockey, it is necessary to develop basic hockey movements in combination with the specific skills of hockey. In *The Science of Hockey*, exercises are laid out for developing speed with stick and ball (pages 207 to 9), training games for improving stamina (pages 212 to 17), examples of the use of the interval method in hockey training (pages 217 to 23), as well as exercises for developing flexibility and dexterity (pages 223 to 27). This connection between the acquisition of technical moves and the process of developing the characteristic movements (or vice versa) is, of course, not exclusive, and one or other is sometimes to be seen as more important.

Note to 3. Developing the ability to compete and play hard must be planned and taken into account just as much as the coaching of skills and characteristics of movement. Developing the ability to compete should aim at the player reaching a stage where he understands how to employ his skills, the physical qualities he has acquired, and his technical ability, as well as the 'psychological' part he is to play in a match, according to the role he has been assigned. Methodical and systematic preparation for matches, therefore, also involves the developing of willpower (see Chapter 6), mental stamina, fighting spirit, decisiveness, the ability to concentrate, self-control etc., and the coaching of tactical awareness (see Chapter 13).

Note to 4. One primary aim of hockey coaching in schools and clubs is to make a lasting bond between the player and the game of hockey, for

Photo 46

'only insofar as he commits himself to the game, can he also derive something from it'. How far the need for regular training and matches grows in a player depends, amongst other things, on whether the coach can make his training sessions interesting, purposeful, happy, inject them with variety, and keep them in line with the player's expectations (see Chapter 25).

CONCERNING ORGANISATION

Taking these four tasks into account, however, does not guarantee good coaching. It is equally important to organise training effectively. Well organised hockey-coaching at school or in a club is distinguished by:

1 The short duration of training.
2 Its high intensity.
3 Careful use of regular repetitions.
4 Giving enough theoretical sports knowledge to put practice in perspective.
5 The teaching methods used.

Note to 1. An afternoon's training at school or in a club should not exceed one and a half hours. If training lasts longer, then the physiological work-load must inevitably be reduced, i.e. that also the effectiveness of training will be reduced. Since a player's attention also relaxes after ninety minutes' training, further coaching will be generally less successful. Faults in technique and tactics can creep in as a result of physical and mental fatigue. In addition, injury becomes more likely the longer training continues.

A training session of two hours' duration is recommended only when organisational considerations require it—e.g. when there are insufficient hockey-balls and flagposts for the number of players, or when the practice area is limited. However, circumstances permitting, a coach should make every effort to shape his training sessions to be brief and intensive.

Note to 2. An afternoon's training is intensive if the ratio of an individual's practice-time to the duration of the training session is as high as possible. Characteristics of modern coaching methods are not only the volume of the total work-load, but also the sufficient intensity of individual physical work-load. A graph of the physical work-load against time, from the beginning till the end of training, should lead to a curve in which peaks and troughs follow regularly.

In order to maintain a high intensity of coaching in even the final stages of a training session, the players can be split into teams with few per side. Games with less than eleven players have a positive effect because of frequent ball-contact on the basic skills of movement, but also further the development of tactical awareness, since extra space is available, which is easier for a player to use than is the more limited space of a full-number game. Even the weakest player, who finds himself in the thick of action in such games, has the chance to score a goal, and that spurs him to greater effort. However, if a weak player is involved with stronger players in an eleven-a-side game on a full-sized pitch, as is unfortunately still to be seen almost everywhere, he will often be put in a position out of the way in which he only touches the ball a few times, making him virtually a spectator. In this way, time which could be spent improving his technical and tactical performance is wasted, and in any case, that player will soon wonder whether he should bother to turn up at all for the next session (see Chapter 24).

A dull ninety-minute training session, with indifferent work-load and repetitive exercises, exhausts players both physically and mentally. Coupled with a sufficient range of exercises and games, a high training intensity level encourages a player's interest in hockey, and reinforces discipline.

Note to 3. Since, as everyone knows, learning is immediately followed by more or less forgetting, training should aim to establish lasting skills and basic moves. In order to make technical moves and tactical match conduct easier to remember, regular repetition must take place, but ringing the changes so that training is never monotonous. A variety of exercises should be involved in the process of making a move automatic, so that the execution of the technical skill or tactical element is further improved by being capable of variation. In this respect, repetition exercises can be interwoven with other moves; they can be conducted as a competition, at increased speed in different circumstances (e.g. instead of having an imaginary opponent, any active or passive opponent can be engaged), or under difficult conditions (e.g. on a very bumpy pitch, with wet or long grass). The repetition of technical and tactical exercises has fulfilled its aim if players succeed in using them in a competitive match in more difficult circumstances.

Note to 4. The game of hockey offers the coach numerous possibilities for combining physiological, physical and simple psychological knowledge with the practice of coaching. In coaching skills (e.g. hitting or flicking), short, clear remarks about the physical basis of a movement can make for greater clarity about the course the move is to take. Even in the development of speed, stamina and strength, a player can often be interested by simple physiological explanations.

Note to 5. During the training session the coach should create situations in order to develop players' capacity to cope. He should encourage a high standard in *all* aspects of practice and play, and this includes: smooth running of training sessions, honesty in competition, self-reliance, practice even when continuous encouragement from the coach is lacking, responsible relations with helpers and umpires, mutual correction of errors, willingness to help, punctuality . . . .

In modern hockey coaching, training and effective teaching must work in harmony; without compliance to the norms of order and disciplined conduct, no team-feeling or cooperation can develop. Discipline and order should not be achieved by the coach shouting or using harsh disciplinary measures, but should be instilled. However, so that players recognise 'conscious discipline', the coach must make his players aware of the necessity for disciplined thinking.

In a certain sense, praise and censure are also educational measures. The acknowledgement of good play by the trainer is, especially for weaker players, a great stimulus to further improvement. However, if the coach praises his better players too often, then arrogance and complacency may result, leading to a decline in the standard of play.

In training and during matches, the coach should not make the mistake of concentrating exclusively on the better players. All youngsters, and especially those of a lower standard, seek the praise of an adult. If the coach sees that a young player insists on 'being noticed', he has at hand the perfect means of developing the child's motivation.

The coach's example often acts like a mirror to a young player, reflecting his own ability or inability. Only if the coach is satisfied with him is the youngster satisfied with himself. Thus a nine-year-old's remark becomes comprehensible when, after a 6-1 defeat, he explained to his parents that the coach had praised the team for their best performance of the season against much older opposition, and was looking forward to victory in the return match next year, if the team continued to take training seriously.

27 Critical observations on the use of visual aids in coaching hockey

One important aim of any sports training is to improve the movements of the person being trained and enable him with this improvement to achieve a better overall performance. Just how well a person understands a new move or movement in sport is of enormous importance in achieving that goal. Based on this fact, audio-visual teaching methods were introduced into sport in the early 70s, though somewhat belatedly, and finally into the sport of hockey also. Because the complexity and speed at which sporting movements are executed did not allow for a clear exposition of moves by the demonstration method which was prevalent at the time, the use of films and slides was used to provide players with a better understanding of sporting movement.

Photo 47 The Dutch defence runs out to defend on artificial turf a penalty corner from Spain 1976 in Utrecht (2:2).

Apart from a very few film loops, sound films and photo series, there has in the past been a severe lack of visual aids which can be incorporated into the process of coaching hockey. Alongside Hugo Budinger's film loops and the FIH Coaching Manual[1] which concern higher standards, a good number

[1] *See and Learn Hockey* by Horst Wein obtainable from Swiss Hockey Association 6030 Ebikon, Kaspar-Koppstr 96, Switzerland.

of coaching films have appeared on the market in the last few years which do little to help the schoolboy to learn the game of hockey, either because they give too much or even false information, or because the order in which points are covered is unsuitable. Positive results are in these cases only to be achieved by coach and players in the area of willingness to learn.

In the production of many of these visual aids, it was not sufficiently understood that the depiction of a move can only fully succeed when players know in advance the content of what they see on the screen, i.e., they have to know before they look at a film or photo series what is particularly important about a move and which parts of a move deserve greater attention. Such introductory information should be contained in an accompanying booklet, rather than in the visual medium itself, so that even a coach of little experience can direct his players' attention accordingly.

In much of the visual aid material already on the market, the speed of presentation is so fast that no schoolboy will be able to retain all the information available to him and put it to use. But by repeating the showing with the help of slow-motion or freeze-frame to demonstrate the particular characteristics of a given move, these shortcomings can be eliminated. In this way, the understanding of moves and the learning of basic movements of hockey can be facilitated.

The ultimate success of audio-visual material depends on how it is employed in a complete training schedule. Sound films, film loops and photo series should only be shown in measured doses according to the coach's wishes. Knowing the right amount of times that a film can be shown and knowing when enough is enough is very important in teaching terms since many films (though not film loops) contain too much information.

One piece of equipment that has become almost indispensible for hockey coaching is the video-recorder. Its possibilities of repeated use with specific aims in mind have broadened the scope of audio-visual techniques of hockey coaching for both player and coach. Its most important asset is the ability to portray action objectively, as is frequently required, since it allows the instantaneous recording of a player's movements. Its use in the realm of technical and tactical training can have the following positive results:

1 Players become aware that they make a lot of mistakes.

2 Players recognise that the coach's instructions are correct and can understand the corrective action he takes. The resultant willingness to cooperate leads to more rapid learning but less actual practice.

3 Recorded on tape are well-executed or faulty moves which can then serve as sources of reference for personal improvement.

4 Increased training activity on the player's part will also motivate his coach.

The use of a video-recorder in competitive matches can bring about improvements in individual and team performances in the following ways:

1 A detailed group study of the opposition can prepare a team more fully for the next match both tactically and psychologically.

2 'Experiencing' and understanding his own mistakes can considerably improve a player's own and therefore the team's overall performance.

3 Making a player aware of his own moves in a match, whether they contain errors or not, will leave a lasting impression in his mind which can only be compared to the experience of real playing conditions, i.e. a player's experience in terms of how best to resolve a given match situation becomes wider and is put to better use by employing a video-recorder.

28 Interesting to note

The effective duration of a hockey match on natural grass at the Second World Cup in Amsterdam 1973 was only 37 min. 16 secs., i.e. for fifty-three per cent of the game, the ball was in play[1]; in the Soccer World Cup in 1974, the ball was in play for sixty-six per cent of the match[2].

The lower the standard of hockey, the less the actual playing time in a match (around thirty minutes during the Intercontinental Cup).

In almost all soccer matches, there is less actual playing time in the second half; in hockey it seems to be the reverse.

Play was stopped by the whistle 120 times in 90 minutes of play at the Soccer World Cup in 1974, which corresponds to 93 interruptions in 70 minutes, with an average duration of 16 seconds[2]. In hockey the average interruption lasts only 8.7 seconds[1], but there are more than twice as many interruptions as in soccer (230 interruptions per match in the Pre-Olympic Tournament at Montreal in 1975 and in the 1st Intercontinental Cup in Rome 1977).

During a match in the Second World Cup in 1973, the average player was in action for only 20 min. 36 sec. (thirty per cent of the match), and covered in that time 5610 metres (i.e. 81 metres per min.). Defenders generally cover less ground (5140 metres), and midfield players more (6360 metres). The player who covered the greatest distance in one observed World Cup match in 1973 was Selwyn Maister (New Zealand), with 8818 metres, 126m per minute[1].

Sixty-one per cent of all movements in hockey last between 0.5 and 2 seconds, only five per cent last more than 7 seconds[1].

The hockey player makes more light movements than strenuous ones (sixty-nine per cent compared with thirty-one per cent). Centre forwards and wing-halves have the highest levels of strenuous movements (thirty-six per cent and thirty-five per cent), whilst midfield players function on average with seventy per cent light movements[1].

[1] See M. Derweduwen *Observation of a Hockey Competition*, scientific study for the First International Coaching Seminar.

[2] See W. Kuhn *Untersuchung zur Problematik der Spielzeit im Fussball*–dargestellt an Hand von 24 Spielen der FUSSBALL-WELT.

The pulse rates of players during a hockey match fluctuate between 106 per min. minimum, and 190 per min. maximum, (measured each five minutes during the matches at the German Interprovincial Tournament in 1976).

	average pulse rate in	
	First half	Second half
First player	163	156
Second player	164	154
Third player	153	142
Fourth player	168	166
Fifth player	163	160

On average, there is a free-hit or push-in awarded every eighteen seconds.

Around forty per cent of all push-ins taken at the First Intercontinental Cup in Rome did not reach a player of the team which took the push-in.

Italy and Mexico, in the first ten minutes of their pool match at the First Intercontinental Cup in Rome, lost possession of the ball eighty-one times. Out of the twenty-three free-hits taken by both teams in these ten minutes, only four reached a player of the same team.

Another memorable match was played in 1970 as part of the Asian Games in Bangkok, between Pakistan and Thailand (Result 0-0). Pakistanis were caught thirty-one times by the well organised off-side trap of Thailand, eighteen times in the first and thirteen times in the second half. In addition to the eighteen offside offences in the first half, the umpires blew the players of both teams twenty-one times for 'sticks' in thirty-five minutes, fifteen times less than in one half of the match between Malaysia and Singapore, in which a 'world-record' was established, of thirty-six stick whistles in one half.

The speed of the head of the stick at the moment of impact rises to between 50 and 70 m.p.h. depending on the speed-strength of the player and the weight of the stick.

In an average hockey match during the Montreal Olympic Games in 1976, only between six and ten shots at the opposing goal were from open play. Shots from penalty corners, long corners and strokes, as well as shots which missed the goal, were not counted. Pakistan, with six, and Germany and India, with five shots per match, kept opposing goalkeepers busier than the other participating countries. From nine shots in open play, two resulted in a goal.

In the same Olympic Tournament, there was a correlation between the age of players and the final ranking. The five eldest teams (averaging between twenty-six and twenty-seven years). Germany, Spain, New Zealand, Australia and Holland, finished in the first six. The youngest team (Argentina) finished last. In previous Olympic tournaments too, the winners were generally older than the average age of all participating players (27.2, against 26.7 years).

There is no significant relation between frequency of goals and the duration of a game, although it seems that there are more goals awarded in the second half than in the first, especially towards the end of the game.

29 Indoor hockey tactics and how to coach them

INTRODUCTION

Because of the reduced number of players in a team compared to field hockey, (five outfield players and one goalkeeper), the even playing surface (of composite blocks, lino, flagstones or concrete) with its four inch-high sideboards, neither hitting nor lifting the ball (except when shooting at goal) being allowed, and the resultant limitation of the various possible match situations, indoor hockey makes greater demands for co-operation and understanding amongst players than does hockey played on grass or artificial turf.

Only a regular training schedule carried out over a period of months, undertaken by all players at the same time (and above all continuing where the training programme of the previous year left off) can produce good understanding and an instinctive awareness amongst the six players of a team who are on the field of play, and also the substitutes. Not only in actual play with team-mates, but also in how they react to the opposition, all players in a team should 'speak the same language', a requirement which generally in indoor hockey is more important to victory or defeat than the level of physical fitness of each individual player, since the rules allow repeated substitutions. Intelligent tactical play, taking both team-mates and opposition into account, can be achieved only when, together with sound physical fitness and technical skills, players are in a position to select the most suitable move to follow any match situation.

In indoor hockey training therefore, technical coaching should as often as possible be combined with tactical instructions, observations and exercises.

Tactical coaching should be a complex teaching process, one which develops all forms of activity simultaneously. Its content ought to correspond to the respective stage of development in each player. In the build-up of tactical playing skills, demands should develop from easy moves to difficult ones, i.e. from simple to complex moves and finally to competitive matches. Only by repeated consideration of such moves, within the structure of an indoor hockey player's training schedule, does the player learn to adapt himself mentally and practically, technically and tactically to the widest possible range of different game situations. But this complex form is not the only one to be considered in tactical coaching. Some tactical moves can also be developed, with simple exercises suited to this purpose.

The following exercises and games should provide the trainer and player with knowledge of the numerous tactical moves possible, and should also give the player, after sufficient practice, the experience that will allow him to resolve recurring match situations. A player's ability to find the correct

Photo 48

solution quickly, and to use it without risk, can be progressively developed by repeated use of the exercises and games set out below.

After studying the propositions in the following pages of defence, attack and various match situations, the coach should decide the general tactics which are most suitable for a particular team, taking into account the individual players' ability. The coach must be able to recognise players' peculiarities (e.g. a player might be speedy and yet impetuous, good at counter-attack, or cool and calculating, less intuitive but with first class skills), turn them to account, and develop them to the team's benefit. He should not only provide his players with general tactical knowledge, but also consider particular aspects more broadly so that a characteristic method of play for the team is developed. In coaching a team's characteristic style, the trainer should always keep an eye on how indoor hockey is developing as a whole.

In the following pages, comments on skills and tactical coaching have been intentionally omitted, unless they are different from field hockey, since these have already been made in detail in *The Science of Hockey*.

THE DEFENCE

In indoor hockey, defence begins even before possession is lost, since not all outfield players are to press forward into attack. Sufficient defenders should always remain in their own half so that a long straight pass, or a long pass via the sideboards to an opposing striker, can be intercepted, and a possible counter-attack by the opposition can at least be slowed down.

The moment the ball is lost to the opposing team, all players should adopt defensive tactics, with the single idea of preventing even a shot at goal by the opposition. Every player should then move as quickly as possible *not* to be where he thinks he can successfully regain possession of the ball for his team, but to the particular part of the field which has been pre-assigned to him in the tactical plan, taking into account his team-mates' positions and the current position of the ball.

As in field hockey, defensive play employs:

a zonal marking;

b man-to-man marking;

c combined marking.

In defence, each player, independent of the proposed marking system, should strive to manage without the help of a team-mate beside or behind him whenever he can. This is because, in coming to his assistance, that team-mate must temporarily leave his position, automatically providing space for an opposing player. In order that this space does not remain empty, thus giving an opponent in that space sufficient time to move freely, a defender who has been beaten should not watch dejectedly and passively as the opposition builds up its attack, but should hurry back decisively to the defence and fill the gap that has appeared in it.

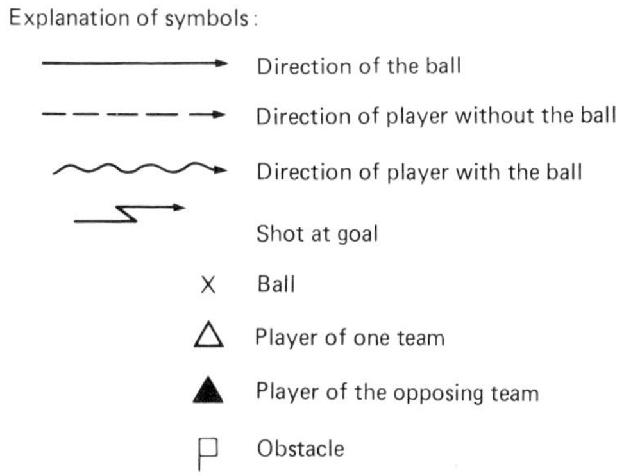

Figure 41

Zonal marking

Zonal marking is the easiest marking system in indoor hockey, to both learn and put into practice. Each player is allocated a certain area to cover in his defending half of the field, for example, the left defender is given the left defensive quarter of his half, the left striker is given the left attacking quarter of his half, the central defender is responsible for the area in the centre between the other defenders' and strikers' zones, etc.

The areas to be covered are in no way fixed zones, but continually alter over the length and width of the field, according to the position of the opposing player with the ball. (See figs. 42, 43 and 44).

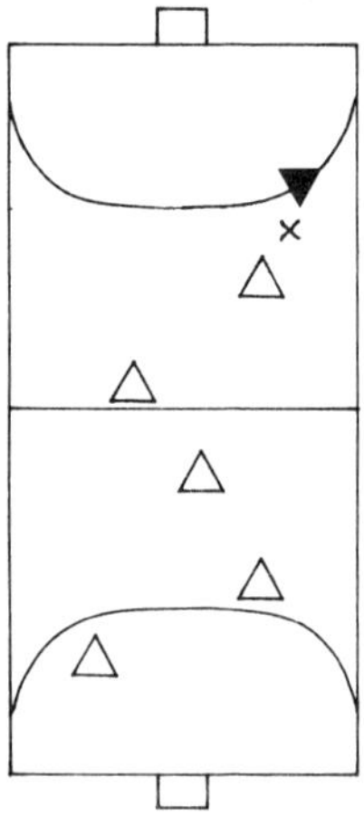

Figure 42

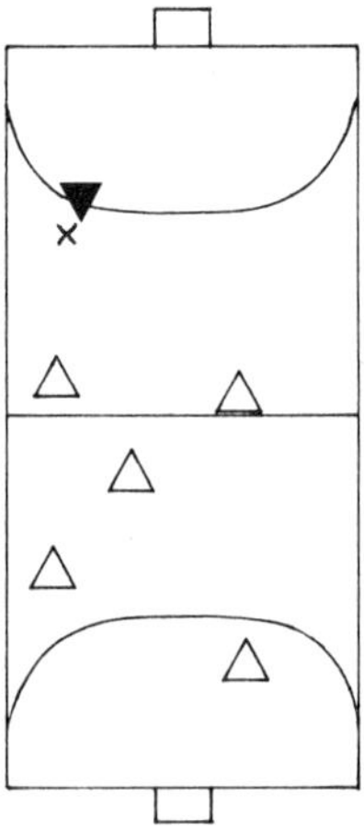

Figure 43

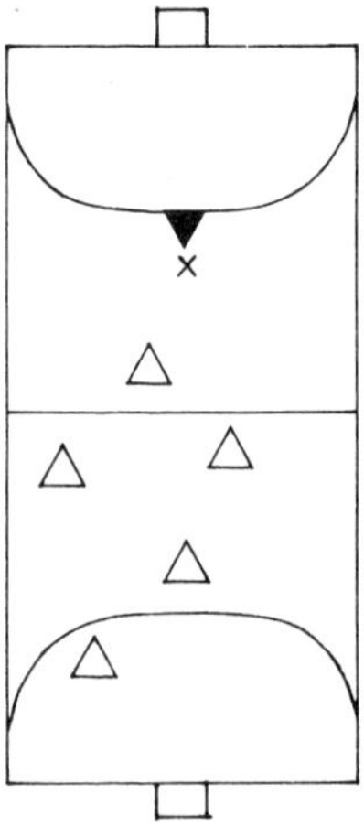

Figure 44

Because of the greater effectiveness of defending on the open side, i.e. on the right-hand side of the body, defenders should position themselves to the left of the ball (particularly if the ball is in the centre strip of the pitch) in order to force an opposing player to attack on the right-hand side of the defending team. Intentionally yielding space in this way saves zonal defenders from making unnecessary changes of position, changes which may disturb defensive cohesion. Furthermore, such yielding makes conditions favourable for anticipating the opposition's attack. Intentionally leaving space free on the right-hand side of the defence leads to more frequent opposition attacks down that side, resulting in the opposing left strikers passing square or diagonally, rather than the more dangerous situation of an attack down the left-hand side of defence, followed by a pass into the circle to a left-striker ready for a first-time shot at goal. In general, left strikers (along with the corner specialists) are the top goal-scorers of any indoor hockey team.

Zonal marking demands less running than man-to-man marking and is preferred particularly by slower and older players when opponents are very quick and inventive, and when man-to-man marking, which does require great physical fitness, holds little hope of success.

Zonal marking continually gives the initiative to the team in possession of the ball, though this is not to say that defenders act passively in zonal marking. By means of frequent dummy-moves in defence, and especially by skilful positional play, they should create favourable conditions for intercepting the ball.

Man-to-man marking

In a man-to-man marking system, each player is given one specific opponent to mark, whom he should, usually, follow like a shadow (either over the whole field of play or only in the defender's own half), and whom he is to harass as soon as that opponent tries to receive the ball. In doing so the defender should always keep his eye on the ball, and make sure that he is nearer the goal than his opponent.

In spite of his task of tightly marking his man, he must not become independent of his team-mates, for a defender who thinks only of marking his specific opponent out of the game has not completely fulfilled his role. In spite of his close marking duties, he also has a responsibility to the rest of the team.

Photo 49

Man-to-man marking not only demands greater running than zonal marking, but also a better understanding between defenders. Only players who can react quickly, retain concentration while playing, and who are mentally agile, can make use of the advantages of man-to-man marking and prevent them becoming disadvantages (see Chapter 15).

Total man-to-man marking over the entire field of play is nowadays used less often in indoor hockey, since experienced strikers are easily able to shake off their opponents for a few seconds by skilful manoeuvering. Apart from a systematic changing of positions over the length and width of the field, man-to-man marking can also be beaten by not taking up certain positions in attack, combined with sudden square passes designed to switch the attack from one side to the other. An attack down the right-hand side in which the left striker also takes part, although marked, by switching over to the right, leaves an unmarked space on the left, into which the left defender or even the central defender can suddenly move up field.

Combined marking

Combined marking is at present the most successful tactic in defence, representing a synthesis of zonal marking and man-to-man marking. As in zonal defence, each player, in his own half of the field, has not only space to cover, but also an opponent who is available for a pass within that zone. In contrast to zonal defence however, the distance between the defender and the opponent within his zone is very small indeed, i.e. man-to-man marking is adhered to in principle but is not limited to one pre-specified opponent. Defenders involved in combined marking exchange opponents far more often, yet still do not basically alter their field of action. In this way, order and cohesion can be maintained in defence.

Since a striker or another player must be left unmarked for a second if the responsibility of marking him is 'passed over' from one defender to another (which means that he would be available for a pass) the defence should always adopt a tight man-to-man marking system (see 'The ninth basic tactical rule', page 194), at free-hits for the opposition in front of the circle.

Defensive and offensive tactics for defenders

Defenders can play with both defensive and offensive tactics. In defensive tactics, the opponent is normally only picked up in the defending team's half of the field (as in handball or basketball) to which all players immediately retire as soon as possession of the ball is lost. In doing so, zonal marking or combined marking is generally employed. After successfully re-gaining the ball, a counter-attack is introduced.

In offensive tactics, which are of particular use against weaker opponents, men are picked up even in their own half of the field, in order to hamper any systematic build-up into attack. With aggressive tackling in the opponents' half, frequent opportunities arise to work a shot at goal or even score.

Whether a team plays with zonal, man-to-man, or combined marking, and with defensive or (far more difficult) offensive tactics in defence, depends upon the team's preferred style of play, upon the physical fitness and technical ability of that team's players, and on those of the opposition. Good teams should be able to master all tactical styles of play, and sometimes employ several of them in the same match.

Since, in contrast to offensive tactics, defensive tactics in defence require less preparation in training, most of the tactical exercises and games below take offensive tactics in defence as the basis.

Photo 50

THE ATTACK

While defence in indoor hockey is organised systematically, attacks generally develop more freely. Especially in finishing off an attack, both in front of and inside the opposition circle, flair must often replace well-practiced, standard moves, flair that is the result of wide experience. By contrast, the build-up of attacks is more likely to succeed if it is systematically varied, rather than merely intuitive every time.

In indoor hockey, we must differentiate between positional attack and the counter-attack.

Positional Attack

A positional attack almost always begins with a push-out at the top of the circle, or a free hit in one's own half. The players concerned (above all, the three defenders) should try to start the attack, minimising the risk of interception so that one of their team-mates can receive the ball near to or even inside the opposition circle. Hard, concealed push-passes, carried out quickly, and continuous organised running into space by players not in possession, are important for the successful introduction, build-up and execution of a positional attack (or of a counter-attack), as are awareness, technical and tactical experience, and the skill to assess the speed of team-mates, opponents and ball.

Positional attack is in the introductory phase, and in its build-up more systematic and calm, and less impetuous or risky than the counter-attack.

Exercises covering the introduction, build-up and execution of a positional attack are laid out in the second, third and sixth basic tactical rules of indoor hockey.

Counter-Attack

Neither the ratio of attackers to defenders, nor the time taken, are decisive criteria in the effectiveness of carrying out a counter-attack in indoor-hockey, which usually unfolds out of deep defence. It is characterised above all by gaining midfield control very rapidly, i.e. overrunning the opposing team with the intention of concluding the attack before the opposing defence has had time to become established.

A counter-attack by one team is always preceded by an unsuccessful attack by the opposition, i.e. the opposing team must have finished its attack with a technical error or a failed shot at goal. Any defender who is able to separate an opponent from the ball, or who gains a free-hit after an opponent's mistake, should aim to start an attack as quickly as possible. A quick hard pass through midfield should be preferred to time-consuming dribbling or short passes (see 'The third basic tactical rule'). The player making such a pass, or his team-mates, then have the important task of covering the ground to the player receiving the ball in the opposition's half, so as to make themselves available for a return pass.

In order that a counter-attack can succeed, not only are anticipation and speed of reaction in switching from defence to attack of importance, but also the basic requirement that the technical skills of stopping the ball, passing and dribbling, have been mastered and can be used at full speed. The higher the standard of play, the more decisive will be technical errors in stopping and passing the ball, exploited by the opposition. If technical skills and tactical ability have been poorly coached, then failures in counter-attacking will depend on the mistakes of the attacking team rather than on good defensive work by the opposition. From this, we can conclude that the success or failure of a counter-attack depends upon the standard to which the players concerned have been coached.

Detailed observations and analyses of counter-attacks show that the number of counter-attacks is about twenty per cent of the total number of attacks in indoor hockey. The winning team clearly executes more counter-attacks than the losing team, and the percentage of goals scored by means of counter-attacks is greater than by positional attacks.

If value is to be derived from the observations made in the last four years, then a greater consideration of the counter-attack is required in the training programme of indoor hockey. Above all, the relative probability of a goal with a counter-attack, compared with other forms of attack, demands that better coaching is given, and more widespread use made of

Photo 51

the counter-attack. In training, therefore, coaches should lay greater emphasis than has so far been the case on creating the necessary physical, technical and tactical requirements for the counter-attack.

If the build-up of a quick counter-attack holds little hope of success, then positional attacks should be used instead. (See exercises concerning the second, third and eighth basic tactical rules.)

Exercises and games involving the counter attack

1 a Solo run from the half-way line into the circle, followed by a shot at goal. The ball must be touched at least four times on the way to the circle. Time is taken, on a stopwatch, from the moment the player crosses the half-way line until the ball hits the net or the backboard. Who takes less than four seconds to dribble and shoot at goal?

b Ditto, but with one defender who stands a yard behind the striker on the half-way line, and has to try to tackle the striker.

2 a The ball is played accurately from the half-way line towards the opponents' goal, so that a striker setting off from the half-way line can reach it before it enters the circle, and follow up his sprint with a shot at goal. The time is taken on a stopwatch. This can also be practised with a goalkeeper.

b Ditto, but with one defender, who stands on the half-way line with the striker and the passer who passes towards the circle. The defender coming once from the left and in another try from the right, must try to prevent a goal being scored after the ball has been passed.

Photo 52

3 a Two strikers combine from the half-way line, and finish their first attack with a shot at goal. Which pair needs the least time to score a goal? At least two passes must be made.

b Ditto, but with a defender waiting behind the pair of attackers. The defender sets off after them from the half-way line in order to tackle back.

4 a A pair of strikers should play out one defender with a combination and score as fast as possible.

b Ditto, but with a defender, 'already beaten', who stands behind the strikers (not timed).

5 a A wing-defender tries to beat an opposing wing-forward near the boards in the opposite half but loses the ball (since for the present his role is passive), whereupon the striker counter-attacks. The stopwatch runs from the time the striker crosses the half-way line to the moment the ball crosses the goal-line.

b Ditto, but with one defender near to the circle, at first passive, then fully involved, who must also be beaten on the route to the goal. As in a, the wing-defender remains passive after losing the ball.

c Ditto, but with one active defender and a goalkeeper.

d As in a, except that both players are fully active, and each of them must try to beat his opponent and, despite his attempts to tackle back on the way to the circle, score a goal. A defender stands on the edge of the circle, and behind him, in the goal, a goalkeeper.

6 a Pass and run. A hit-out team of three players stands in the circle, while an outfield team of three players lines up in a good tactical formation behind the half-way line, prepared to control the ball as quickly as possible when it is pushed by the first member of the hit-out team and to score a goal. After the ball is pushed out, all players in the hit-out team must run towards the half-way line, touch it, and then try to reach the circle again (see fig. 45) before the ball enters the goal. When this happens, the coach blows his whistle. The hit-out team is awarded one point each time one of its players succeeds in reaching the circle before a goal is scored by the attacking outfield team. Only the hit-out team can score points. When all players in the hit-out team have played the ball once, the teams change sides.

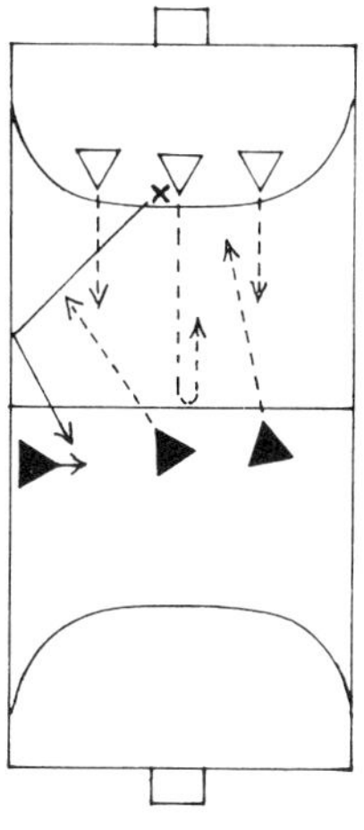

Figure 45

The push-out does not count if the ball goes out over the sideboards in front of the half-way line. A successful return to the circle by the hit-out team is of no value if the attackers are actively hindered in their counter-attack.

b Ditto, but with a neutral goalkeeper.

c As in a, except that the ball can be passed once before it is pushed towards the half-way line. The pass should always be made parallel to the goal-line. The player who then pushed the ball towards the half-way line has had his turn.

d Ditto, but with a neutral goalkeeper.

e As in a. The player who pushes the ball stays in defence as 'sweeper', while his team-mates must run towards the half-way line (they do not try to defend).

f As in c, except that the two players involved in pushing the ball out remain in defence, while only one player must run in order to score points.

g As in a, except that the player pushing out must run, while his two team-mates try to stop the outfield team until the runner is back in the circle. This is played without a neutral goalkeeper.

7 Four defenders line up in their own half against three or four strikers and it is their job to prevent a quick pass from the defenders to a team-mate running in space in the other half of the field. How many seconds does the defending team need from the taking of the push-out to a goal being scored by their team-mate? The strikers are not allowed to set foot in their own defending half of the field.

Exercises aimed at improving a rapid switch from defence to attack and thereby building up a counter-attack

1 Two against two in one half of the field, without restrictions or conditions. Which team can keep possession of the ball for the longest period?

2 a Two against two with one neutral player, who always assists the team in possession of the ball.

b As in a, except that the neutral player may no longer be tackled by the two defending players.

3 Two against two, each team having one neutral player. Neither neutral player is allowed to defend, but should try to combine with either their team *or* with the other neutral player, so as to surprise their fellow players. Following a sudden pass to the other neutral player, the team on the defensive goes into attack.

Passes between the two neutral players should be made very frequently, so as to instil in the players the meaning and aims of the exercise, which are to improve the rapid change from defence to attack.

This exercise can also be organised as a competition: the game is played in one half of the indoor pitch. The team in possession of the ball must try to cross the opposite 20-yard goal-line (either the goal-line or the half-way line) with the ball, without being tackled by a neutral player during the attack. Neutral players are basically there to act as receivers and distributors of the ball. Goals scored by them do not count.

THE BASIC TACTICAL RULES OF INDOOR HOCKEY

1 Because of the reduced number of players, and above all because of the higher speed at which the game is being played, attackers and defenders cannot be strictly differentiated. Attackers must frequently defend, and defenders often go into attack.

The usual formation today is for two strikers and three defenders to play in front of a goalkeeper. While the central defender regularly supports his attackers from a position mid-way between attack and defence, the wing defenders generally stay back and mark in defence, attacking only when a neglect of their defensive duties will have no decisive effect upon the game.

2 The three defenders should never stand in a straight line, when in possession of the ball, and should hold the ball until a good upfield pass is available, or until a gap appears for a dribble.

3 Defenders should play long or short passes according to the match situation and the defensive tactics employed. Long, hard passes out of defence to a striker running into space are preferable to dribbling or short passes (especially in defence by offensive moves), because:

a the ball moves more quickly than the fastest player;

b long passes require less effort and, in terms of the whole game, are more economical;

c the opposing strikers can be outplayed more quickly and with greater effect;

d opposing markers can be deceived more easily.

4 Push-passes should always be made as hard as possible, straight onto the stick of a team-mate, to his right foot, even when the player receiving the ball is only a few yards away. A hard pass makes it more difficult for an opponent to intercept the pass, and generally speeds up play.

5 As often as possible, the ball should be deflected without first stopping it. A first-time or wall-pass speeds up play, and allows the opposition less time to organise themselves in defence.

6 In making a long pass, when a straight pass to a team-mate is not possible the sideboards should be included in the move as a passive team-mate. Because of the high demands of both effort and accuracy a pass via the side-boards requires (the ball must always strike the sideboards level with an opponent), and because an opponent can lay his stick at full length along the ground and intercept such a pass, using the sideboards for passing is

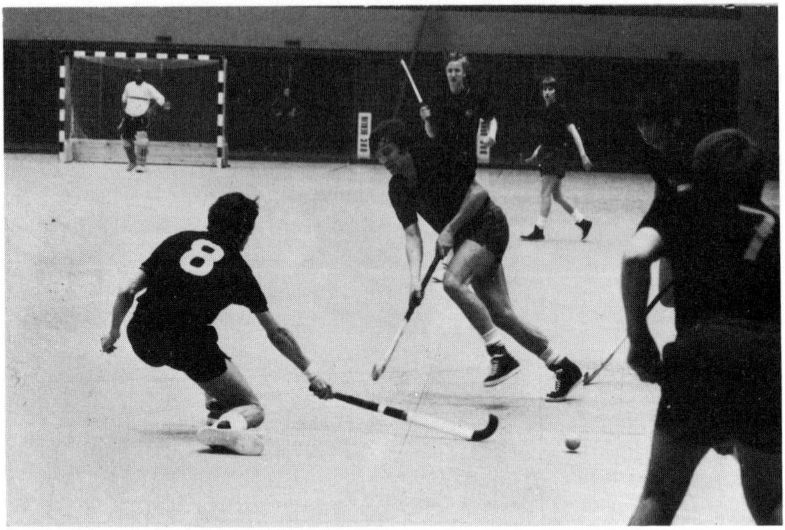

Photo 53

more difficult and less successful nowadays than it used to be in the early 70s. The use of the boards for beating an opponent, especially on the right-hand side of the field, is far more successful than use for passing.

7 Two strikers should rarely play square of each other. Careful tactical consideration suggests that one of the strikers runs back and forth in mid-field, and the other makes himself available for a long pass into one corner of the circle (usually on the same side as the ball), an offensive method of play would push both strikers up into the corners of the pitch to create space for the defender following up. If they are skilful at running into space (in particular running towards the ball), the strikers can make themselves available for a pass for a few seconds.

8 If a defender can see that a long pass from him will reach his striker running into space near to or inside the opposition's circle, either he or another defender should sprint forward as quickly as possible in support as soon as a pass is made, to make himself available for a return pass.

9 At a free hit for the attacking team in front of the circle, a maximum of four players should be in attacking positions. The fifth player should cover at the back and prevent any possible counter-attack by the opposition. The more players there are in the circle, the less space there is available for a good pass.

If the free hit cannot be taken quickly, so as to surprise the opposition (i.e. no team-mate is available for a pass), then the player making the pass should take his time, and carry out a move that has previously been practised with the other players. Basically, because of its surprise effect, running into space should be from a standing start. Only when a team-mate has freed himself from man-to-man marking should a hard and accurate pass be made. It is better if the strikers, when running into space inside the circle, sprint from inside the circle outwards, rather than vice versa.

10 A ball played at full speed towards the goal should never be stopped in the opposing circle by the strikers, but deflected first time into the goal. In doing so, the striker should take up a position side-on to the goal with his stick horizontal, and should try to play the ball on his open side as often as possible.

11 When possession of the ball is lost, every outfield player should watch that the man in his zone is not nearer to the goal than he is, i.e. he should always position himself so that he has his man directly in front of him, or so that no member of the opposition is standing behind him. When a free hit is awarded to the opposition in front of the circle, four defenders should mark man to-man, while one defender covers space.

12 An indoor hockey team is usually composed of two goalkeepers, three wing defenders, one central defender (middle-man) and three strikers. Players should be substituted only when the ball goes out over their own team's goal-line. Because of his decisive role in the game, the middle-man should be substituted as little as possible.

Photo 54

Indoor hockey coaching methods for carrying out the basic tactical rules.

Exercises and games for basic rule no. 2

The three defenders should never stand in a straight line when in possession of the ball, and should hold the ball until a good up-field pass is available, or until a gap appears for a dribble.

1 Three defenders form a triangle at the top of the circle, so that the central defender stands as far as possible behind the two wing defenders. The ball should be passed round the triangle in any order. Outside the circle, first-time passing is desirable, but inside the circle, because of the danger of lifting the ball, this should be avoided as far as possible. Once the ball is played, each defender should run immediately into space.

2 Ditto, except that one opposing forward should try to intercept the ball as it is passed round the triangle (fig. 46).

3 After a minimum of three successive passes around the triangle, the three defenders, in combination (or one defender on a solo run), should try to dribble the ball over the half-way line. An opposing forward has the job of preventing one of the defenders taking the ball over the line (fig. 47). This exercise is designed to teach the three defenders to hold the ball as long as possible until an up-field dribble can be executed in complete safety.

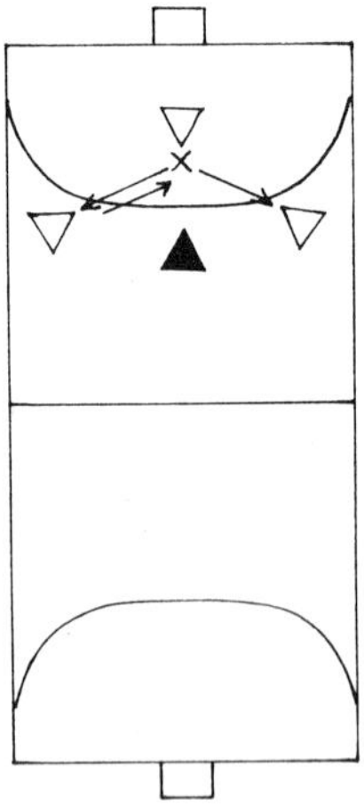

Figure 46

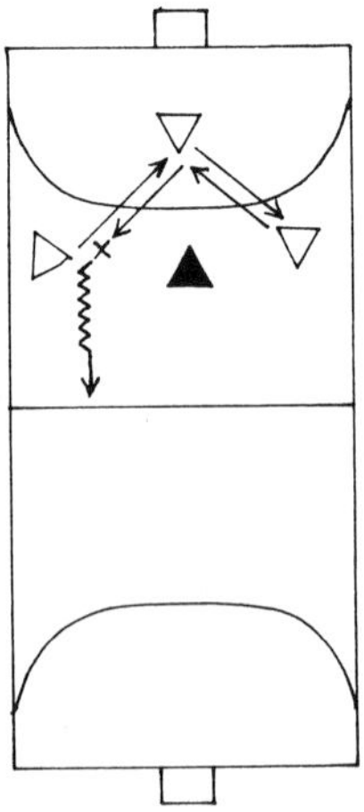

Figure 47

4 Three defenders take on two opposing strikers in their own half. If the three defenders are able to make four (or eight) successive passes, without

breaking the rules of hockey, then they score one point. If the two attackers gain possession of the ball, then their tackle earns them one point. Which team is the first to score ten points? The exercise starts with a free hit on the edge of the circle, taken by one of the three defenders. The game is played in only one half of the pitch (fig. 48).

5 Three defenders take on two attackers in their own half, and after a free hit at the top of the circle, try to beat the two strikers, so that one of the defenders is able to dribble the ball over the half-way line (fig. 49). This is designed to teach the defenders to hold the ball until a safe pass is possible, or until a gap appears for a safe up-field dribble over the half-way line.

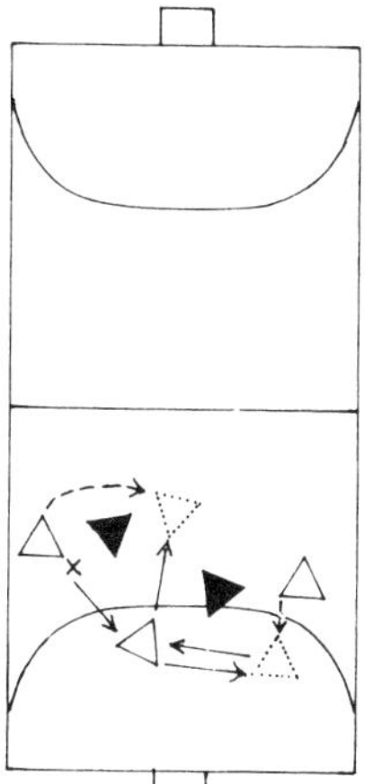

Figure 48

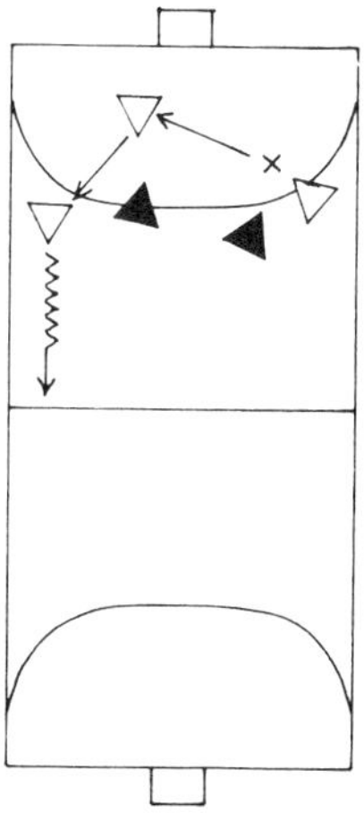

Figure 49

6 Three defenders plus a goalkeeper play in their own half against three opposing attackers. The game begins with a free hit to the defence at the top of the circle. By taking the free hit skilfully, possibly making use of the goalkeeper, the three defenders must try to combine and score a goal (one point) against the strikers, who mark either man-to-man or zonally. If the attacking team, marking offensively, gain possession, and can shoot at goal, they receive one point, or two points if a goal is scored.

In order to take the free hit successfully, and to build up their attack, the defenders and the gaolkeeper have several possibilities:

a a concealed pass to a team-mate running into space behind an opposing attacker;

b a pass via the sideboards to a team-mate who runs into space behind an opposing attacker;

c the player on the ball runs away from the ball at the moment he recognises a marked team-mate's intention to take the free hit from his place;

d a team-mate who is marked suddenly takes a few quick steps towards the ball, immediately receives a pass without obstructing his opponent, and plays the ball straight back to the player who has taken the free hit without stopping it;

e inclusion of the goalkeeper as the man taking the free hit;

f diagonally forward of the defender taking the ball, no. 1, stands a team-mate, no. 2, who is marked, but who suddenly runs into space on the other side, by means of a curved run behind no. 1. Because of the direction in which no. 2 is running, and because of no. 1's position, the attacker's path is blocked as he tries to follow no. 2, such that for a few seconds his man is unmarked. At this moment, no. 2 receives the pass directed diagonally forward by no. 1. In order to avoid an obstruction as the free hit is taken, the ball should always be played in the direction of the opposing goal (fig. 50).

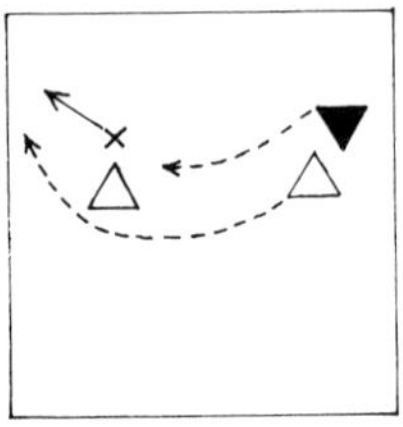

Figure 50a

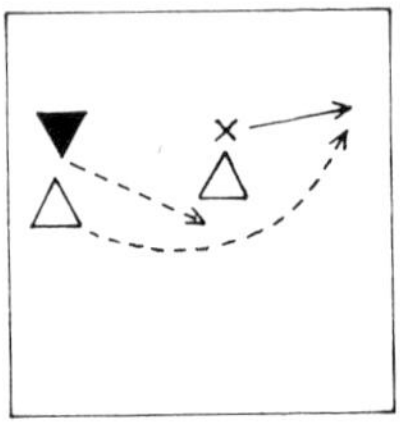

Figure 50b

Exercises and games for basic rule no. 3

Defenders should play long or short passes according to the match situation and the defensive tactics employed. Long, hard passes out of defence to a striker running into space are preferable to dribbling or short passes (especially in defence by offensive moves), because:

a the ball moves more quickly than the fastest player;

b long passes require less effort and, in terms of the whole game, are more economical;

c the opposing strikers can be outplayed more quickly and with greater effect;

d opposing markers can be more easily deceived.

1 a Three defenders play two attackers, and after taking a free hit at the

top of the circle, try to pass the ball past the two strikers over the half-way line at a suitable moment, so that it can be met by a fourth member of the defending team (fig. 51). Each successful tackle by the two attackers, and each mistake by the defending team earns the attackers one point. The attackers also score one point if the pass to the fourth player of the defending team is so inaccurate that it cannot be stopped. If, however, the ball reaches the team-mate behind the half-way line without being intercepted by the attackers, then the defenders are awarded one point. Which team is the first to reach ten points?

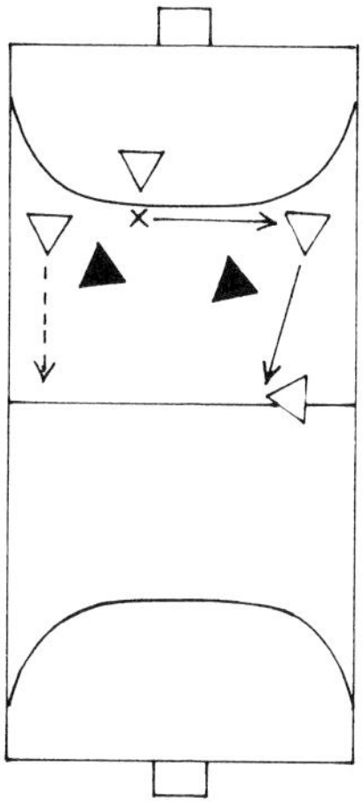

Figure 51

b Three against two in the defending half of the field, with the intention of passing the ball to one of two team-mates running in space in the attacking half, who have only one opponent to beat (i.e. two against one in the attacking half of the pitch).

2 Three defenders try to play a long pass out of their own half to their attacker in the other half, either using the sideboards or not as circumstances dictate. In doing so, they are pressurised in both halves by one opponent (i.e. three against one in the defending half and one against one in the attacking half).

3 Three defenders must try to beat two opposing attackers in their own half, so that a pass is possible to a team-mate running into space in the other half of the pitch, but who is marked by one opponent (fig. 52). Each time the ball is received by the fourth player in the attacking half, the defending team scores one point. Every time the two attackers or their team-mate make a successful tackle, they score one point.

Photo 55

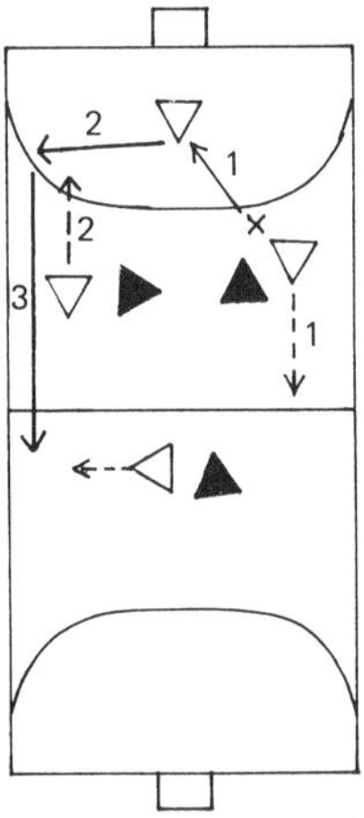

Figure 52

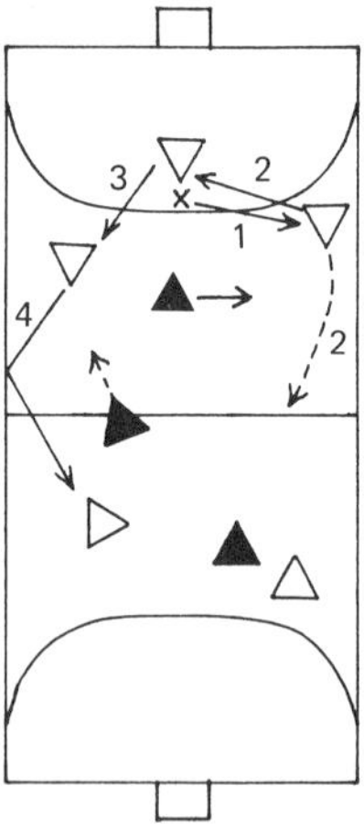

Figure 53

4 Three against one in the defending half, and two against two in the attacking half, whereby one of the two marking players in the attacking half may set foot in both halves of the pitch. No remaining players may leave their own half (fig. 53).

5 Three against two in the defending half, and two against two in the attacking half.

6 Three defenders play with one team-mate running into space in the attacking half, against three opposing attackers whose intention is to break up, by offensive man-to-man marking, combination play between the defenders and their free attacker. If the opposing attackers gain possession and work a shot at goal, they score one point, or two points if a goal results. The defending team gains a point only with a goal scored. As in the preceding games, the game is started with a free hit in or at the top of the circle.

7 Indoor hockey, three against three in the defending half, and two against one or two in the attacking half. Both goals are defended by a goalkeeper. The game is played as in 6.

Games and exercises for basic rules nos. 4 and 6

Push-passes should always be made as hard as possible, straight onto the stick of a team-mate, to his right foot, even when the player receiving the ball is only a few yards away. A hard pass makes it more difficult for an opponent to intercept the pass, and generally speeds play up.

In making a long pass, when a straight pass to a team-mate is not possible, the sideboards should be included in the move as a passive team-mate. Because of the high demands of both effort and accuracy a pass via the sideboards requires (the ball must always strike the sideboards level with an opponent), and because an opponent can lay his stick at full length along the ground and intercept such a pass, using the sideboards for passing is more difficult and less successful nowadays than it used to be in the early 70s. The use of the boards for beating an opponent, especially on the right-hand side of the field, is far more successful than the use for passing.

1 a Standing still, players push a stationary ball across the field through a goal one yard wide set up in the middle of the pitch. The winner is the first player to score ten goals. In pushing the ball, players should keep it flat on the ground, pay attention to the powerful use of the arms, and, because of the accuracy required, try to keep the stick in contact with the ball for as long as possible. To stop the ball, in contrast to the position adopted in field hockey, the stick should be held horizontal.

b Ditto, but pushing the ball on the reverse side.

2 The exercise is now carried out by three players; each player pushes the ball at the goal, and then follows his pass, taking up the receiver's position on the opposite side of the pitch (fig. 54).

3 As in 1. The goal is now extended to 5 yards wide and is defended by a third player. The two players in front of and behind the goal try to score a goal with a hard push-pass (as concealed as possible in order to deceive the

goalminder) from an agreed distance (8 to 10 yards). Who is the first to score ten goals? Alternatively, whoever scores a goal becomes goalminder. Which player, after an agreed length of time, was most often goalminder? When stopping the ball on either side of him, the player in goal should lay his stick flat on the ground.

4 One player dribbles the ball parallel to the sideboards. From a distance of 5 or 6 yards, he pushes it, from moving, at the sideboards, and practises control as it rebounds (fig. 55). Variations are possible as follows:

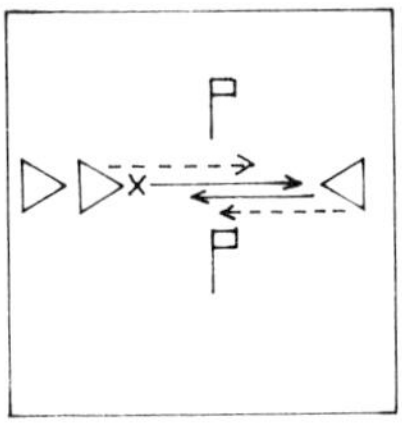

Figure 54

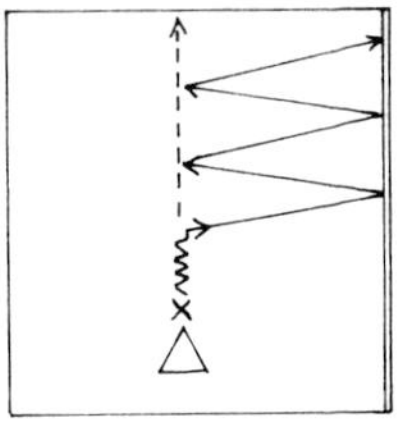

Figure 55

a With a reverse-stick pass to the right-hand boards. Receiving the ball can be with either open stick or on the reverse, depending on the position of the body.

b With an open-side pass to the right-hand (or left-hand) boards, with or without stopping the ball first.

c With a preceding feinted pass in the direction of the middle of the pitch.

d With one passive defender who blocks the attacker's path at a distance of 4 yards from the sideboards. The defender, who remains constantly on the same spot, is to be beaten with or without the use of the side-boards.

e With one semi-active defender.

f With one fully involved defender who is to be beaten with or without the use of the sideboards, inside an area 6 yards wide.

5 a Two players pass a ball between them off the sideboards. No. 1 plays the ball so that it rebounds accurately to no. 2 and vice versa. This can also be practised without first stopping the ball, or by continually changing the position of the player receiving the ball. The important thing is that the ball should always rebound from the boards at such an angle that the other player can receive the pass without difficulty.

b Two players pass the ball between them over a distance of 20 or 30 yards (according to their standard) with or without the use of the sideboards. A third player stands between them in a goal (5 yards wide) set up near the sideboards (fig. 56) through which the ball must be pushed to the second player. Who is the first to score fifteen goals? On tactical grounds, the player making the push-pass should immediately follow his pass as soon as he realises that it will reach the second player.

6 a An attacking defender stands on the half-way line approximately 6 yards from the sideboard. He takes a free hit from there against the left-hand sideboard, such that the ball strikes it level with the top of the circle and rebounds to a team-mate standing on the opposite goal-line (fig. 57). After the latter has controlled the ball, he passes it back via the sideboards to the attacking defender. A flagpost representing a defender is set up approximately 4 yards from the sideboards. If the ball is played hard and accurately onto the sideboards level with the flagpost, then an actual defender has no chance of intercepting.

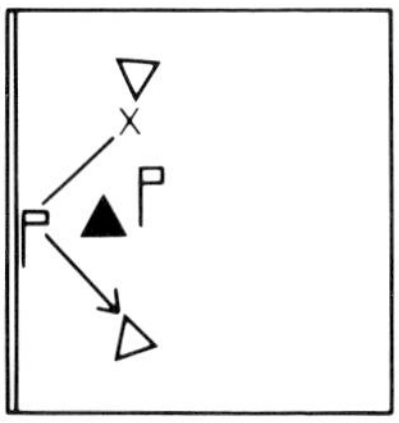

Figure 56

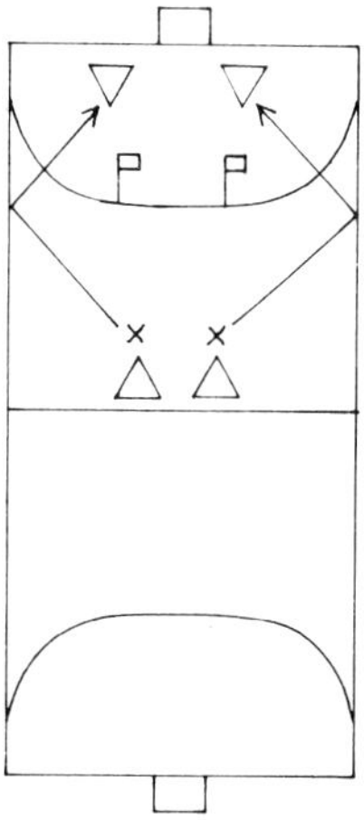

Figure 57

b Ditto, but with a concealed pass to the left, i.e. feint as if to make a straight pass parallel with the sideboards, but at the last moment, by turning the upper part of the body through 45 degrees, play a pass off the sideboards.

c As in a, except that the ball is played off the right-hand board.

d Ditto, but with a concealed pass to the right.

7 All the exercises laid out in exercise 6 concerning passes off the side-boards are now carried out with one active defender, who stands where the flagpost previously stood. The defender should stand 4 yards from the side-boards, level with the top of the circle and may only move towards the ball

to intercept it once the free hit has been taken. In order to deceive the defender, the ball should often be passed straight, i.e. without using the sideboards.

8 a Shuttle relay with five players in each team. Inside the first half of the pitch, the ball must be dribbled, but as soon as the half-way line is crossed, the ball may be pushed, from moving, to the next player in the team, who is waiting behind the goal-line at the other end. After this push-pass, the player takes his place in the opposite line (fig. 58). The competition finishes when each player has pushed the ball four times, and the first player has received the ball for the fifth time.

b The dribble may only be made alternately on the open side and on the reverse ('Indian dribble').

c The ball may only be lead on the reverse-stick side.

d The push-pass must be made on the reverse-stick side.

e After dribbling to the half-way line, the player concerned must pass the ball via the sideboards to his team-mate waiting on the goal-line.

f On the way to the half-way line, a flagpost or marker is established level with the top of the circle, which must be dribbled around to the right (or to the left). After crossing the half-way line, the ball is pushed hard against the sideboards level with the defender in the other half, so that it rebounds accurately to the player waiting on the goal-line.

9 A player stands in the middle of the pitch, and pushes the ball straight against the boards. By turning round as the ball comes back, the player can push it against the opposite board without first stopping it. From there it rebounds to the middle of the pitch for the next push-pass. Several players compete against each other. Running towards the ball is not allowed. Which player is in the lead after one minute's practice, or who is the first to make fifteen push-passes?

10 Several pairs of players stand two or three yards from the sideboards, near to one another. The players in possession of a ball push the ball as hard as possible over the width of the pitch and off the opposite boards, so that it rebounds over the pitch-width again to the player standing next to them. Players are not allowed to step over a pre-determined line, this is to prevent them from trying to receive the ball more quickly (fig. 59). The higher the players' standard of pushing the ball, the further back towards the sideboards should the line be drawn. Which pair is the first to make ten push-passes off the boards?

11 a A player positions himself on the goal-line with three balls on the spot from which corners are pushed out. He should pass the ball

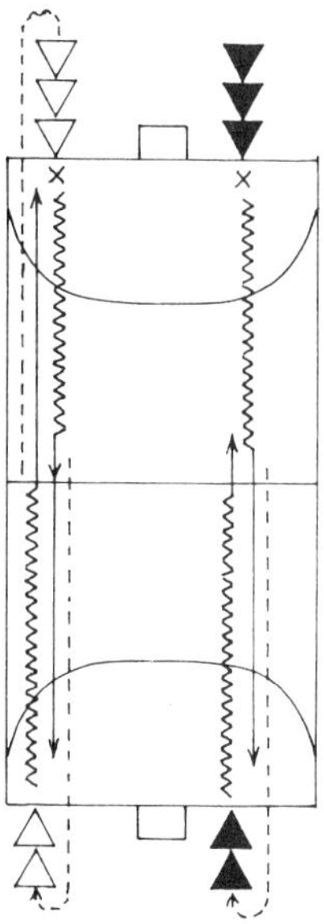

Figure 58

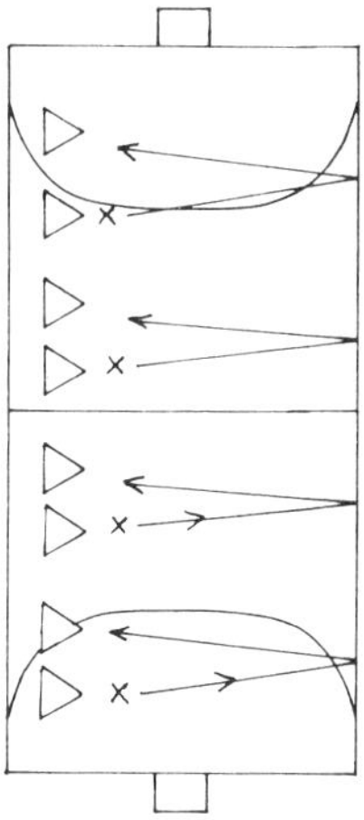

Figure 59

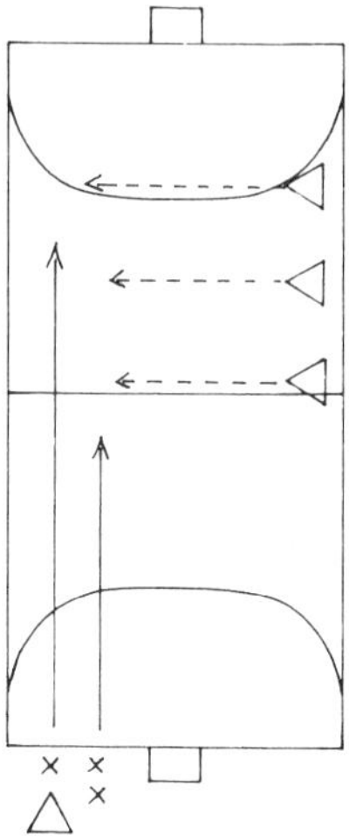

Figure 60

parallel to the sideboards in the direction of the opposite goal-line at such a speed that his opponents, who are standing by the opposite sideboards in the other half of the pitch, cannot reach the ball by sprinting across the pitch. The position of the defenders inside the pitch depends on the standard of the player pushing the ball. The defenders begin by standing near the boards on the half-way line. If they cannot reach the ball as it is pushed hard towards the opposite end, then they take up positions further down the pitch, or further into the field of play (fig. 60).

b Successful interception by the defenders is made more difficult if passes are made via the sideboards.

c In order to prepare defenders for all game situations, defensive practice should be alternated on the right- and left-hand sides, i.e. the pass must be intercepted both on the open side and on the reverse (near the sideboards, it is best to lay the stick parallel with the floor, so that the fingers of the left hand touch the floor, and the head of the stick touches the sideboard).

12 a The idea of this exercise is to push the ball over the opposition's goal-line. The game is started with a push-pass from the top of the circle. Wherever the ball is stopped dead by an opponent, he then pushes it back towards the opposite goal-line. If the ball bounces, then according to the rules, possession is given to the other team. No more than three players are in each team, although if two balls are used, five

players are allowed in each team. In deciding the winner, either the number of points scored in a particular time can count, or the game can be played until a certain number of points is reached.

b Variation: the ball must not be held for more than two seconds. Before it is pushed towards the opposite goal-line, it can be passed to a team-mate standing to the right or to the left, but the pass cannot be used to gain any ground!

13 The pitch is divided into three areas of equal size, each of which contains three players. The two outer teams pass the ball between them so that the three members of the middle team are unable to intercept the pass (fig. 61). Using the sideboards for passing makes the middle team's task more difficult. Each successful pass between teams A and B scores them one point, as does intercepting the ball for team C. Which team is the first to score fifteen points? Each team must take its turn in the middle. The players of the outer teams are allowed to pass the ball between them, in order to create a more favourable position for passing to the team opposite, as long as they do not set foot in the middle area.

14 As in 13, except that there are now four teams of three players each in four areas of equal size. Each pass between the players of team A or B scores one point. Which team is the first to reach fifteen points (fig. 62)?

Games and exercises for basic rule no. 8

If a defender can see that a long pass from him will reach his striker running into space near to or inside the opposition's circle, either he or another defender should sprint forward as quickly as possible in support as soon as a pass is made, to make himself available for a return pass.

1 a A defender standing on the half-way line 5 yards from the sideboards takes a free hit and plays the ball off the sideboards to a team-mate waiting on the opposite goal-line. An opponent standing 4 yards from the sideboards, level with the top of the circle, has to try to intercept the pass by moving towards the ball as soon as the pass is made. If the ball strikes the sideboards level with the opposing defender, and if the push pass is made with sufficient power, then the opposing player will have no chance of intercepting it. As soon as he has taken the free hit, the defender should run straight to the edge of the opposite circle, to wait for a pass from his team-mate and to try to score a goal (fig. 63). The opposing defender should not at first try to prevent the pass back to the edge of the circle. Players should practise passing off both right and left sideboards, as well as concealed passes to right and left.

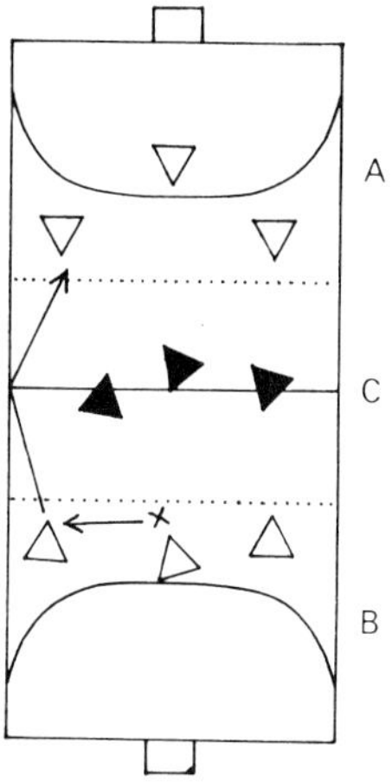

Figure 61

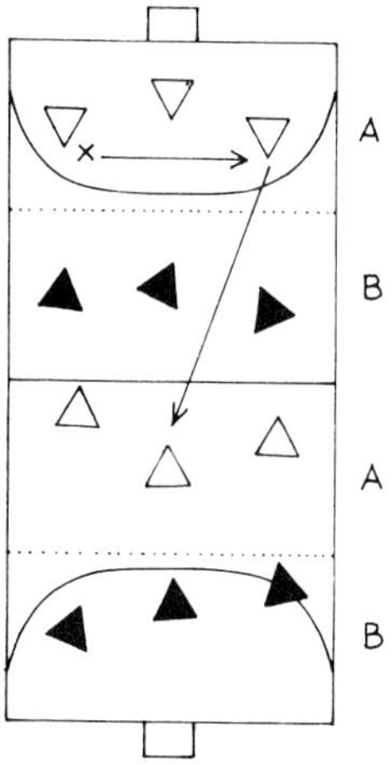

Figure 62

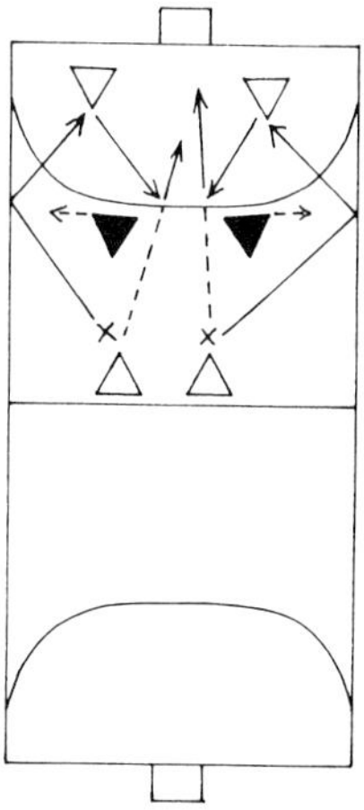

Figure 63

b As in 1, except that an opponent standing approximately 4 yards from the sideboard and 4 yards in front of the half-way line must first be dribbled round. The striker should not now, as in 1a, stand waiting on the goal-line for a pass off the sideboards and then play the ball back, but should continually change his position, moving in different directions in order to play the received ball back (either immediately or after first stopping it quickly) to his attacking defender, who is running forward.

2 a Two against one on the right-hand side (or left-hand side) of the defending half of the field. The two defenders should try to beat the opposing attacker, so that one of them can push the ball at full speed from near the half-way line to a team-mate running free in the corner of the attacking half of the field.

b Variation: instead of the two defenders, the opposing attacker standing on the half-way line is given the ball. He should try to beat the two defenders with a solo run on the right-hand (or left-hand) side of the pitch. If one of the defenders can make a successful tackle, then he should switch from defence to attack as quickly as possible. According to the situation, he will then either make a long, hard pass up-field to the team-mate running free in the opposite circle and then immediately follow in support, or he will push the ball to his defending team-mate, who is in a better position to pass the ball quickly to his striker up-field.

The game is played first without a defender marking this striker, then with a passive defender, and finally with a fully involved defender who should follow the defenders' team-mate like a shadow. These two players, as with the three players in the other half of the field, are allowed to move only on the right- (or left-) hand side of their half of the field.

3 a Three defenders play in their own half against one opposing attacker who tries to intercept passes made from near the half-way line to one of their two strikers waiting on the goal-line. The attacker in one half of the field is supported by two full-backs, who stand in their own half of the field approximately 4 yards from the sideboards on the right- and left-hand side level with the circle. Their job is to intercept the passes played off the sideboards by the defenders towards their attackers in the circle, but without leaving their positions. After passing the ball off the sideboards, the defender concerned should immediately sprint towards the top of the circle to make himself available for a return pass from his team-mate (fig. 64). The pass-back to the edge of the circle should only be intercepted by a full back if the previous passes off the sideboard and back from the goal-line have been carried out faultlessly.

Note: The defender's pass to his forward should be made off the nearest sideboard. If the pass is made from a position 3 or 4 yards from the sideboards, it is very difficult for an opponent to intercept it, if the pass is concealed well, because of the narrow angles involved.

b Played as in a. If the right (or left) attacker thinks that he will not receive the ball, he should leave the corner and make himself available for a straight pass to the penalty-flick spot. In doing so, he is marked by a fully involved player of the opposition (unlike his fellow strikers).

c Played as in a. Both attackers are allowed to move wherever they like in the attacking half of the field. One of them is tightly marked, while the other has a better chance of receiving the ball when not under pressure, since his opponent is marking zonally. The upfield pass out of defence should always be to this player.

4 a Three against two in the defending half of the field, with two against two in the attacking half; the two players marking the two strikers use zonal marking (fig. 65). Only if a return pass to the top of the circle has a good chance of success should the defender who gave the long pass make himself available.

b Three against two in the defending half of the field, passing up-field to one of two strikers marked man-to-man. As soon as the player making the pass can see that it will reach his team-mate, he or the other defender must support the attack and make himself available for a return-pass, which will be necessary by a first-time pass. No more than five players are allowed in either half. The fifth player comes from the team with the ball.

5 a Three against three in the defending half of the field, passing up-field to one of two strikers. Played as in 3a, b and c.

b Three against three in the defending half of the field, passing upfield to one of two strikers marked man-to-man.

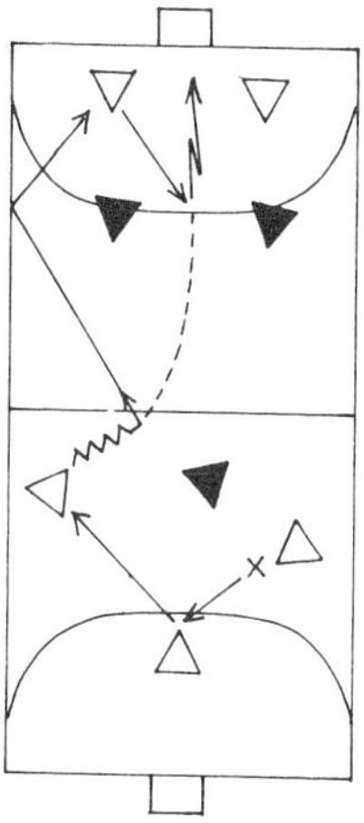

Figure 64

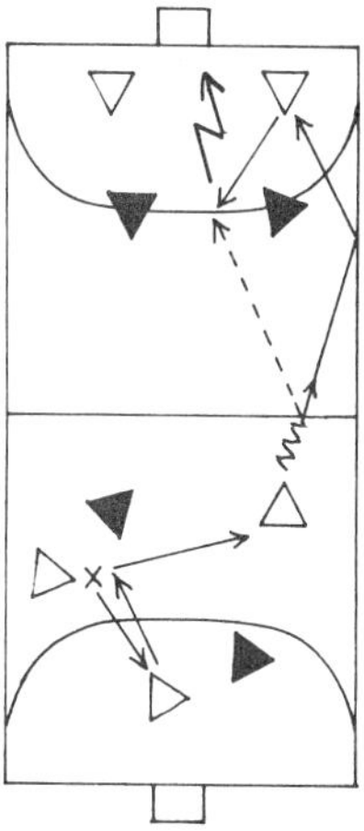

Figure 65

Photo 56

Games and exercises for basic rule no. 5

As often as possible, the ball should be deflected without first stopping it. A first-time or wall-pass speeds play up, and allows the opposition less time to organise themselves in defence.

1 a First-time passing with a partner standing 10 to 15 yards away. In passing the ball first time, make sure that the upper part of the body is

over the ball, that the right hand is further down the stick than usual, and that the stick is as horizontal as possible, so as to increase the area covered by the stick.

b First-time passing with a partner running 10 yards away. This exercise is carried out from goal-line to goal-line. How many mistakes does the pair make there and back? How long does the best pair need for these two lengths of the field? (The ball should be played at best six times in each direction). The attack is not valid if there is a stopping error, or if an inaccurate pass is made.

The ball should always be played to the left-hand man towards his back-leg, since he can only play the ball first-time if the ball is a little behind his body. By contrast, the ball should always be passed to the right-hand player into his path (i.e. slightly in front of him).

In order to force players to lift their eyes from the ball while dribbling or passing, runs should be instigated from both goal-lines simultaneously.

2 a Three players in a triangle pass the ball first-time between them; the distance between players should never be less than 6 yards. How many first-time passes can be made without a mistake (inaccurate passing, stopping, or lifting the ball)? Which team of three achieves the best results in three minutes' play?

b As in a. Players are not allowed to stay on the same spot for more than three seconds, and after playing the ball should immediately make themselves available for a return pass by running into space.

c Ditto, but with a definite direction of attack, and concluded by a shot at goal.

d Ditto, but three against one in the defending half of the field. Each first-time pass to a team-mate scores one point, while stopping the ball first scores nothing. If the ball is lifted or touched by the attacking defender, then the player who has made the mistake must defend in the middle. Which three-man-team can score the most points?

e As in d, but played in one direction three against two. The two defenders, who may only tackle in their own half, must be beaten one after the other by the team of three in possession of the ball, who must use first-time passes in the direction of the opposite circle. The ball may only be stopped three times. How many attacks do the three strikers need to score a goal?

f As in d, but played four against two. If the ball is inside the team's own circle, it should not be passed first-time, because of the risk of lifting the ball, but should be passed quickly to an unmarked team-mate once it has been stopped.

g As in d, but played five against three the latter defending over the whole field. A game with use of the sideboards can be introduced.

3 Game with three teams.
Two teams of three players fight for the ball inside a tennis-court drawn on the floor. A first-time pass between two players of the same team, or between one of them and one of three players of a third team always ready for a pass outside the tennis-court, scores one point (fig. 66). Which of the two teams inside the tennis-court is the first to score ten points?

Further games and exercises designed to coach first-time passing can be taken from the exercises devised for rule no. 9.

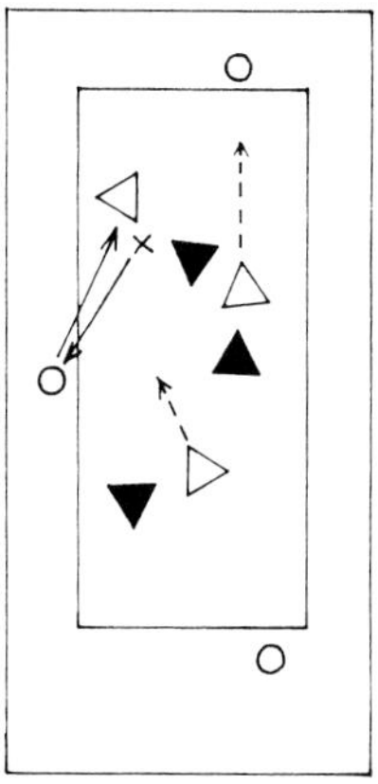

Figure 66

Games and exerises for basic rule no. 9

At a free hit for the attacking team in front of the circle, a maximum of four players should be in attacking positions. The fifth player should cover at the back and prevent any possible counter-attack by the opposition. The more players there are in the circle, the less space there is available for a good pass.

If the free hit cannot be taken quickly, so as to surprise the opposition (i.e. no team-mate is available for a pass), then the player making the pass should take his time, and carry out a move that has previously been practised with the other players. Basically, because of its surprise effect, running into space should be from a standing start. Only when a team-mate has freed himself from man-to-man marking should a hard and accurate pass be made. It is better if the strikers, when running into space inside the circle, sprint from inside the circle outwards, rather than vice versa.

1 One particularly successful method of taking the free hit is to push the ball into the circle to a suddenly unmarked attacker, who immediately passes it straight back to the player having taken the 'free hit' (who is not usually marked), and who can then flick at goal without first stopping the ball (fig. 67).

Photo 57

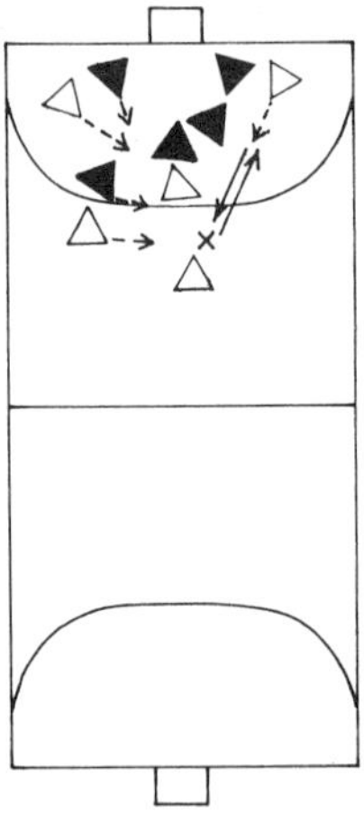

Figure 67

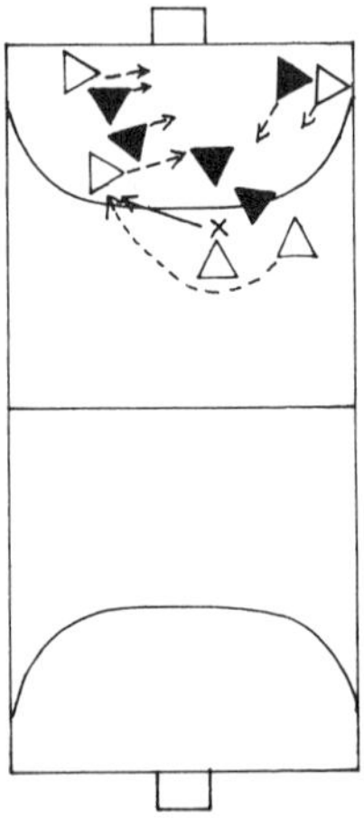

Figure 68

2 Another possibility begins when all strikers in the circle run into space on the same side of the field, so as to create a gap into which a further member of the attacking team can suddenly sprint from behind (fig. 68). Only then should a pass into the circle be made. The ball should not be stopped, but should be pushed or flicked at goal first-time if possible.

If the player receives the ball in space, but in an unfavourable position to score, then a shot at goal should be avoided, and he should aim at a mistake by the opposition, to force a corner.

3 A forward who is marked on the right-hand side of the circle makes a sudden run out of the corner towards a team-mate preparing to take a free hit near the edge of the circle. As soon as the latter recognises his intention, he runs away from the ball some four yards to the left, where he receives a quick pass from the player who now actually does take the free hit, and flicks first-time at goal. If this move fails, against a team that marks very tightly, then it should be carried out twice, or perhaps varied, by including a different player (fig. 69).

4 A player stands diagonally in front of the player taking a free hit but suddenly makes a curved run behind the player with the ball to the opposite side, whereby he gains one or two seconds on his opponent, and can thus receive the ball (fig. 68). Because the free hit is played diagonally forwards, obstruction of the marking defender is avoided.

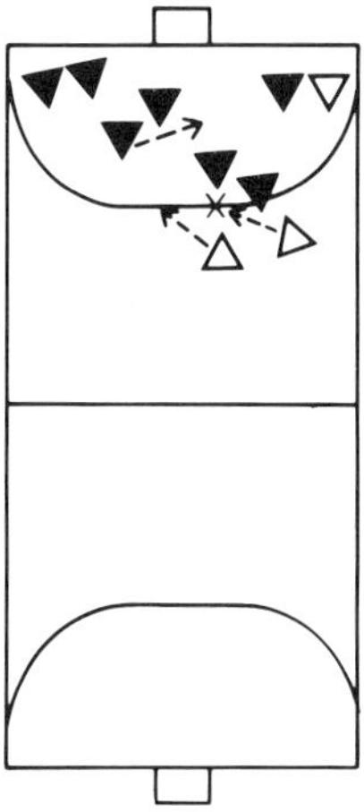

Figure 69

5 One striker takes up a position on a line approximately a yard from the left-hand post, at any distance from the goal-line, but within the circle. He must position himself relative to his marking defender such that he will not obstruct as he receives the ball (i.e. side-on with his left shoulder facing the direction in which the pass will come). At the moment that he runs towards the player with the ball at the edge of the circle, a hard pass is made, aimed at the left-hand post. The striker should try to get his stick in the way of the ball, so as to deflect it at goal by changing its direction and lifting it.

Games and exercises for basic rule no. 10

A ball played at full speed towards the goal should never be stopped in the opposing circle by the strikers, but deflected first time into the goal. In doing so, the striker should take up a position side-on to the goal with his stick horizontal, and should try to play the ball on his open side as often as possible.

1 a From various positions on the edge of the circle, hard passes are played to the penalty-flick spot, or 2 yards from the left-hand post. A hard pass should always be made when a striker in the inside-right position makes a run towards the middle of the goal, or towards the left-hand post, so he can deflect the ball, as it comes towards him, into the goal.

b Ditto, but with a goalkeeper.

c Ditto, but with a goalkeeper and one defender.

2 a A ball played from the half-way line into the circle near the left-hand post should be deflected straight into the goal by a player running from right outside the circle into that area (fig. 70).

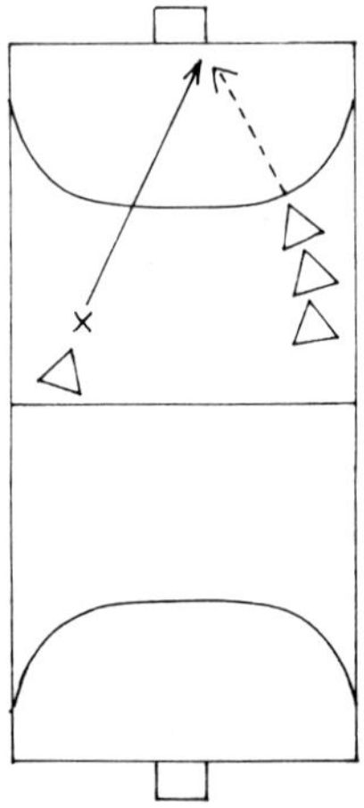

Figure 70

b This can also be practised with a goalkeeper, but he many only leave his line at the moment that the pass is made.

c As in b, but without restrictions to the goalkeeper's movements.

3 See exercise 2, except that the pass from the half-way line is played now from the right-hand side towards the right goalpost, and the attacker begins by standing on the left at the edge of the circle. The striker should try to deflect the ball into the goal on his open side.

Photo 58

Games and exercises for basic rule no. 11

When possession of the ball is lost, every outfield player should watch that the man in his zone is not nearer to the goal than he is, i.e. he should always position himself such that he has his man directly in front of him or so that no member of the opposition is standing behind him. When a free hit is awarded to the opposition in front of the circle, defenders should mark man-to-man, while one defender covers space.

1 An attacker tries to lose a defender by reversing the direction of his running, and using body-feints and changes of speed between the half-way line and the goal-line. In each phase of the exercise, the defender should take up a correct position relative to the man he is marking, in order to avoid his running free. If the forward is able to free himself for a second from the defender, then the ball is passed to him by a second forward standing at least 6 yards away on the half-way line (fig. 71). The ball should be taken without breaking the rules, i.e. without obstructing. The defender and the forward compete against each other: each successful tackle by the defender (he has to play the ball back to the player originally passing the ball), and each goal scored by the forward, earns one point.

2 Two strikers, right and left, try to run free of their tightly marking defenders and shake them off. In every situation, the two defenders should try to take up a good position relative to the players they are marking (positional play). They should always have their man in front of them, and stand on a line between the middle of the goal and the opposing player. If

one of the strikers is able to get free of his defender for a few seconds, then the ball is played to him from at least six yards away by a third striker on the half-way line (fig. 72). If possession is gained by the defence and one pass is made between the two players, or if a striker obstructs as he receives the ball, then the defenders are awarded one point. If the strikers can score a goal after successfully receiving the ball, they are awarded two points. Which is the first team to score ten points?

There are several different methods for successfully passing the ball to the forwards, covered in rule no. 2, exercise 6.

3 Three forwards try to free themselves from their marking defenders. A fourth forward should feed the ball to one of his team-mates so that he can receive the ball under no pressure from a pursuing defender (fig. 73). After a few minutes' practice, this exercise is continued as a competition. Points are awarded as in 2.

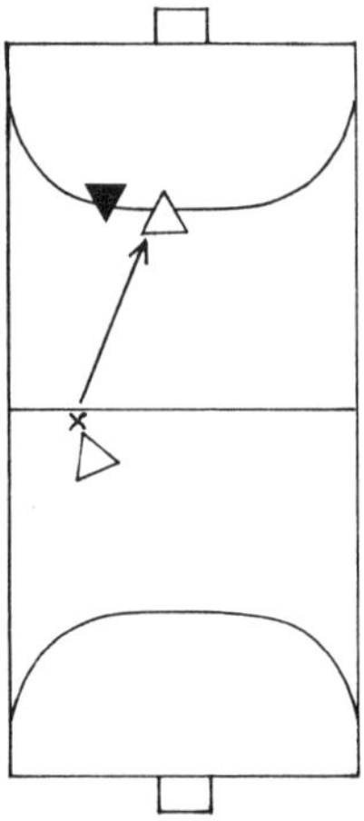

Figure 71

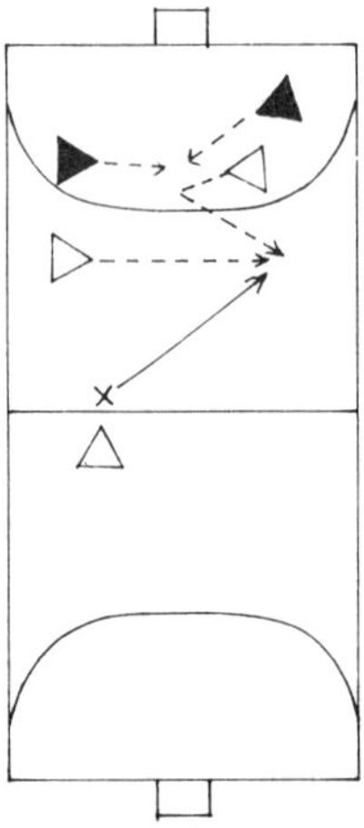

Figure 72

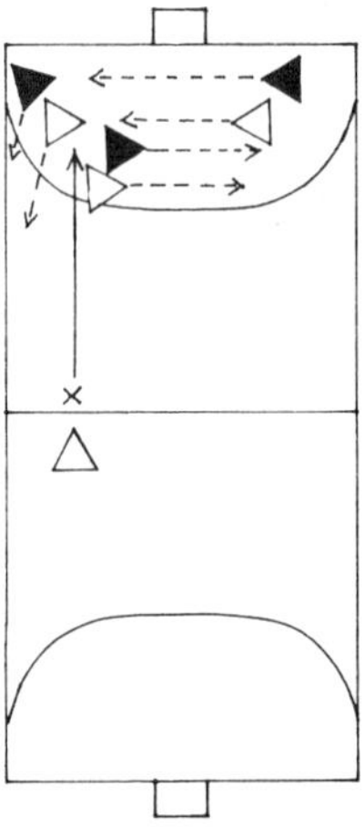

Figure 73

4 See 'Exercises aimed at improving a rapid switch from defence to attack', page 192.

THE THEORY AND PRACTICE OF SHORT-CORNERS

The goalkeeper in indoor hockey has an even more important role than in field hockey, because of the higher ratio of the size of the circles to the size of the pitch, and because of the reduced number of players in a team. He is the centre of the action, especially at short corners.

There are four different short-corner variations in general use by attackers, and these are listed and depicted (fig. 74) below, according to their frequency of use.

Photo 59

1 A first-time flick or push after a hand-stop (photo 60).

2 A pass to the left (photo 61).

3 A pass back to the pusher-out.

4 Beating the first player running out on his reverse-stick side, especially if the ball was inaccurately pushed out too far towards the middle of the circle.

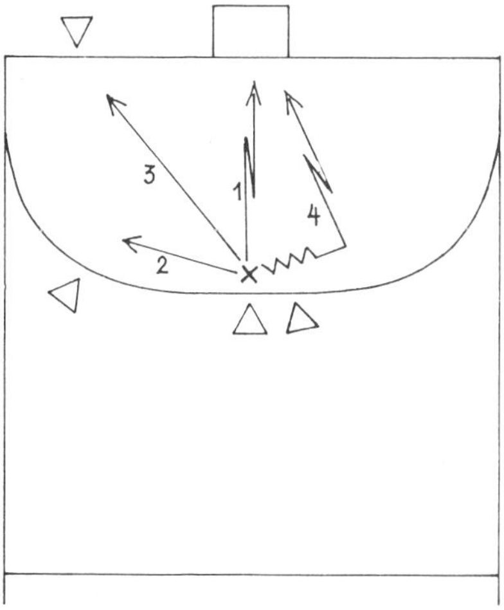

Figure 74

Photo 60

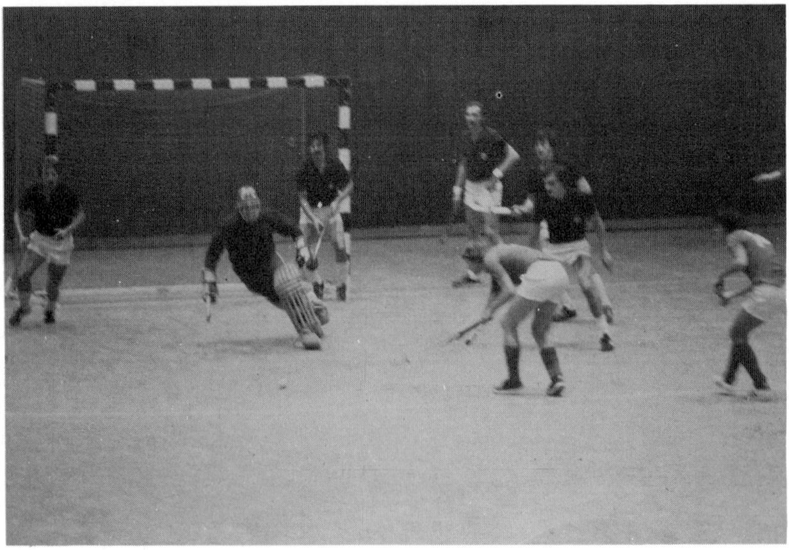

Photo 61

A tactical response to these four different short-corner variations leads to the following tasks for the defenders (fig. 75).

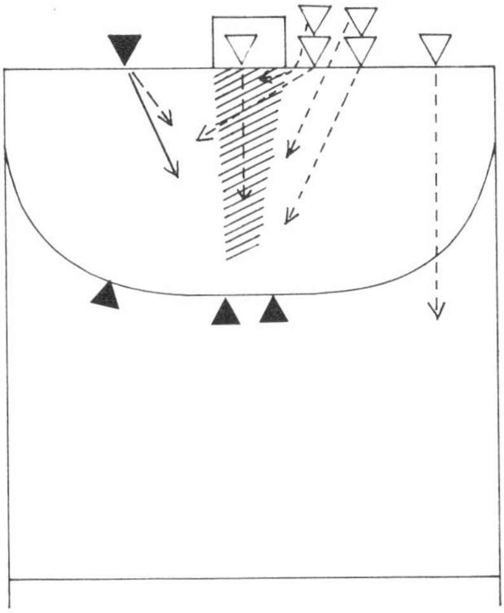

Figure 75

1 The goalkeeper should frequently sprint out of the goal so as to stop the flick at goal as early as possible; at least he will narrow the flicker's angle. The goalkeeper is always accompanied by another defender (photo 62).

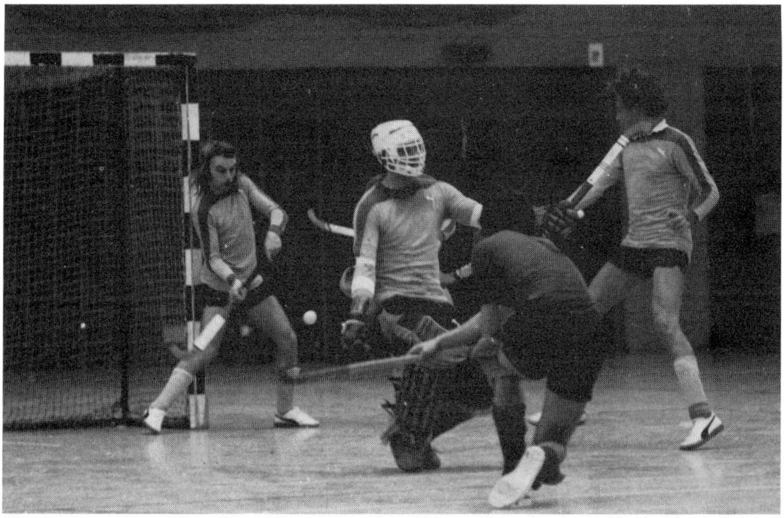

Photo 62

2 The first player standing by the left-hand post runs behind the goalkeeper to the pusher-out.

3 The player standing in the second row behind him hurries into the goal approximately two feet from the left-hand post (photo 63).

Photo 63

4 A third player runs out with the goalkeeper to his left in order to intercept any attempt to beat the goalkeeper on his reverse side.

5 A fourth player follows behind the goalkeeper, so that he can clear any ball that is deflected or saved by the goalkeeper.

6 The fifth player runs straight out of the circle, and prepares for a counter-attack if the ball is successfully cleared (photo 64).

Photo 64

Despite improved standards of goalkeeping and defending, every third corner results in a goal, with good teams. If the goalkeeper stays on the line, the attacking team convert, on average, every other corner, but if he runs out and narrows the angle, the conversion rate is reduced to one in four. Although these figures taken from the West German indoor hockey championships in 1979 would speak in favour of the goalkeeper running out in combination with his defenders in a tactically sound formation, it is still true that in approximately fifteen per cent of all corners, the goalkeeper stays on the line.

With the goalkeeper on the goal-line, fifty per cent of all corners lead to a goal, twenty per cent are saved by defenders and fifteen per cent by the goalkeeper himself or through mistakes by the attacking team. It can be deduced from these statistics therefore, that the chances of saving a shot if the goalkeeper runs out with the other defenders are double those if the goalkeeper stays on the line.

Of course, more corners would be converted today if the practice of the goalkeeper running out, together with a sound formation of defenders (first used in 1968 by the author's club team) had not been discovered to be effective. The goalkeeper tries to run as far as possible towards the hand-stopper so as to narrow the angle of the shot. If he can get to within two yards of the ball as it is stopped, he can narrow the angle completely, while at a distance of three yards from the ball at the moment of impact, only seventy-five per cent of the goal is covered.

Since the goalkeeper has only one second to run out—pushing the ball out to the handstopper takes approximately 0.7 seconds, and a further 0.3 seconds generally elapse before the ball is flicked by the corner taker—it is normally impossible for him to completely narrow the angle of the shot, unless he runs out from the line too soon.

The shortest route for the goalkeeper is to start from the right-hand post, moving straight towards the handstopper, who has to stand directly in front of him when the push-out is taken. By running from the right-hand post, the goalkeeper automatically covers the right side of the goal, which another defender could only cover with difficulty, because of the time involved.

Ideas which may decrease the number of goals scored from corners.

Special sprint training (only rarely undertaken by goalkeepers at present); staying upright for as long as possible in running out; lighter and safer goal-keeping equipment; intelligent running out of outfield players; better coaching of the player standing in the goal, by training with tennis balls, will lead to a reduction in the percentage of goals scored from corners, despite improvements in speed and accuracy on the part of the specialist goal-scorers.

What an indoor hockey goalkeeper must particularly watch out for.

Further important notes for goalkeepers indoors:

a if the ball is in the other half of the field, the goalkeeper must sometimes take over the role of a defender supporting the attack, by marking the opposing goal-hanger in the circle (see exercises for rule no. 10);

b at a free hit from the circle, if all players are marked, he should make himself available for a pass, or better still take the free hit himself (see the last exercise for rules no. 2 and 3);

c many corners result from the goalkeeper kicking a bouncing ball off the ground after saving a high shot—special exercises help to solve this problem; and

d finally, all variations of games involving numerical superiority for the attacking team are the best exercises for the goalkeeper.

Further comments, exercises and notes on exercises and games designed to improve the goalkeeper's and other players' skills, tactical appreciation and physical preparation can be found in the author's coaching manuals, *The Science of Hockey* (revised edition, 1979) and *See and Learn Hockey* (published 1978) as F.I.H. Coaching Book by the Swiss Hockey Association.